FASHION AS COMMUNICATION

'one of the best compact intros to this fascinating topic'   *i-D* magazine

What kinds of things do fashion and clothing say about us? What does it mean to wear Gap or Gaultier, Millet or Moschino? Are there any real differences between Hip-Hop styles and Punk anti-styles? In this fully revised and updated edition, Malcolm Barnard introduces fashion and clothing as ways of communicating and challenging class, gender, sexual and social identities.

Drawing on a range of theoretical approaches from Barthes and Baudrillard to Marxist, psychoanalytic and feminist theories, Barnard addresses the ambivalent status of fashion in contemporary culture. He looks at the producers, consumers and critics of fashion, exploring the tensions between *haute couture* and high culture, and asking how meanings are generated, and by whom.

Examining concepts such as culture, meaning, class, gender, reproduction and resistance, Barnard demonstrates that fashion is not an innocent form of communication, and uncovers the ways in which clothing can be used both to create and critique identities. The new edition features six new illustrations, a glossary of key terms and suggestions for further reading and research.

FASHION AS COMMUNICATION

Second Edition

Malcolm Barnard

Routledge
Taylor & Francis Group

LONDON AND NEW YORK

First edition published 1996
by Routledge
11 New Fetter Lane, London EC4P 4EE

Simultaneously published in the USA and Canada
by Routledge
29 West 35th Street, New York, NY 10001

Reprinted 2001

This second edition first published 2002

Reprinted 2004

Routledge is an imprint of the Taylor & Francis Group

© 1996, 2002 Malcolm Barnard

Typeset in Times Ten by RefineCatch Limited, Bungay, Suffolk
Printed and bound in Great Britain by
Biddles Ltd, King's Lynn, Norfolk

British Library Cataloguing in Publication Data
A catalogue record for this book is available from the British Library

Library of Congress Cataloguing in Publication Data
A catalogue record for this book has been requested

ISBN 0–415–26017–5 (Hbk)
ISBN 0–415–26018–3 (Pbk)

CONTENTS

LIST OF FIGURES

ACKNOWLEDGEMENTS

Most of the words in this book were written in the autumn semesters of 1994 and 2001, something that would have been impossible had it not been for the Cultural History and Critical Theory Research Centre, at the University of Derby, relieving me of my teaching duties.

Most of the works referred to in this book were obtained for me to read, via the Inter-Library Loan system, by the hard-working and under-resourced staff of the Library and Learning Resources Centre at Britannia Mill. I am very grateful to them.

And most of the ideas, topics and approaches covered in this book either would not be here at all, or would be here in even more garbled and distorted forms than they are, had it not been for the many comments and suggestions made by my colleagues in the Department of Historical and Theoretical Studies at the University of Derby. While I would like to thank Robert Burstow, Mary Cunningham, Gail Day, Mark Durden, Giles Peaker, Janet Sleath and Rhiannon Williams for their help, I owe an especially ironic debt of gratitude to Steve Edwards, who, while disagreeing with and disapproving of most of the things I say, has probably helped me most of all. Caroline Evans, of Central Saint Martin's College of Art and Design, and Taylor & Francis/Routledge's anonymous readers have also contributed useful, perceptive and improving suggestions and I am grateful to them.

Thanks to Morrison McConnell and Coats plc for the Tattersall shirt picture, to Vivienne Westwood Ltd for the body-stocking picture, www.adbusters.org for their Hilfiger spoof, *The Guardian* and Stephen Bates for the newspaper article concerning the Queen.

I would also like to thank Principles for allowing me to use their advertisement and Siân Mitchell for providing a print of the advertisement. Debbie Sinfield and Martin Durrant of the V&A, Luigi DiDio at Hulton Deutsch, Tim Clifton-Green at Vivienne Westwood Ltd and Nina Hodson of Morrison McConnell and Coats plc were also extremely helpful in finding and providing illustrations. And, finally, I must thank Sally Edwards, Simon Birkett and Richard Richards at the University of Derby for providing photographic and digital images suitable for reproduction here.

ACKNOWLEDGEMENTS

Every effort has been made to trace all the copyright-holders, but if any have been inadvertently overlooked the publishers will be pleased to make the necessary arrangements at the first opportunity.

PREFACE TO THE
SECOND EDITION

The first edition seems to have been of some assistance to students who are interested in beginning the critical analysis of fashion and clothing. To that extent, it has worked. The second edition is intended to provide even more support to such students. In order to provide such support, and guided and reassured by Routledge's anonymous readers (who generously commented upon the first edition), I have not tried to write a different book. By clarifying the obscure, updating the outdated and filling in the lacunae, I have tried to improve the existing work. Many of the trickier concepts are introduced and explained as simply as I know how to in a glossary. Other ideas are developed a little more in the text. The references throughout are brought up to date and there are entirely new sections on hip-hop, 'kinderwhore' and 'fashion, art, performance, masquerade', for example. There are even some new illustrations. I hope it all helps.

INTRODUCTION

TWO VIEWS OF FASHION AND CLOTHING

In Britain and the USA, as in many other western capitalist countries at the beginning of the twenty-first century, fashion and clothing present curious and ambiguous profiles. From one side, the profile looks attractive and seductive. Newsagents' shelves groan under the weight of style and fashion magazines, which offer glossy advice, to both men and women, young and old, on what to look like and how to look like it. The High Streets and malls of these countries are filled with more or less confident fashion and clothing franchises, staffed by more or less snooty assistants offering more or less exclusive gear to the more or less discerning consumer. Online versions of companies such as Lands' End provide the chance to construct a virtual 'you', kitting yourself out with potential purchases (go to 'My Model' at *www.landsend.co.uk* and *www.landsend.com*). Television shows with tricky graphics, eclectic taste in music and enthusiastic presenters offer make-overs in provincial shopping malls and interviews with glamorous-looking fashion designers. Other television productions, often with 1920s' or 1930s' graphics and music to match, have offered frock design as serialised, if not always terribly high, drama. Between the shows, companies like Gap and Nike advertise their clothes with swinging choreography and pop groups. The world of fashion design made one of its periodic appearances in Hollywood film in 1995 when *Prêt à Porter*, a story of designers, models and consumers, was released. Daily newspapers, conservative and liberal alike, set aside whole pages and employ journalists to offer their opinions concerning the ideal size of female models or to present the latest in latex. And, inevitably, in their turn, some of these models, presenters and journalists become household names, fit to offer their endorsements of other household names in magazine and television advertisements.

From the other side, however, the profile looks much less attractive and, although it is still seductive, it is so in quite a different sense. The glamorous stores, television and magazine ads are tarnished by the knowledge that Gap, Tommy Hilfiger, Nike and the rest depend upon exploiting sweated child

Figure 1 Adbusters.org Tommy Hilfiger spoof 'Follow the Flock'

labour in developing countries (Klein 2000: 46, 212, 327, 331). Tommy Hilfiger is so affected by the opprobrium they have attracted as a result of their practices that it will not allow Hilfiger advertisements to appear in academic texts such as this one, in case they are used to disgrace the company even further. From another angle, Sapir has noted that 'the term fashion may carry with it a tone of approval or disapproval' (Sapir 1931: 139). In as early a work as the dialogue known as the 'Greater Hippias', for example, which some attribute to Plato, writing around 400 BC, clothes are linked with beauty. However, they are linked with beauty in the context of a fraud that is perpetrated on those seeking the beautiful (Plato 'Greater Hippias' 294a-b in Hamilton and Cairns (eds) 1961: 154–7). And as modern a work as *i-D* magazine, for example, points out that, for some people, 'to be fashion conscious or "fashionable" is still deemed to make you "fickle", "dumb", "ephemeral" [and] "fascist"' (*i-D* magazine 1985/6). The ways in which clothing, fashion and textiles feature in everyday colloquialisms reflect this view, a much less welcoming and trusting view. In many everyday figures of speech, fashion, clothing and textiles are associated with triviality and deceit. These phrases may be thought of as part of some collective unconscious; they are the slips of the tongue that whole cultures make, which give away that culture's actual feelings about a topic.

Examples of everyday phrases suggesting the deceptive nature of clothing or dress abound and Valerie Steele (2001: 73) suggests that the notion of fashion as deceit stems from eighteenth-century usage. When, for example, one wants to say that someone is dressing in a way that is too young for them, one says that they are 'mutton dressed as lamb'. Whether or not this phrase applies as easily to men as it does to women (and it is unlikely that it is ever applied to men), the idea that the notion of clothing conveys here is that of deceit. Clothes here are being used to 'pull the wool over one's eyes', to fool one. People also speak of someone being a 'wolf in sheep's clothing'. Indeed, this phrase was the only copy in a series of ads for wool in the early 1980s (compare Imrie 1986, for example). Again, the idea is that a person (and here it is unlikely that the phrase is ever applied to a woman), who is one kind of person uses clothes to appear as another, less threatening, kind of person. The idea which dress is used to convey here, again, is deception.

The well-known children's story concerning the Emperor's new clothes, in which the Emperor is himself fooled by two conmen, and in which he in turn fools most of the population, clearly works on the basis of clothes being bound up with the idea of deceit. Slang gives other senses; to dress a hat is to commit a robbery, for example. To dress for the part is to be hypocritical in theatre slang. Oscar Wilde's claim, that only a fool would not judge by appearances, gains its satirical force by countering the popular wisdom that one should not judge a person by their clothes. Popular wisdom being well aware, only presumably, of just how beguiling clothes can be. There are probably other phrases which, like these, associate fashion or clothing with deception, but these give the flavour.

It seems that there are fewer phrases that associate fashion or dress with the trivial (although there is plenty of anecdotal evidence to suggest that modern western culture does just that and Angela McRobbie (1998: 15) writes of the 'trivialised status' still enjoyed by fashion in the late 1990s). Sapir, for example, points out that 'a moralist may decry a certain type of behaviour as a mere fashion' (Sapir 1931: 139). Fashion is used here to give the sense of something that is not very significant, a 'mere' thing. Similarly, people will speak of someone as a 'fashion victim', meaning, partly at least, that they spend too much time or money on fashion. The implication is that they will follow the fashion unquestioningly when, in reality, there are other, much more important things to be attended to. The idea of someone being a slave to fashion also shares in this sense that fashion is not the sort of thing that should be overvalued, that it is not particularly important.

Anecdotal evidence of fashion and dress not being taken as seriously as it could or should be is not hard to find. One need only ask fashion or textiles students what their peers taking other subjects at college and, occasionally, their families, think of them pursuing such a career to confirm the popularity of this prejudice, especially if those peers are male. It is a common prejudice that fashion and textiles students will be only too happy to shorten a pair of trousers or run off a scarf, for example, because that is what they do, that is what their subjects are about. The idea that fashion and textiles are not

3

perhaps as serious or as important as other subjects is often not one that junior education ministers of government do much to combat. Timothy Eggar, for example, who was Minister of State for Education and Science in October 1990, suggested on Radio Four's *Today* programme that 'able children' should study proper subjects like Classics or a second language in the National Curriculum, while 'less able children' should study design (Clough 1990: 3).

While the adoption of small-minded prejudice as Conservative government policy may surprise no one, the contrast between these two sides or profiles of fashion probably will. From one side, fashion and clothing represent objects that are desirable and sexy and practices that are both glamorous and respectable. From the other side, they represent deceitful, exploitative trivia to be pursued only by the intellectually challenged. This seems to be a clear case of double standards: creative production, art if you like, is given both positive and negative valuations. (There is another double standard, operating 'within' this one, which determines that men's involvement in fashion and clothing is valued differently from, and valued above, that of women. This will be discussed in more detail in chapter five and see Buckley 1986: 4–5). However, one ought not to be surprised by the curious and ambivalent position allotted to fashion and dress by this culture. There are various explanations offered for the phenomenon, some of which will be examined in more detail in the following chapter. Williams points out, for example, that this dichotomous response to creativity or cultural production has a long history and may be found in both 'high theory and low prejudice' (Williams 1961: 35). The creativity of artists and designers has long been both admired and despised by societies. Wilson suggests that this 'cultural ambivalence' is the result of what she calls the 'blatant consumerism' of fashion and clothing 'shocking' the culture that we live in, while simultaneously expressing the 'heart' of that culture, saying something essential or true about it (Wilson 1990: 209).

The ambivalence of this culture's response to fashion and dress does not arise by chance and the effects of such ambivalence cannot simply be dismissed as irrelevant or accidental. They cannot be dismissed because, systematically and thoroughly, these issues and their implications work their way through even the definition of the word 'fashion' as well as its relations to other words like 'style' and 'clothing'. In order to examine how these issues affect the meanings of words like these, chapter one will begin by studying the etymology of the word fashion.

This introduction has tried to introduce some of the concerns of the rest of the book by considering the cultural status enjoyed by fashion and clothing in contemporary western society. They are seen to have an ambivalent status, at once both positive and negative. In chapter one, that status will be related to the similarly ambivalent status of creative or cultural production in general, and it will be seen to be further complicated by a relation to gender. This ambivalence will be shown to cut across many of the other words which are used as synonyms or near synonyms for fashion and dress. So, while etymology will be used to shed a little light on the matter, it will be argued that the context in which these words appear must always be taken into consideration when deciding whether a garment is being understood or used as an item of fashion or clothing. The ideas of fashion and anti-fashion will be used in chapter one to try to illuminate the problems involved in rigidly defining these terms.

The following chapters will take up and develop these ideas and themes. Chapter two will continue to consider fashion and clothing as cultural phenomena; it will explain various conceptions of culture and attempt to decide which is most appropriate for the study of these topics. While the French phrase *haute couture* might translate loosely as high quality fashion design, does that mean it is necessarily high culture? Does it make any sense to speak of fashion as a cultural phenomenon if 'culture' is taken to mean a process leading to a final, perfect, point? Are fashion and clothing more properly thought of as popular or mass culture? Is fashion art, or is it, as most colleges have it, design? This chapter will also establish fashion and clothing as communication. It will explain various conceptions of communication and try to decide which one best fits the workings of fashion and dress. The idea that our clothes say something about us has become a commonplace, but what sort of communication is it and what sorts of 'somethings' does fashion say? It is clearly not spoken or written communication (even when our clothes have slogans and labels on them), but does it make any sense to speak of misunderstanding someone's clothes or of wondering what they mean by wearing those particular clothes? Chapter two will finally introduce the idea that it is not an innocent or a neutral form of communication; it will argue that power and ideology are involved.

Chapter three will develop the idea of fashion and clothing as communication. Having considered the argument that the primary, or material, functions of clothing are protection from the elements and modesty, the chapter will then look at the cultural or communicative functions of clothing. However, given that members of different cultures assume different ways of protecting themselves from the elements, might it not be the case that even these material functions have communicative aspects? Similarly, it might be that, as members of different cultures have different standards of modesty, these standards might also be communicative. A concern with the display or otherwise of the body does not preclude that display, and that body, being thoroughly meaningful and available to semiological analysis.

Having established that fashion and clothing are communicative phenomena and having explained some of the things that they communicate, chapter four will begin to explain how meanings are generated and communicated. How are we to explain that a Tattersall check shirt, for example, is smarter or more formal than a T-shirt but not as smart or formal as a plain white shirt?

The chapter will look at various potential sources of meaning (the designer, the wearer, a spectator, for example), and it will examine two types or levels of meaning, denotation and connotation. Chapter four will then argue that it is the socially agreed, and coded, differences between garments, colours, textures and so on that generate meanings. Who says that the combination 'blue and green should ne'er be seen', for example? How is it that men wearing light grey suits with brown shoes inspire such a mixture of pity and contempt? The nature of these differences and the combinations they enter into will be explained as the sources of meaning. The nature of the social agreement, the workings of power and ideology will be examined in more detail here in order to take into account the workings of hegemony, the ways in which dominant groups in society maintain their dominance.

The parts played by fashion and clothing in establishing and maintaining, or reproducing, social status will be developed in chapter five. The ways in which fashionable dress has been used to construct and establish class and gender identities and the ways in which those identities have been reproduced will be examined. Clearly, different classes and genders have different positions within society; they have differing amounts of power and they are of higher or lower status. Fashion and clothing are profoundly political as they are among the means by which those inequalities have been maintained and reproduced from one generation to the next. The ways in which Veblen sees class superiority being constructed, signalled and ensured by means of conspicuous consumption and waste of dress, for example, will be described here. And, beginning from Berger's account of the situation in which men act while women appear, the ways in which women are reduced to appearances, signs of their husband's wealth, will also be described.

To suggest that fashion and clothing are the only ways in which class and gender identities are constructed and reproduced is obviously to grossly oversimplify matters. It is simply not the case that dominant groups, be they class, gender or any other kind of group, are only dominant or are only maintaining their positions of dominance by virtue of the things they wear. These groups are always in opposition to other, subordinated, groups; they meet resistances and fashion and clothing are pre-eminently among the ways in which subordinate groups may contest and challenge prevailing identities and positions. What people wear is political in the sense that what people wear is a means of contesting and challenging class and gender identities. Chapter six will look at a number of examples of fashion being used to contest identities. For example, Punk may be seen as an attempt to oppose and challenge a dominant, middle-class view, or ideology, of beauty in women and value in jewellery. The chapter will also look at claims that working-class women in the 1950s appropriated middle-class fashions for themselves. And it will consider the ways in which women have attempted to counter or refuse what has been called 'the male gaze', challenging gender identities by means of fashion and clothing.

Chapter five considers the reproductive aspects of fashion, the ways in which what people wear constructs and maintains their identities. Chapter six considers the revolutionary, or challenging, aspects of fashion, the ways in which what people wear can contest those identities. Chapter seven will attempt to present the postmodern aspects of fashion and clothing, in which it can be argued that reproductive and revolutionary elements co-exist at the same time. This chapter will first provide a working definition of modernism and modernity and it will explain the position of fashion within these terms. It will then use the work of Jameson and Baudrillard to construct a basic account of postmodernism and postmodernity and explain the position of fashion in their terms. Derrida's notion of intertextuality will be used to argue that fashion and clothing are 'undecidable', their meanings and values (as reproductive or revolutionary, for example) being produced and destroyed at the same time. The intertextual constitution of the meanings and values associated with the stiletto heel will be used to illustrate how an item of fashion may be both enslaving (as reproductive) and liberating (as revolutionary) at the same time.

Finally chapter eight will reconsider the curious and ambiguous profiles presented by fashion and clothing and attempt to provide another explanation of them using the perspective of undecidability developed in chapter seven. It will also assess the consequences of the postmodern analyses of chapter seven for the notions of fashion and communication.

FURTHER READING

- At the end of each chapter will be found a series of bullet points, these are recommendations for further reading. They will generally be of two kinds: first, suggestions for following up the references in the text with more difficult material and, second, suggestions for authors or topics that could not be covered in the text. The **bold text** will give a clear and quick idea of what the bullet point contains.
- Elizabeth Wilson's (1985) *Adorned in Dreams: Fashion and Modernity*, Virago, is a good source of the **ambivalencies of fashion**; it is a theme that crops up throughout the book.
- The reference to **Hollywood and fashion** may be followed up by looking at Part Three of Bruzzi, S. and Church-Gibson, P. (eds) (2000) *Fashion Cultures: Theories, Explorations and Analysis*, Routledge. Classic Hollywood films and film-stars are covered, as well as more contemporary examples.
- The **global and disreputable side of fashion** may be pursued in Naomi Klein's (2000) *No Logo*, Flamingo. The websites at *www.nologo.org* and *http://adbusters.org* contain examples of how unscrupulous fashion companies and ads may be subverted.

1

ETYMOLOGIES AND DEFINITIONS OF FASHION AND CLOTHING

ETYMOLOGY

Etymology is concerned with the origins and development of the meanings of words. It is not a fashionable topic and is sometimes described as 'dry', but it is useful in that it can bring out or remind language-users of senses and meanings that words once had but which are now half-forgotten and only dimly perceived. Etymology is important in that it is useful to know what the words one is using mean and how they have come to have those meanings (see the section on fashion, clothing, power and ideology in the next chapter). An idea of the situation that can arise if one uses words without concentrating upon their different meanings can be gained from Breward (1995). On the first page of his Introduction, he uses 'adornment', 'clothing', 'fashion', 'dress', 'costume', 'style' and 'decoration' as synonyms or near synonyms for the phenomenon he is to deal with. Some will say that this does not matter, that we all know what the author means, but the use of seven different words with different meanings and associations in an opening paragraph cannot go unremarked. There is no doubt that these words are near synonyms; the purpose of the present chapter is to bring out their similarities and dissimilarities and to show how and why they are near synonyms. Etymology will show the background of words and leave users feeling that they know the word a little better because they know its background.

For an introduction to the etymology of the meaning of the word 'fashion', the *Oxford English Dictionary* is as good a place to start as any. The etymology of the word relates it back via the Latin *factio*, which means making or doing (and from which we get our word 'faction', with its political sense), to *facere*, which means to make or to do. The original senses of fashion, then, referred to activities; fashion was something that one did, unlike now, perhaps, when fashion is something that one wears. The original sense of fashion also refers to the idea of a fetish, or of fetish objects, *facere* also being the root of the word 'fetish'. And it may be that items of fashion and clothing are the most fetishised commodities produced and consumed within capitalist society. As commodities, items of fashion and clothing appear to be the clearest example of the way in which 'a definite social relation between men . . . assumes . . . the fantastic form of a relation between things' (Marx 1954: 77). Every day we make decisions about the social status and role of the people we meet based on what they are wearing: we treat their clothes as 'social hieroglyphics', to use Marx's term (1954: 79), which conceal, even as they communicate, the social position of the wearer. Fashion and clothing, that is, may be the most significant ways in which social relations between people are constructed, experienced and understood. The things that people wear give shape and colour to social distinctions and inequalities, thereby legitimating and naturalising those social distinctions and inequalities. Various ways in which what Marx called the 'fetishism of commodities' appears and is experienced will be covered in later chapters.

The *OED* lists nine different senses of the word 'fashion', ranging from 'the action or process of making', 'a particular shape or cut', 'form', through 'manner or demeanour' to 'conventional usage in dress'. These nine senses may be reduced to two main senses, the noun and the verb and, although it is difficult to be certain, both senses appear well established in English by the middle of the sixteenth century. As a noun, 'fashion' means something like a kind or a sort, or a particular make or shape, as in the definition of 'manner or demeanour' noted above. 'Fashion' here may be considered as synonymous with the word 'way' or 'manner', familiar to us in the French phrase *façon de parler*, a 'manner of speaking' and in the phrase 'Don't speak to me in that fashion'. In *King Lear*, for example, Shakespeare has Lear say to Edgar 'I do not like the fashion of your garments' and asks him to go and change them *(King Lear* III vi 1.79, in Shakespeare 1951). He means that he does not like the kind or the style of the clothes and indeed refers to them as 'Persian'.

As a verb, 'fashion' has the sense of the activity of making or doing. It is probably the case that people do not use it as a verb as often as they use it as a noun. In response to questions like, 'What are you doing?', one is more likely to receive the answer 'I am making a box pleat' than 'I am fashioning a box pleat'. This sense of the word may be found in *Othello*, for example, where Iago says that he will 'fashion' Cassio's leaving of a certain premises at a certain time. He means that he will make or cause Cassio to leave the place (*Othello* IV ii 1.236, in Shakespeare 1951). It may be that this sense of the word now has only a poetic or archaic usage, occurring occasionally in poor advertising copy or as a journalist's witty conceit (Freeman 2001: 8).

However, the situation regarding the meaning of the word 'fashion' is far from clear. In addition to the positive and negative values that may be given to the idea and practice of fashion, noted above, Polhemus and Procter have pointed out that 'in contemporary Western society, the term "fashion" is often used as a synonym of the terms "adornment", "style" and "dress"' (Polhemus and Proctor 1978: 9). There are also those who use the word as a synonym of 'clothes' or 'clothing'. It should also be pointed out that, even where it is not used as a synonym of these words, the word 'fashion' exists within a network of relations to these words, and to other words. These relations to other, different words more or less subtly shade and change the meaning of the word 'fashion'. If this chapter is to begin to define what is meant by the word 'fashion', then the relations between these terms, what it is that makes them suitable for use as synonyms, and what it is that makes them different, ought to be examined.

FASHION, STYLE, CLOTHING, DRESS

It will have been noticed that, like the word 'fashion', the words 'adorn', 'style', 'dress' and 'clothing' can also be used as either verbs or nouns. They all refer both to an activity and to either the items used in an activity or to the products of that activity. For example, one may dress oneself or somebody else in a particular way; here the word 'dress' is used as a verb, it refers to an activity. And one may put a certain dress on somebody; here the word 'dress' is used as a noun, it refers to something used in that activity. Similarly, one may wear one's hair in a certain style, where the word 'style' operates as a noun, and one may style one's hair, where it operates as a verb. This exercise can be performed with all the words noted above, and the fact that they can be used in these ways may encourage people to believe that these words are somehow more synonymous than they really are.

Consulting the *OED* again, 'dress' as a verb is defined in terms of dressing oneself 'with attention to effect' and in relation to adornment and array. As a verb, early seventeenth-century usage relates 'dress' to clothing and costume, 'Not merely to clothe but also to adorn'. And Daniel Defoe is referred to as using the word to mean to till, to cultivate and to tend crops; he writes of 'dressing the vine'. Cloth and clothing are likewise found in noun and verb forms: they are defined in terms of dressing and covering as with a garment and in terms of fabric or textiles. While there is no sense of adornment or decoration, or of dressing for effect in the entry for 'cloth'/'clothing', as is found in the entry for 'dress', it is clear that the words are to a large extent defined in terms of each other.

For it cannot be denied for very long that there is something akin to what the philosopher Ludwig Wittgenstein calls a 'family resemblance' between these words (Wittgenstein 1958: §§66–7). While there is no single meaning or sense that is common to them all, each of the terms will have something in common with at least one of the others. So, it could be said that, while all clothing is an adornment, not all adornments are fashionable. Some adornments might be terribly unfashionable. It could also be said that, while all clothing is an adornment, not all clothing is fashion, and that while all fashion is dress, not all dress is fashion, for the same reason. And it could be said that, while all fashion is adornment, not all fashion is clothing. Some fashion is tattooing or cicatrisation. Similarly, while every item of dress will be in a particular style, not every style will be the fashion, as styles go in and out of fashion. And, while every item of dress will be after a certain fashion, not all fashions will be stylish; it is well known that some fashions set out to be anti-style. It could, finally, be said that, while all fashion is in style, not all fashion is an item of dress; as noted, some fashion involves changing the colour or shape of the body.

The permutations of these terms could be multiplied and the differences in their senses explored further. But the above should give some idea of the 'complicated network of similarities overlapping and criss-crossing' that Wittgenstein refers to as family resemblances. It should also give us some idea of the difficulty involved in, if not the impossibility of, trying to provide a final or rigid definition of the meanings of any of these words. An example of the attempt to provide such a definition may be found in Roach-Higgins *et al* (eds) (1995). Here, Roach-Higgins and Eicher try to provide a 'specific' definition of the word dress. However, they are forced to define the word by distinguishing it from a network of other words like 'fashion', 'appearance', 'clothing' and so on (1995: 7–10). The point here is that there is no stand-alone definition; any and all definitions will refer to other words and gain their meaning from their place in that network, or structure, of relations. Joanne Entwistle (2000) makes another attempt to define 'fashion' and 'dress'. She defines dress as 'an activity of clothing the body with an aesthetic element (as in "adornment")' and she defines fashion as 'a specific system of dress' (2000: 48). Anne Hollander provides the same definition, suggesting that while

> everybody has to get dressed in the morning and go about the day's business . . . [w]hat everybody wears to do this has taken different forms in the West for about seven hundred years, and that is what fashion is.
>
> (Hollander 1994: 11)

Again, there is no stand-alone definition; each of the terms is defined by its relations to the other terms in the structure. There is no single sense or meaning that is common to all of the words used, in the same way that there is no one single feature that is shared by all members of a family. The differences existing between those family resemblances, which Wittgenstein neglects, prevent any simple or straightforward substitution of one of the words for another, and oblige us to investigate the context in which a word is being used before ascribing it a meaning. Wilson points out, quoting Martin, that 'It may well be true that fashion is like all "cultural phenomena, especially of a symbolic or mythic kind, [which] are curiously resistant to being imprisoned in one . . . 'meaning'"' (Wilson 1985: 10–11). It may well also be true that other words in this network like 'adornment', 'dress' and 'style' are similarly resistant.

For these reasons, it has to be said that this book is about all these things; it is about fashion, clothing, dress, adornment and style. It is simply not the case that these ideas and concepts can always be easily distinguished or separated from one another and studied discretely, apart from their relations to each other or outside of the context in which they are found. It must be our responsibility, as students of these matters, to ascertain which sense of 'fashion' or 'clothing', for example, is being used, and with what connotations, each time the words are encountered.

FASHION AND ANTI-FASHION

While it may not always be easy, or even possible sometimes, to distinguish clearly between the senses of fashion as dress or clothing or style, it may be worthwhile looking at the distinction which some commentators have tried to maintain between fashion and non-fashion, or between fashion and anti-fashion. The distinction may help to shed light on what is meant by fashion, as opposed to dress or style, by looking at what people have held fashion not to be. By looking at the differences between the terms, it may be possible to get a better idea of any positive meanings that we may already have. The distinction between fashion and anti-fashion is explored by Ted Polhemus and Lynn Procter (1978) who trace it back to the psychoanalytical approach of John Flügel, writing in 1930. It may, however, also be found in the work of the sociologist Georg Simmel (1971), writing in 1904.

In Simmel's account, 'two social tendencies are essential to the establishment of fashion' and, should either of these tendencies be absent from or lacking in a society, 'fashion will not be formed' (Simmel 1971: 301). The first of these tendencies is the need for union and the second is the need for isolation: individuals must possess the desire to be part of a larger whole, society, and they must also possess the desire to be, and to be considered as, apart from that larger whole. These conflicting needs are central to Simmel's account of fashion, as indeed they are central to his account of all social phenomena: the whole history of society, he says, is reflected in the conflict between 'adaptation to society and individual departure from its demands' (Simmel 1971: 295). Should one of these forces be absent, there will be no fashion. In fact, on Simmel's account, it is unlikely that anything like society could exist if one of these forces were absent.

As far as fashion is concerned, this is not a very startling claim. Simmel seems to be referring to the need which people have to be both part of a larger social group and yet not to be so bound up in that group that they possess no individuality. People appear to need to be social and individual at the same time, and fashion and clothing are ways in which this complex set of desires or demands may be negotiated. This is the paradox which Wilson points out when she writes that 'we want to look like our friends but not to be clones' (Wilson 1992a: 34). The point being that fashionable clothing is used in western capitalist societies to affirm both membership of various social and cultural groups and individual, personal identity. Indeed, as Wilson says, it may be that the need to distinguish oneself from everyone else is perhaps strongest with regard to the group 'to which one has the strongest affiliation' (Wilson 1992a: 34).

Thus Simmel argues that, in societies where one of these forces is absent, there is no fashion. Societies in which the 'socialising impulse' is more power-fully developed than the 'differentiating impulse', what Simmel calls 'primi-tive societies', will have little if any fashion. The 'modes of primitive races are much more stable than ours', he says, because in such societies the socialising forces which encourage individuals to adapt to the demands of society are stronger than they are in our own society (Simmel 1971: 301). There will be little encouragement to express an individuality if that individuality is subju-gated to the values and beliefs of the wider society. Consequently, there will be relatively few changes in what people wear 'because the need of new impressions . . . is far less pressing' (Simmel 1971: 302). Thus, what people in these societies wear is not fashion, it cannot strictly be called fashion on this account and should perhaps be referred to as something more neutral, like adornment or dress.

In more complex societies, with a number of clearly defined and segregated groups, presumably, the forces encouraging members of that society to sub-mit to the demands of that society are countered more strongly by the desire for individuation, and fashion can develop. What people wear can be used to express that individuality, that difference from others and other groups within society. As Simmel says, 'segregation by means of differences in clothing . . . is expedient only where the danger of absorption and obliteration exists, as is the case among highly civilised nations' (Simmel 1971: 301). While Simmel's insistence on opposing 'civilised' and 'primitive' nations, when he means either more or less complex societies (that is, societies that either are or are not made up of a number of identifiable sub-groups), is unfortunate and offensive to modern readers, the general point should be clear. What people wear in those simple societies is not fashion. It is not called non-fashion or anti-fashion by Simmel, but it is clearly not fashion as the word is used to describe what people wear in the more complex societies.

Flügel's version of this distinction is between 'fixed' and 'modish (or fash-ionable)' types of clothing and, like Simmel, he relates them to a 'certain differences of social organisation' (Flügel 1930: 129). According to Flügel, the differences between these two types of clothing may be most clearly understood in terms of their opposite relations to time and space. This is neither as difficult nor as complicated as it sounds. Basically, fixed costume 'changes slowly in time . . . but varies greatly in space' and modish costume 'changes very rapidly in time . . . but varies comparatively little in space' (Flügel 1930: 129–30).

Fixed costume varies in space because it is associated with a particular locality and with separate social bodies in their different localities. This type of dress, according to Flügel, is more likely to be found 'outside the sphere of western influence'. Because it is associated with separate social bodies, it is fairly permanent, it does not change in time to any great extent. As fixed, 'its whole value depends . . . upon its permanence' (Flügel 1930: 129). Modish costume, however, is the type of costume which 'predominates in the western world' and it does not vary in space as it is diffused throughout that western world very quickly. In that it spreads in this way, it is said to change quickly in time but not in space.

Thus, societies outside the influence of western civilisation do not wear fashion, they wear fixed dress. It is fixed in that it does not change in time and in that it is closely associated with a particular place. Western societies, however, do wear fashion. They wear fashion in that what they wear may be found all over western civilisation at one time: their clothing does not vary so much in space, as every fashionable westerner will be wearing much the same thing, the fashion. But it will vary rapidly in time: what the modish westerner is wearing will soon be replaced with something else.

Braudel presents a version of this thesis in volume one of *Civilisation and Capitalism*. He says that where society 'remained more or less stable, fashion was less likely to change' (Braudel 1981: 312), and presents China, India and the Turkish Empire in support of his case. The silk costume pictured by Father de Las Cortes in 1626, with gold embroidery and silk boots, he says, was the same as that found in eighteenth-century engravings. A traveller to China at the end of the eighteenth century remarked that 'dress is seldom altered in China from fancy or fashion' and expressed surprise that even the ladies did not follow fashion. Another late eighteenth-century traveller, Mouradj d'Ohsson, writes in the *Tableau générale de l'empire ottoman* that 'fashions which tyrannise European women hardly disturb the fair sex in the east; hair styles, cut of clothing and type of fabric there are almost always the same' (Braudel 1981: 312). Braudel's case also includes the poor. The above examples appear only to include the nobility of the particular country, but Braudel suggests that if the entire world were poor, there would likewise be no fashion. 'No wealth, no freedom of movement, no possible change. To be ignorant of fashion was the lot of the poor the world over. Their costumes, whether beautiful or homespun, remained the same' (Braudel 1981: 313). The clothes worn by the women Cortez would have seen in New Spain, long embroidered tunics, were still being worn in the eighteenth century, for example, and the Peruvian Indian's *poncho* may be seen being worn today, as it was two hundred years ago (Braudel 1981: 314).

Polhemus and Procter develop these ideas still further. They explicitly identify fixed dress with anti-fashion and modish dress with fashion. They drop all the value-laden and potentially offensive references to whether a culture is western or non-western. And they develop the analysis of the political connections between fashion, anti-fashion, different social and cultural groups, and different conceptions of time. These ideas are introduced and pursued by looking at two gowns that were the objects of much attention in 1953, Queen

Elizabeth II's coronation gown (Figure 2) and a gown from Dior's 1953 collection (Figure 3).

The Queen's coronation gown, they suggest, is 'traditional, "fixed" and anti-fashion . . . designed to function as a symbol of continuity' (Polhemus and Procter 1978: 12). Dior's 'tulip line' dress (Figure 3), however, was fashion. It 'announced that a new season had arrived' and, in being different to the 'princess line' which had preceded it in 1951, functioned as a symbol of discontinuity and change. Items of anti-fashion, like the Queen's robe, are meant to stress continuity, in this case the continuity of the monarchy and the British Empire. They are concerned with the maintenance of the status quo. Items of fashion, like Dior's dresses, are meant to emphasise discontinuity or change, and Polhemus and Procter show how the New Look of 1947 was replaced by a whole series of new looks. They show how 1951's 'princess line' was replaced by the 'tulip line', which was replaced by the 'H line' in 1954, which in turn was replaced by the 'A' line and 'Y' line of 1955 and so on (Polhemus and Procter 1978:13). Polhemus and Procter relate these two gowns and their functions to the understanding of time that they reflect. 'Time', they say, drawing on the work of the anthropologist Evans-Pritchard, 'is a socio-cultural concept which reflects and expresses a society's or a person's real or ideal social situation' (Polhemus and Procter 1978: 13). The concept of time itself can be used to express a culture's views about the world and its contents. The analyst can see, then, in a person's or a society's understanding of time, how that person sees or would like to see him/herself and how that society sees or would like to see itself. That understanding of time is itself expressed or reflected in dress: 'traditional, anti-fashion adornment is a model of time as continuity, (the maintenance of the status quo) and fashion is a model of time as change' (Polhemus and Procter 1978:13).

Consequently, it is not surprising that the Queen, who (as a direct result of her social, political and economic position) has an interest in things staying largely as they are, 'should have worn a gown that proclaims a message of continuity over hundreds of years' at her coronation. And it is not surprising that someone who wants to move up a social scale 'will use the latest fashions to reinforce and project an image of time as change and progress' (Polhemus and Procter 1978: 13). That these matters are still of interest to the British press and European public may be seen by the article from *The Guardian* newspaper, published in October 2000 (Figure 4). The headline suggests that the Queen is a 'fashion icon', while designer Mariuccia Krizia says that she 'is above fashion . . . not really a fashion lady'. Overall, the argument is that the Queen would like to see things stay the way they are and she uses anti-fashion which changes slowly, if at all, in time to express this. The social climber would like to see their position change and uses fashion, which changes rapidly in time, to express this. In this way, then, the political relations between social groups are expressed and reflected in fashion and anti-fashion in terms of their different preconceptions of time.

15

Figure 2 Queen Elizabeth II's coronation gown, 1953

It is tempting to consider other members of the English Royal family in the context of these ideas. Whatever other differences they may have had, it is tempting to consider the abundant and substantial sartorial differences between Prince Charles and Princess Diana, for example, in terms of fashion and anti-fashion. Throughout her career as Princess of Wales, Princess Diana was associated (in the British press, at least) with fashion; she was continually photographed wearing it, she created it and, indeed, was touted as a one-woman walking advertisement for, or personification of, the British fashion industry. In 1984, a book entitled *The Princess of Wales Fashion Handbook* appeared (James 1984). This book was a guide to adapting her various and

Figure 3 Christian Dior's 'tulip line' dance dress, 1953

It might not appear immediately obvious to her subjects but this woman is now regarded as a fashion icon

Wowing them in pastels and pearls

Stephen Bates in Milan

Figure 4 The Guardian newspaper article by Stephen Bates, 20 October 2000. Copyright *The Guardian*

numerous 'looks' for everyday wear by 'ordinary' women. Few things would be more unlikely than the Prince of Wales being the subject, or the object, of a similar book. On the contrary, the Prince has been associated (again in the British press, at least) with tradition, with, precisely, anti-fashion. He is always photographed wearing traditional and traditionally tailored clothing, whether it is a double-breasted suit, with light-coloured shirt, or something more sporty for the country. The Prince wears anti-fashion, and is photographed wearing anti-fashion. This fits in with his image of a traditional, land-owning aristocrat with an interest in things staying pretty much the way they are now or, indeed, were in the past. The Princess wore fashion and was constantly photographed wearing fashion. This was consistent with her image (if she may have been said to have had just one) of an upwardly mobile, modern, non-traditional young woman with an interest in changing and improving things, through her charity and humanitarian work, for example.

On this account, then, it may not be possible to define a particular piece of clothing or a specific garment as an item of fashion, but it should be possible to ascertain whether a particular piece of clothing is functioning as fashion. In the same way as a binliner, for example, is not an item of dress until someone wears it, so a garment is not an item of fashion until someone uses it to indicate their actual or ideal place in a social structure. There is no essence that a garment must partake of in order to be fashion; on this account, it may be fashion, and fashionable, at one point in time but not at another. There is nothing common to all fashion or fashionable garments, just as there is nothing that is common to all the near synonyms noted above: fashion, clothing, dress and adornment. It is only the context that allows the identification of a garment as fashion or nonfashion, as it is only the context that allows the identification of the correct meaning of these words.

Consequently, context must be used to determine whether a garment is being referred to as fashion, in the sense of indicating the wearer's desire to improve their social position in a complex, class-based society, or whether it is being referred to as clothing or dress, in the more 'anthropological' sense. Dress or clothing, while they may be used to indicate or construct membership of a social class or a person's position within a society, are not used to indicate a desire to improve that class position. They are not used to construct membership of a social class that is perceived as having a higher status.

With fashion and anti-fashion defined and explained in this way, however provisionally, these definitions and explanations may be used to analyse and explain all forms of fashion and clothing. In order to exist, fashion demands a certain kind of social organisation. That social organisation needs to be one in which there are different social classes. Those classes need, moreover, to be unequal in terms of power and status; they must exist in a hierarchy. And, as Flügel points out, social mobility, usually upward movement from class to class, needs to be both possible and desirable (Flügel 1930: 140). This is not to say that anti-fashion cannot exist in such a society, nor is it to deny that fashion can turn into anti-fashion; Polhemus and Procter spend a lot of time illuminating the ways in which anti-fashion can and does exist in complex societies. The issues surrounding fashion and social class will be dealt with in more detail in chapters five and six.

FASHION, CLOTHING AND TRIVIA I

Having thus defined fashion and distinguished it from its near synonyms, clothing, dress and adornment, this section will return to the charge that such pursuits are somehow either fraudulent or trivial, or both, fit only for the intellectually disenfranchised. Clearly, the intellectually disenfranchised are to be found in all walks of life and, until the sociologists say otherwise, the assumption that they have a particular affinity for fashion or textiles should be resisted, however attractive it may seem. There are a number of arguments against these charges. This section will examine three arguments against the triviality charge and two against the deception charge.

The idea that fashion and clothing are trivial pursuits is just one popular prejudice. Writing in the *Guardian* in 1992, Wilson notes how, 'every so often, a letter appears in The Guardian's Women's Page'. The writer of the letter is always different but, she says, the letter is always the same and it always argues that fashion is 'irrelevant to serious-minded persons' (Wilson 1992a: 34). The idea, clearly, is that there are concerns that are proper to these serious minds and that fashion is not among them; fashion is trivial and ridiculous and serious minds need not be detained by it.

Perhaps the most obvious argument against this sort of case would be to say that fashion seems to be necessary or inevitable, given the social and economic organisation of most of the world. It would be quite a feat to claim that an inevitable thing, something that appears to follow from socio-economic reality, was trivial. It would, at least, be quite a different sense of 'trivial' from what most people would understand. On Simmel's, Flügel's and Polhemus and Procter's accounts, fashion is a product of a society with more than one class in it and where upward movement between classes is both possible and desirable. Thus it would seem that, as soon as this kind of society exists, as soon as modern, capitalist society exists, fashion exists. Consequently, fashion follows, almost by definition, from this kind of socio-economic organisation and, insofar as this kind of socio-economic organisation covers increasingly large parts of the world, it is hardly appropriate to call fashion trivial.

There is another sense in which fashion is not trivial. In this sense, clothing and dress are also not trivial. That is the sense invoked in the argument that there are other, more important things to be concerned with than the shape, colour and cut of one's frock. Social justice, the starving millions, and whales are some of the things that are often held to be more important than fashion and clothing. Clearly, on one level, things do not come much more important than these, and the person who says, for example, that they would rather have a new frock than social justice is, among other things, confusing levels. However, the cut of the frock is not trivial in the way that social justice, the starving millions and whales are not trivial, in that they are all or may all be treated as cultural phenomena. They are all ways in which a group can identify and constitute itself as a cultural group: they are all topics or areas in terms of which a group may express its hopes, fears, beliefs about the world and the things in it. How a group responds to the starving millions is just as much a cultural response as the way in which it responds to the cuts of frocks, and the relative importance that it gives to these things.

The third way in which fashion, dress and clothing are not trivial concerns the idea of decoration. The notion of decoration as a function of clothing or dress will be dealt with later, in chapter three, as will protection and modesty; this section is concerned only with their use in constructing a criticism of fashion and clothing. The criticism goes along the lines that, once the real work of protection and decency has been taken care of, all fashion and clothing can do is to decorate or prettify the body. There are at least two arguments against such a criticism. The first argument is that this criticism presupposes that protection and decency are the 'real work' that clothing does and that protection and decency are the same wherever clothes are worn. Both of these presuppositions are mistaken: some people living in inhospit- able places wear so little clothing that it seems to offer no protection at all, and different cultures have different ideas of what constitutes modesty, for example. If this is the case, then modesty and protection cannot be the real work or the real reason for wearing clothes. The second argument is that this criticism presupposes that decoration or 'prettification' are also the same wherever clothes are worn. It is rather the case that what counts as decoration and 'prettification' varies from culture to culture: different cultures will give different meanings to the different things they do to decorate themselves. What one culture will call decoration, for example, another will call mutila- tion. As a cultural phenomenon, then, as a way in which a group constitutes itself as a group and communicates its beliefs, hopes and so on to other groups, decoration is not trivial.

FASHION, CLOTHING AND DECEPTION

The criticism that fashion and clothing are deceptive has two aspects. The first is that fashion and clothing are in the business of dressing something up as something else, that they take the body and disguise it or present it as something that it is not. It is the claim that fashion and clothing impose meanings on a raw material that either does not originally have any meaning or which has a sort of natural meaning. The second is that fashion and clothing may be used to mislead, to make people respond in ways that they would not or should not. The difference between these two aspects may become clear only when the responses to them are considered.

The first criticism presupposes either that there is some original, pure and meaningless thing that fashion and clothing then come along and turn into something else, or that there is some natural meaning to this original thing that fashion and clothing distort. The original, pure and meaningless thing that is intended is the body. The flaw in the claims that either the body has no meaning, that it is pure and 'neutral' in some sense, or that it has some natural meaning that is always and everywhere the same, shows up most clearly when looking at photographical or art-historical studies of the nude. As Hollander (1993), Clark (1956), and any of Mapplethorpe's collections of photographs (1983) will testify, the nude or naked human body is deeply, and sometimes shockingly, meaningful. Moreover, the meanings that are ascribed will change in time; Renoir's nudes, Man Ray's nudes, Titian's nudes, Bonnard's nudes – all mean different things. It is, therefore, very difficult to uphold the idea that there is first of all a meaningless thing that fashion and clothing then adorn and make meaningful. And it is very difficult to uphold the idea that there is any natural meaning to the body that is everywhere and always the same.

The second criticism, that fashion and clothing are deceptive in that they may be used to mislead, applies equally well to all means of communication. Dressing one thing up as another thing is, after all, not unknown in television, radio or the print media. However, it is no defence of fashion and clothing to say that everyone else is doing it, except insofar as it may be impossible to conceive of a means of communication that did not do it. If it is the lot of human communication to have to use one thing (a word, a sign, a picture, or a sound, for example) to stand for another thing, then dressing one thing up as something else seems to be a definition of communication. And, until thought transference is offered along with GCSE Level English Language, representation (using one thing to stand for something else) seems to be the lot of human communication.

A less flippant-sounding defence of fashion and clothing would be to point out that the charge of misleading and disguising one thing as another presupposes the possibility of some pure essence that could be communicated if only it were not for all those clothes and fashions. As noted above, the existence of this pure and unadorned essence is unlikely, given that even nudity and nakedness are cultural constructions, the meanings of which vary from place to place and from time to time. It also presupposes the possibility of some channel of communication that is itself neutral, that could transmit a message without transforming that message in some way. The next chapter will examine different models of communication, and the possibility of such a channel or model of communication will be seen to be remote. It will be argued that the designer, the buyer, the wearer and the audience all contribute to creating and transforming the messages that are communicated by means of fashion and clothing.

THE STUDY OF FASHION AND CLOTHING

It is tempting to try to explain the curious cultural profile enjoyed by fashion and clothing noted above. And it is tempting to suggest that the positive valuations are the result of viewing the profile from one direction, while the negative valuations are the result of viewing it from another. Before this metaphor gets out of hand, it could be claimed that fashion and clothing touch on or are relevant to the concerns of many disciplines, that they occupy or straddle many areas of study. It could then be claimed that, because of this, it is not surprising when fashion and clothing present different profiles. Because fashion and clothing impinge upon the concerns of so many disciplines, they must be studied in terms of those disciplines. But because they impinge on so many disciplines, it is hardly surprising that they look different when viewed in terms of them.

Braudel, Tickner and Wilson are all agreed that fashion and clothing are highly relevant to the concerns of many disciplines. What they do not agree on is which disciplines. Braudel, for example, suggests that 'The history of costume is less anecdotal than it would appear. It touches on every issue: raw materials, production processes, manufacturing costs, cultural stability, fashion and social hierarchy' (Braudel 1981: 311). He seems to stress the relevance of fashion and clothing to the economic and social sciences. Tickner argues that fashion is 'a rich and multidisciplinary subject, and a point at which history, economics, anthropology, sociology and psychology could be said to meet' (Tickner 1977: 56). She envisages a much wider, or at least a more detailed, list of disciplines. And Wilson tries a different metaphor, but with the same intention:

> The attempt to view fashion through several different pairs of spectacles simultaneously – of aesthetics, of social theory, of politics – may result in an obliquity of view, even of astigmatism or blurred vision, but it seems we must attempt it.
>
> (Wilson 1985: 11)

Even allowing for the fact that Braudel says that he is thinking in terms of what he calls costume, rather than of fashion or clothing, this is an enormous range of disciplines in terms of which fashion and clothing may be studied. The study of these topics is obliged to range from issues concerning production and manufacturing, to issues concerning aesthetics and politics, taking in all of the social sciences on the way. Because fashion and clothing touch on all of these disciplines, each discipline must be employed in the analysis and explanation of fashion and clothing. Yet, at the same time, because fashion and clothing touch on all these disciplines, it is to be expected that they look slightly, or even very, different when explained and analysed in terms of them.

Thus, it could be the case that a positive valuation of fashion and clothing is more likely to result from looking at them in terms of the economics of production, say, where their positive benefit to the balance of payments budget, for example, may be taken into consideration. That is, if these areas are studied in terms of their 'hard', financial role in national and world economics, it is conceivable that they will appear to be attractive propositions

23

to a certain type of person. In such cases, fashion and clothing would be likely to receive positive valuations. And it could be the case that a negative valuation of fashion and clothing is more likely to result from looking at them in the terms of history, for example, where the seemingly meaningless succession of forms for its own sake would immediately become apparent. That is, if fashion and clothing are studied in terms of their liberal, humanities relations to what is perceived, by some, as a 'soft' social science like history, then it is not unlikely that they will receive a negative valuation.

Another way of beginning to explain this cultural ambivalence may be found in the work of Raymond Williams. Creative or cultural production, he points out, 'may be valued as revelation or transcendence or dismissed as mere fancy' (Williams 1961: 35). Western thought in general, he suggests, is unsure whether to view creativity, or cultural production, as a good thing or a bad thing. Consequently what artists, or creative people in general, produce may be seen either as delusions or as illuminating a superior reality, as fancy or as revelation. This is the view of Theseus, in Shakespeare's *A Midsummer Night's Dream*, who believes that 'the lunatic, the lover and the poet/Are of imagination all compact'. He believes that they share the same imaginative or creative faculties. The lunatic sees 'more devils than vast hell can hold', the lover 'sees Helen's beauty in a brow of Egypt' and the poet gives shape, name and location to the 'airy nothing' that his imagination produces or engenders (*A Midsummer Night's Dream* V i 2–22, in Shakespeare 1951). Creativity, then, is seen as potentially dangerous lunacy and as desirable poesy at the same time; the lunatic and the lover may be dismissed as mere fancy and the poet may be fêted as transcendent for doing much the same sort of thing.

It was noted above, in the introduction, that operating within these double standards is another set of double standards, concerning gender: common sense or popular wisdom will have it that the study of clothing, fashion and textile design is an even less proper subject for male students than it is for female students to study. As Wilson points out, 'fashion is, rightly or wrongly, primarily associated with Woman' (Wilson 1990: 209). It may be argued that fashion and clothing are therefore accorded a similar profile to that enjoyed by women, that the cultural valuation given to women and feminine values is transferred, as if by metaphor, onto fashion and clothing. That is, that they are either worshipped unreasonably or dismissed as secondary. Barthes refers to this phenomenon by saying that fashion 'reproduces, on the level of clothing, the mythic situation of Women in Western civilisation, at once sublime and childlike' (Barthes 1983: 242). These are the two options open to women, sublimity or childishness, and these two options are reproduced or carried over into the realm of fashion and clothing.

They are reproduced, or carried over because, as Wilson says, fashion is commonly associated with 'Woman'. Without wishing to commit oneself to any essentialising fetishes that might be contained within the notion of 'Woman', this might be unpacked a little. It is certainly true to say that

24

women are, or the feminine is, presented in contemporary society as being close to the cosmetic arts, associated with surface display and concerned, if not continually obsessed, with appearance (Oakley 1981: 82). This is true to the extent that boys and young men who are concerned with what they look like, who worry what sort of face they present to the world, will be accused by their peers of effeminacy, if not outright homosexuality. Whereas, of course, it is perfectly acceptable in this society for women to carry mirrors everywhere in their handbags, to spend every spare moment in pubs and clubs in front of the mirror with their girlfriends and to be late every time for dates because they are still doing their hair. Car manufacturers recognise this phenomenon and have long catered for the 'always-female' passengers of their cars by inserting what is referred to as a 'vanity mirror' on the non-driver's side sun-visor. Clearly, while not always possible to take entirely seriously, the commonsense or ideological association of femininity with appearance and with looking nice is a difficult one to escape.

There are another couple of aspects to this profile which have not yet been touched upon. The first is to do with gender again and concerns the problem of what to call a genius who is a woman. The second is to do with the ways in which, in Europe at least, different activities have at different times been called art or design. Furthermore, these two aspects are not unconnected. The history of what has and has not been called art and design since the Renaissance is complicated. Sometimes a practice will be called art, or an art, and at other times it will be called design, depending on who was doing the calling and on whether they wanted to increase or decrease the status of the practice in question.

At present, it would probably be agreed that art enjoys a higher status than design in European culture. Were this not the case, there would be no need for older designers in advertising agencies to inflate their status by calling themselves artistic or creative directors. Fashion design, as a design activity, therefore enjoys a lower status than any of the so-called fine arts. Wilson has suggested that 'fashion is the degraded or unacceptable face of art' (Wilson 1990: 209); again, this is the idea that fashion and fashion design seem to present two faces, one acceptable and one not. The best thing that fashion design could do to improve its status would be to call itself an applied art, perhaps, which would at least have the benefit of getting the word 'art' into the designation. The problem, however, is that many people, including fashion designers, consider fashion design to be an art and in no need of a change of name. Angela McRobbie notes, for example, that 'the designers I interviewed all perceived themselves as artists' (1998: 6). It may be that this ambiguous status contributes to the ambivalent response of society, which is unsure whether to exalt it as art or denigrate it as design.

This ambiguity of status is related to the first aspect that was noted above, that there is a problem as to what to call a woman, artist or designer, who is a genius. The problem is alluded to in the title of Pollock and Parker's art historical work *Old Mistresses* (1981): the point they are making in using this title is that there is no simple female version of the reverential title applied to male artists and designers who are deemed to be the best. Simply reversing the title of 'Old Master' does not work as the connotations of 'mistress' are not the same as the connotations of 'master'. 'Genius', similarly, seems to be a title which does not transfer from male to female very easily in this culture. So, the concept of genius is found more often in the realms of art than of design and sits more happily on the shoulders of men than of women. Consequently, when men are engaged in cultural production, it is more likely to be referred to and valued as transcendence and revelation, and when women are engaged in cultural production, it is more likely to be dismissed as mere fancy. When men are engaged in cultural production, the results of that production are more likely to be called art, and when women are engaged in it, the results are more likely to be called craft or design (see Buckley 1986 for more on this).

CONCLUSION

The Introduction tried to raise some of the concerns of the rest of the book by considering the cultural status enjoyed by fashion and clothing in late twentieth-century western society. Fashion and clothing were seen to have an ambivalent status, at once positive and negative. In this chapter, that ambivalent status was related to the similarly ambivalent status of creative or cultural production in general, and was seen to be further complicated by a relation to gender. This ambivalence was shown to cut across, or affect, many of the other words which may be used as synonyms or near synonyms for fashion and clothing. So, while etymology was used to shed a little light on the matter, it was finally argued that the context in which these words appear must always be taken into consideration when deciding whether a garment is being understood or used as an item of fashion or clothing. Chapter two will continue the account of fashion and clothing by considering them in terms of the concepts of culture and communication.

FURTHER READING

- On **fashion and royalty**, see Cecil Beaton's essay, 'Fashions of Royalty' in Roach, M. F. and Eicher, J. B. (eds) (1965) *Dress, Adornment and the Social Order*, John Wiley.
- On **fashion, anti-fashion and non-fashion**, see also pp. 14–24 of Anne Hollander (1994) *Sex and Suits*, Kodansha International.
- For more on **definitions of dress, fashion** and so on, see Mary Ellen Roach-Higgins and Joanne B. Eicher's chapter 'Dress and Identity' in Roach-Higgins *et al.* (eds) (1995) *Dress and Identity*, Fairchild Publications.
- General fashion websites which can be investigated for information on fashion, designers and how fashion is viewed include the following:
  www.southam.com/nmc/guide/fashion.html
  www.firstview.com

2

FASHION, CLOTHING, COMMUNICATION AND CULTURE

INTRODUCTION

This chapter will begin to investigate the connections between the concepts of fashion, communication and culture. Now, for many readers, and despite what has been seen in the Introduction and chapter one, the concept of fashion will seem already to be well known and not in need of any further elucidation. Many other readers may feel the same way about the concept of communication. And there will be those who feel that the connections between fashion, communication and culture are simply too obvious. Any ten-year-old, they may say, can tell you what fashion is, communication is about sending messages, different cultures wear different fashions and if you wear bright colours, it means you are cheerful. Such might be the everyday or commonsense reactions to some of the central concerns of this chapter.

However, part of the brief of this book is to unpack or, to use a more appropriate metaphor, to unpick, what is involved in everyday or commonsense notions like fashion, clothing, communication and culture to see what is contained within them, to see how they have been constructed or put together. The words and concepts which people use to talk about fashion, dress and textiles, like items of fashion and dress themselves, are often more complicated than they at first appear. They will, for example, almost certainly have long histories of which one is not fully aware and, as Laver has pointed out in another context (in Lurie 1992: 7), the difference between appearing quaint and appearing ridiculous is but thirty years. And these words and concepts may have picked up associations in that history which commit one unawares to saying or implying things that one would not necessarily want to say or imply. So, conscientious and wise students of fashion and textiles will want to unpick, to analyse, the words and concepts used to talk about fashion just as they will want to analyse, even if they are not always allowed actually to unpick, items of fashion themselves.

This chapter, then, will elucidate the idea that fashion and clothing are means of communication. As Davis notes, 'That the clothes we wear make a statement is itself a statement that ... has virtually become a cliché'

(Solomon 1985: 15). This chapter must examine what sorts of statements clothes make, and what kinds of communication are involved. It will also critically examine different models of culture; if clothing and fashion are cultural phenomena, of what kind or model of culture are they the phenomena? And it will argue that clothing and fashion, as communication, are cultural phenomena in that culture may itself be understood as a signifying system, as the ways in which a society's experiences, values and beliefs are communicated through practices, artefacts and institutions. In order to introduce these concerns, the next section will consider the problem whether fashion is more properly thought of as art or as design: the creative and cultural aspects of fashion seem to ally it with art but the communicative and quasi-functional aspects of fashion seem to associate it with design. The limitations of both alliances will be brought out by the discussion of fashion as communication and as culture and these themes will be picked up again in chapter seven's section on fashion, art and performance.

FASHION, ART AND DESIGN

It is a paradox that the college and university subject that people study when they study fashion is more often than not called 'Fashion Design' while, as noted in chapter one, the people studying it, in art schools, more often than not perceive themselves as artists (see McRobbie 1998: 1, 6). McRobbie defines fashion design as

> the application of creative thought to the conceptualisation and exe-
> cution of items of clothing so that they can be said to display a
> formal and distinctive aesthetic coherence which takes precedence
> over function.
>
> (Ibid.: 14 and see also p. 107)

One gets a clear sense here of fashion design involving 'creative thought', a concern for the 'aesthetic' and the precedence of form over function, all the things commonly held to be peculiar to art. On this view, fashion design is as much of an art as painting or sculpture, for example. However, it is difficult to deny for long that fashion, and especially clothing, entail functional and communicative intent: Louis Sullivan's phrase 'form follows function' has long been taken as a standard definition of what constitutes design. To complicate matters, communication may be thought of as one of the functions of fashion and clothing (see the following chapter). Artefacts where the functional takes precedence over form are commonly called design and fashion design is therefore as much of a design activity as graphic- or furniture-design. For the moment, as this is not an issue which can be resolved here, it may be assumed that the communicative and functional aspects of fashion and clothing lend them the status and appearance of design activities while the aesthetic and creative aspects lend them artistic status and appearance.

The following sections will consider fashion and clothing as communication and as culture in an attempt to deal with this ambivalent status.

FASHION, CLOTHING AND COMMUNICATION

Although Davis considers that the statement that the clothes we wear make a statement to be a cliché, it is not, of course, literally true. The clothes we wear do not sit upon us or wait in the wardrobe shouting 'I'm cheerful!' or 'Open the door for me!' Nor do they whisper seductive nothings from the depths of the lingerie drawer. Davis uses Chast's 1988 cartoon from the *New Yorker Magazine* in which the hat worn by Rhonda Perlmutter III 'says' 'My favourite food is tuna' and her dress points out that 'My mother lives in Sacramento' to make the point effectively (Davis 1992: 7). Most obviously, then, fashion and clothing are forms of nonverbal communication in that they do not use spoken or written words. (It is not difficult to understand that even when garments are covered in words, as brand names or slogans for example, there is still a level of nonverbal communication that exceeds the literal meaning of those slogans or brand names. Martin's essay 'Wordrobe' considers many examples of words being used on clothing and fashion, plotting their relations to graffiti, punk, foreign languages, puns, calligraphy and the Dada and Surrealist movements, for example. The connotational meanings of the word 'Stussy' on children's clothing, for example, are entirely different to those of the words 'North Face'. Connotation will be dealt with in chapter four, as a kind, or level, of meaning.)

The question immediately arises as to whether, given that they are nonverbal forms of communication, fashion and clothing may be treated as being in some way analogous to spoken or written language. When Umberto Eco claims to be 'speaking through' his clothes, for example, he presumably means that he is using clothes to do the same sorts of things as he uses the spoken word to do in other contexts (Eco 1972: 59). Resisting the temptation to suggest a parallel with the English phrase 'speaking through one's hat', Eco's metaphor seems to suggest that clothes are assembled into something like sentences, the outfit or ensemble, in much the same way as words are assembled into sentences. In *The Language of Clothes*, Lurie appears to believe that there is a direct analogy. She says that there are many different languages of dress, each having its own vocabulary and grammar (Lurie 1992: 4). On this sort of account, clothes are the equivalent of words and may be combined into 'sentences'. Lurie suggests that a sharecropper, for example, having very few clothes, will be able to create only very few '"sentences" . . . expressing only the most basic concepts', whereas a 'fashion-leader . . . may have several hundred words at his or her disposal' and will be able to 'express a wide range of meanings' (Lurie 1992: 5).

If such a thing is possible, Lurie seems to take the metaphor of clothing being a language literally. She is of the opinion that language consists of

words, grammar and syntax and that language is only there to express concepts and meanings. This is a mechanistic view of language and meaning, and
it leads to a mechanistic account of meaning in fashion and clothing or as a
language, is not unproblematic and should not, perhaps, be pursued too far.
These aspects of meaning will be returned to and dealt with in more detail in
chapter four.

It is also unclear, from what both Eco and Lurie say in these sources, which
model of communication is being used. As Fiske points out, there are two
main schools in the study of communication and, while each would subscribe
to a general definition of communication as 'social interaction through messages', each understands that definition in a slightly different way (Fiske
1990: 2). Neither Eco nor Lurie says enough in the texts mentioned so far to
make it clear which of these two schools they favour. It was noted above that
any ten-year-old could tell you that communication is about sending
messages. Unfortunately, it is not as simple as that: in order to understand
fashion and clothing as communication it is not sufficient to understand
communication as the simple sending of messages.

It is as the sending and receiving of messages, however, that the first of the
two schools described by Fiske understands communication. The following
sketches are heavily indebted to Fiske's account of these two schools of
communication and for more detail Fiske (1990) is thoroughly and
unreservedly recommended. The first of these two schools may be referred to
as the 'process' school, as communication is conceived of as a process in
which someone says something to someone else in one or other medium or
channel with some or other effect. On this account, a garment, an item of
fashion or clothing, would be the medium or channel in which one person
would 'say' something to another person with the intention of effecting some
change in that other person.

The garment, on this account, then, is the medium in which one person
sends a message to another person. It is by means of the garment that one
person intends to communicate their message to another person. The message, on this account, is the sender's intention and it is this that is transmitted
by the garment in the communication process. The message is also, of course,
what is received by the receiver. The sorts of thing that are most important on
this account of communication are the sender's intention, the efficiency of
the transmission process and the effect on the receiver.

In this kind of account, the sender's intention is important; it is the
message, after all, and it must be in principle retrievable or discoverable. A
message that remains forever unavailable is not strictly a message and communication cannot take place under such a circumstance. The efficiency or
effectiveness of the transmission process is also important; if the message does
not arrive at the receiver or if it arrives in a different or distorted form, then a
part of the communication process, maybe the medium, is seen as having failed
in some way. And the effect on the receiver is important in that it is the effect on

the receiver that constitutes social interaction on this account; social inter-action is defined here as 'the process by which one person ... affects the behaviour, state of mind or emotional response of another' (Fiske 1990: 2).

In terms of fashion and clothing, this model may have some immediate, commonsense appeal. It seems intuitively correct to say that one sends messages about oneself with the fashions and clothes one wears. Everyday experience, in which clothes are selected according to what one will be doing that day, what mood one is in, whom one expects to meet and so on, appears to confirm the view that fashions and clothing are used to send messages about oneself to others. There are various problems with this model, however. There is the question as to who is the sender of the message. Common sense might suggest that it is the wearer of the garment, but the designer might also be said to have a claim, in that it was their intentions that informed the production of the garment in the first place. The notion that wearer and designer constitute a sort of co-sender raises more problems than it solves, in that the process in which an agreement with regard to intentions could be reached does not seem to exist.

It is also difficult to understand what might be meant by the idea of a communication failure or breakdown when considering clothing and fashion. It could be claimed that, even if the intention of the designer or the wearer does not reach the receiver, that receiver will always manage to construct some meaning for the garment or outfit. It does not seem to be the case that anyone ever thinks that someone else is wearing something meaningless. Nor does one look at someone's clothes and think, 'I wonder what they mean by that?'. And, while the idea that social interaction is about the reciprocal affecting of behaviour by individuals has a certain everyday plausibility, it does presuppose that those individuals are already, or have already become, social members of a community, before or outside of that mutual affecting of behaviour. As Cherry says, 'A group of people, a society, a culture, I would define as "people in communication"' (Cherry 1957: 4).

It is on this latter point, perhaps, that the second school or model of communication differs most clearly from the first. This second model may be called 'semiotic' or 'structuralist' (O'Sullivan *et al.* 1994: 50), and, as Fiske points out,

> semiotics ... defines social interaction as that which constitutes the individual as a member of a particular culture or society.
>
> (Fiske 1990: 2–3)

That is, communication makes an individual into a member of a community; communication as 'social interaction through messages' constitutes an individual as a member of a group. Rather than a member of a group communicating with other members of the group, as in the first model, it is communication between individuals that 'first' makes them into members of a cultural group. Douglas and Isherwood suggest, in *The World of Goods*, that man needs goods for communicating with others and for making sense of what is going on around him. The two needs are but one, for communication can only be formed in a structured system of meanings.

(Douglas and Isherwood 1979: 95)

They imply, first, that fashion and clothing may be used to make sense of the world and the things and people in it, that they are communicative phenomena. Second, they imply that the structured system of meanings, a culture, enables individuals to construct an identity by means of communication.

The two models differ also on the matter of what communication is. It was noted above how the process model saw communication as the sending and receiving of messages; the semiotic or structuralist model understands communication as 'the production and exchange of meanings' (Fiske 1990: 2). The difference here is entirely analogous to the difference noted above. On the process model, meanings pre-exist the process of communicating them. On the semiotic model, it is the process of communication that produces or generates meanings. As Fiske points out, the semiotic model 'is concerned with how messages, or texts, interact with people in order to produce meanings' (Fiske 1990: 2).

On this model, the role of the sender or transmitter of messages is less important than it is in the process model; it should probably be said that, strictly, there is no sender until the sender, like the receiver, is constituted in the production of meanings. Any idea of the sender is gained only from the interaction of texts and readers. In this sense, the semiotic model concentrates on the negotiation of meanings rather than the receiving of messages and, consequently, there is a rather different significance given to the notion of misunderstanding or communication breakdown. If the production of meanings is the result of negotiation between senders, readers, their cultural experiences and texts, then it will hardly be surprising if different readers from different cultural backgrounds produce different meanings or readings of texts. Nor will those different readings be seen as evidence of communicative failure; they are only to be expected on the semiotic model.

In terms of fashion and clothing, this model also seems to possess some plausibility. For example, taking the point concerning communication as social interaction constituting an individual as a member of a cultural group, rather than that individual being a member of a group and then interacting socially, it seems clear that wearing 'cropped hair, braces, short, wide, Levi jeans or functional sta-prest trousers, plain or striped button-down Ben Sherman shirts and highly polished Doctor Marten boots' (Hebdige 1979: 55) constitutes or produces one as a late 1960s skinhead. It is not the case that an individual is first a skinhead and then wears all the gear, but that the gear constitutes the individual as a skinhead. It is the social interacting, by means of the clothing, that produces the individual as a member of the group rather than vice-versa, that one is a member of the group and then interacts socially.

32

Youth groups of the late 1980s, like Raggas, Goths, Bendies, Ravers and Casuals, may also be used to exemplify this process. It is the wearing of the baggy, rolled up trousers, puffa jacket, baseball cap and expensive trainers that constitutes someone as a Ragga rather than that one is a Ragga and then goes out to get the clothes.

The semiotic model also seems more plausible on the matter of how meanings are generated. In using negotiation to explain the generation of meanings, this model escapes the problems noted above with regard to the process model. It is no longer the case that either the designer or the wearer or the spectator of the garment is the source of the intentions that provide the meanings; on the semiotic model, meanings are the result of negotiation between these roles. It cannot be a literal negotiation, of course, with the various readers sitting around a table. And the effects of the different readers in the 'negotiation' being in positions of dominance and subservience with regard to each other must not be forgotten. But that is in effect what happens as each reader (who can, in effect, be either the designer, the wearer or a spectator) brings their own cultural experience and expectations to bear on the garment in the production and exchange of meanings. Meanings are generated, then, and positions of relative power established in and through the process of communication.

To say that the meanings of a piece of clothing are the result of a constantly shifting negotiation, and that they cannot escape the influence of differing positions of dominance and subservience, seems intuitively to reflect more accurately what happens when people talk about the meanings of garments. This production and exchange of meanings may be seen quite clearly in the process whereby *haute couture* or catwalk creations are adopted and adapted by high street chains and eventually by the manufacturers of home sewing kits. It is clearly the case here that the meanings of the original garment are given numerous interpretations by numerous cultural producers and that the garment ends up with a set of meanings different from those it began with. If it were the case that the meaning was already in the garment and that the wearer used the garment simply to transmit that meaning, this kind of appropriation and reinterpretation would not be possible.

FASHION, CLOTHING AND CULTURE

Many of these issues will be considered in a little more detail in chapter four, but the previous section attempted to show that fashion, dress and clothing are forms of communication. It also tried to give some idea as to what sort of communication they are and to show that the matter is not as simple as saying that communication is about sending messages. At present it is as much, if not more, of a commonplace to say that fashion, clothing and dress are cultural phenomena, as it is to say that clothes make a statement. This section must look at different conceptions of culture in order to be able to say what kind of cultural phenomena fashion, clothing and dress are.

In *Keywords*, Raymond Williams suggests that 'culture is one of the two or three most complicated words in the English language' (Williams 1976: 76). In *Culture*, he distinguishes three senses of the word. The first is the sense in which one speaks of 'a cultured person' and refers to the developed state of mind. The second is the sense in which one speaks of culture and means specific cultural activities or interests. And the third refers to the means of these processes, in which sense one speaks of the arts and intellectual works (Williams 1981:11). The list of senses to be found in *Keywords* is slightly different to that found in *Culture*, and does not necessarily overlap exactly with it, a fact which may well bear out Williams' claims regarding its complicatedness.

Ultimately, the word 'culture' comes from the Latin word *colere*, meaning to inhabit, to cultivate, to protect and to honour with worship. From this word, the word *cultura* developed. *Cultura* referred mainly to the ideas of cultivation and tending; the earliest uses of the word 'culture' in English in the early fifteenth century, stressed this idea of looking after crops or animals. It seems to have meant what is meant today by agriculture, *ager* and *agri* being the Latin words for field/s or land/s. It is fascinating to note that, even at this early point in the history of the word, there is a metaphorical connection being made in people's minds between the notion of dress and the notion of culture. It will be recalled from chapter one how Defoe uses the word 'dress' to refer to the tending of plant growth, in this case vines.

The ideas that are central to this conception of culture are those of process, production and refinement. These early senses of culture, in the more familiar sense of agriculture, refer to a process: there is a beginning, when the seeds are sown, a middle, when the seeds develop and grow, and an end, when the crop is mature and ready for harvest. They also refer to the notion of production, with the emphasis either on the process of production or on the end product of that process. It is as if the whole process of production makes sense only in terms of the end product, the thing or things that are produced. This emphasis may still be seen in modern uses of the phrase 'garden produce'. And these early senses cannot avoid the implication of 'deliberate tending of "natural" stock to transform it into a desired "cultivar" – a strain with selected, refined or improved characteristics' (O'Sullivan *et al.* 1994: 69). Bearing in mind another warning from Williams that the changes in the meaning of the word 'culture' are both complicated and intricate, it seems that this sense of culture was 'extended to a process of human development' (Williams 1976: 77).

Williams claims that from the early sixteenth century the word 'culture' began this metaphorical slide from one area of human experience to another. Where people were used to the idea of the word 'culture' relating to tending crops and animals, they began to get used to the idea of 'culture' relating to the 'process of human development'. Thus the earliest uses of 'culture' in the sense of human culture were metaphorical; the familiar use of a word was coopted to describe something with which people were less familiar. It is important to note that the central ideas of that conception of culture were also transferred from one area of experience to the other. Thus, when people began talking of culture as human development, the idea of process, of production, they stressed the end products of that process and the idea of refinement and improvement. The latter is something still found today when people speak of 'improving' literature, for example, or of 'refining and improving one's mind' or manners, or of a 'cultured person'.

Consequently, a particular conception of human culture became common and Williams suggests that it was dominant from the sixteenth century until the early nineteenth century. This conception of culture combines elements from what Williams elsewhere calls the 'ideal' and the 'documentary' conceptions of culture (Williams 1961: 57). On the 'ideal' model, culture is conceived in terms of a process, of having more or less developed or mature forms. Culture here is a 'state or process of human perfection' (Williams 1961: 57). It is conceived in such a way that an end point, an ideal, may be thought of and in terms of which all other cultures may be measured and judged. This point is worth emphasising: the presence of an end point, a point at which development can go no further, in the conception of culture makes possible the comparison of cultures. The culture which is held to be at that end point may be used as the standard by which to judge others as either deviant or immature. On the 'documentary' model, culture is conceived as a set of what may be termed 'edited highlights' from that process. All the best, most interesting and illuminating pieces of art, literature and music are collected together on this view and called 'culture'. As Williams says, on this conception, culture is 'the body of intellectual and imaginative work' in which human experience is recorded (Williams 1961: 57).

On this view of culture, it is unlikely that fashion, dress or indeed any form of adornment would count as culture. Certainly, if the word 'fashion' is intended in the sense of 'the fashionable' then there seems very little chance that it could be considered as culture when 'culture' is used in the sense of a final point in a process of increasing refinement or cultivation. The sense of perpetual change, which some would discern as being essential to the very idea of fashion, appears by definition to rule out the idea of fashion having reached such a final point. Ulrich Lehmann, for example, argues that 'fashion ... does not follow an evolutionary path progressing from one form to a higher incarnation' (1999: 301); if it does not follow such a path, then there can be no end point to fashion. In a fascinating discussion, Baudrillard describes fashion as a perpetual cycle, an endless process of innovation, explicitly relating it to culture in general in this very regard (1981: 79). Others might argue that fashion, dress and adornment are simply too trivial or unimportant to be considered as cultural phenomena. On this view of culture, it would be only too easy to rule out fashion and adornment as culture on the grounds that they are hardly intellectual or imaginative works which illuminate the dark recesses of the human condition. The argument here is the deeply elitist one that fashion and adornment are not art; they are not painting, sculpture, literature or music and thus cannot be counted as the highest and most refined products of the human mind. (Parenthetically; they are the easiest of targets, but Ernst Gombrich's *The Story of Art* and Kenneth Clark's *Civilisation* both fail to discuss fashion, dress, costume or clothing, even when what the people in the paintings and sculptures are wearing is the most obvious and striking thing about the paintings and sculptures. Both of these authors employ an elitist and in Clark's case, explicitly idealist, concept of culture: see chapter one of Barnard 1998 for more on this).

There is, however, another conception of culture, one which Williams suggests was introduced in the late eighteenth century but which did not become fully established until the early twentieth century (Williams 1976: 79). This is the conception of culture associated with the name of Herder. Herder argued that nothing was more 'deceptive' than the application of the word 'culture' to all nations and periods because it implied that culture was the same sort of thing, consisting in the same sort of activities and to be judged by the same standards in all these different nations and periods (in Williams 1976: 79). He was arguing against what Williams calls a unilinear conception of culture and in favour of a multilinear conception of it. What Herder thought had happened by the end of the eighteenth century was that eighteenth-century Europe believed itself to be at the end point of culture. Conceiving its own culture as the final and most refined, the most mature point of a process, eighteenth-century Europe therefore thought itself to be in a position to judge all other cultures in terms of its own standards.

The metaphor of human culture as a process, involving a growth to maturity along a proper line of development, had committed the late eighteenth century to a particular way of thinking. If the model is one of development, other cultures may be criticised for being retarded or immature in their development. If the model is one of proper progression along a line of development, other cultures may be condemned for not developing along that proper line; they may be censured for being deviant. Late eighteenth-century European culture had such a model or conception of culture, thus it could condemn other cultures as either immature or deviant.

Thus Herder argued that it was necessary to speak of many different lines of cultural development. He was proposing a multilinear conception of culture, where each line was as valid and as interesting in its own terms as any other. As Williams says, Herder argued that it was necessary to speak of cultures

> in the plural: the specific and variable cultures of different nations and periods, but also the specific and variable cultures of social and economic groups within a nation.
>
> (Williams 1976: 79)

On this conception of culture, culture is a 'way of life'. It may be the way of life of different nations or times. Or it may be the way of life of different

36

groups existing within a nation or a time. Clearly, this conception is in some conflict with the previous conception. It is not possible, for example, to use the conception of culture as a way of life as a standard of excellence by means of which to judge other cultures (Hebdige 1979: 7). The plurality of this conception means that each culture has activities and standards that are specific to it, and the standards of one cannot be used to judge the activities of another. This opens up the possibility of including many more practices and activities as cultural practices and activities than was possible on the unilinear conception. The idea is that all these cultures are relative to one another; there is not one single culture that supposedly stands outside of those relations and acts as a standard or measure for all the other cultures.

There is another feature of this conception that should be noted. It is that according to this pluralist conception of culture,

> culture is a description of a particular way of life, which expresses certain meanings and values, not only in art and learning but also in institutions and ordinary behaviour.
>
> (Williams 1961: 57)

The multilinear conception of culture not only encompasses different lines of cultural development, but it also includes a wider range of things as culture than does the unilinear conception. Whereas the unilinear conception included only the best of the arts, fine art, music and literature, what Arnold called 'the best that has been thought and said in the world' (Arnold 1964: 19), the multilinear conception includes 'institutions and ordinary behaviour' as well. Thus this conception does not consist only in the 'edited highlights' that characterised the unilinear conception but it also includes ordinary, everyday behaviour, performed by ordinary, everyday people. Thus, it includes not just what has been called, by a privileged minority, the 'best' that has been produced in a few limited areas of human experience, but also the whole range of what has been thought of as ordinary and everyday experience.

On this multilinear conception of culture, therefore, fashion, dress and adornment certainly would count as culture. If, as T. S. Eliot says, culture

> includes all the characteristic activities and interests of a people Derby Day, Henley Regatta, Cowes, the twelfth of August, a cup final, the dog races, the pin table, the dart board, Wensleydale cheese, boiled cabbage cut into sections, beetroot in vinegar, nineteenth century Gothic churches and the music of Elgar
>
> (Eliot 1975: 298)

then it would be hard to understand how fashion, dress and adornment can be left out. Indeed, it is curious to note that Eliot omits fashion and dress from his list. Similarly, the idea that there is no final and fully mature point from which other cultures may be judged is consistent with the idea of fashion and dress being a potentially endless series of creative responses and variations in clothing. The ideas of change and difference, which may be seen as elements of any definition of fashion and dress, are compatible with the definition of culture as a way of life which changes and differs both between and within different social and economic groups. And, given Eliot's quote above, fashion, dress and adornment cannot be left out of this definition of culture on the grounds that they are not one of the fine arts, because none of the things in that list is one of the fine arts either.

It was noted above that the term 'culture' was descriptive of 'a particular way of life, which expresses certain meanings and values' (Williams 1961: 57). This, however, is to neglect an important element in the conception of culture. In the same way that fashion and dress were seen above, not simply to express messages, but rather to be constitutive of social relations, so culture and cultural practices are not simply expressive of meanings and values but, as Williams says, they are rather constitutive of a social order. These practices and products are not 'derived', as Williams has it, from a social order that is already there. Rather, these practices and products are 'major elements in its constitution' (Williams 1981: 12–13). It is not the case that there are social groups already existing in positions of relative power who then use cultural practices and production to reflect those positions. Those practices and production constitute them as social groups and in those positions of relative power.

Culture, on this view is 'the signifying system through which . . . a social order is communicated, reproduced, experienced and explored' (Williams 1981:13). Fashion, dress and adornment are now to be conceived as some of the signifying practices of everyday life (along with the arts, philosophy, journalism and advertising, for example), which go to make up culture as a general signifying system. Fashion and clothing are some of the ways, then, in which the social order is experienced, explored, communicated and reproduced. As noted above, it is not the case that there is already in existence a society with different cultural groups, who are already in positions of relative power, who then use fashion, clothing and dress to express or reflect those positions. Fashion, clothing and dress are signifying practices, they are ways of generating meanings, which produce and reproduce those cultural groups along with their positions of relative power.

These issues will come up again later, in the chapter on class. But it is worth stressing here that fashion and clothing are not used simply to indicate or refer to social and cultural positions; they are used to construct and mark out that social and cultural reality in the first place. As such, the conception of fashion and clothing explored here bears similarities to the notion of material culture, explained by people like Daniel Miller (1987) and Tim Dant (1999). For Dant, material culture is conceived as the things in the world 'incorporated into social interaction' and embodying the social structures within which we all live (1999: 2). He argues that society cannot be understood independently of the material culture, including fashion and dress, used within it and that 'there is a system of relationships between ideas and values, material things (clothes) and people' (Ibid.: 107). He also argues that things we live with, products and objects, tie us to others in society, 'providing a means of sharing values, activities and styles of life' (Ibid.: 2) (See his chapter five, 'Wearing it Out: Written and Material Clothing' for more on this). The work of Veblen will be seen, in chapter five, to describe how fashion and clothing may be used to indicate social position. The point here is that it is through fashion and clothing that we are constituted as social and cultural beings, that we decode our social and cultural milieu.

Thus this section has argued that clothing and fashion, as communication, are cultural phenomena in that culture may itself be understood as a signifying system, as the ways in which a society's beliefs, values, ideas and experiences are communicated through practices, artefacts and institutions. In this case, fashion, clothing and dress are the artefacts, practices and institutions that constitute a society's beliefs, values, ideas and experiences. According to this view, fashion, dress and clothing are ways in which people communicate, not only things like feeling and mood, but also the values, hopes and beliefs of the social groups of which they are members (see O'Sullivan *et al.* (eds) 1994: 74–5 for more on this). They are, then, the ways in which society is produced and reproduced: it is not that people are first members of groups and then communicate their membership, but that membership is negotiated and established through communication. Fashion, dress and clothing are thus constitutive of those social groups, and of the identities of individuals within those groups, rather than merely reflective of them.

FASHION, CLOTHING, POWER AND IDEOLOGY

Fashion and clothing have been explained or 'unpicked' as forms of communication. And they have been explained or 'unpicked' as forms of cultural production. While communication has been explained in terms of social interaction and with reference to negotiation and interpretation, it is still tempting to view communication as an innocent activity. And while cultural production has been explained in terms of different ways of life and with reference to the constitution of social, cultural and individual identities, it is still tempting to see cultural production as a neutral enterprise. It is possible, that is, to view these different interpretations, ways of life and identities as happily co-existing, as all being equally valid and accorded equal respect. It is possible, therefore, to view the designing and wearing of fashion and clothing as innocent forms of communication or as neutral cultural activities. And it is even possible, therefore, to see the designing and wearing of fashion and clothing as enabling the peaceful co-existence of different interpretations and ways of life.

There are a number of reasons why taking these views and falling into these temptations would be mistaken. Even the etymology of the word 'fashion' should warn against these views and temptations. It was noted above in chapter one that the word 'fashion' is related to the Latin word *factio*, from which the modern word 'faction' derives. 'Faction' has an obviously political sense; it already refers to conflict between groups and to the possession and exercise of power by different groups. It may even have connotations of an avant-garde, a radical sub-cultural group who do not necessarily agree with the larger or mainstream culture and who struggle against it. This may seem to some to be highly appropriate, given that the subject here is fashion and clothing. While arguments from etymology conventionally receive a poor reception, the presence of such a political sense in the family of the word 'fashion' should not be ignored. It is in the sense of already containing reference to the operations and workings of power that fashion and clothing as communicative and cultural phenomena are said to be not innocent or not neutral.

More convincing, perhaps, is the argument proposed by Douglas and Isherwood, who say that 'goods are neutral, their uses are social; they can be used as fences or bridges' (Douglas and Isherwood 1979:12). This is the argument that, while individual items of fashion or clothing may be neutral or innocent, the uses to which they are put, the functions they fulfil, are not. The uses and functions of garments are social and cultural and therefore neither neutral nor innocent. Douglas and Isherwood reduce the uses or functions to two basic forms, fences or bridges. These metaphors are presumably meant to express the combinative and the divisive aspects of goods and may be compared with Simmel's 'differentiating' and 'socialising' forces noted above in chapter one. Clearly, fences are there to separate territories or to keep people apart, they are employed to ensure that difference remains difference. Bridges, however, are there to join or connect territories, they enable people to meet, to merge and to share identities. Thus, considered as fences, items of fashion and clothing delineate one group from another, they ensure that one identity remains separate from and different to another identity. And considered as bridges, items of fashion and clothing enable members of a group to share their common identity, they provide a way or place of meeting. Although Douglas and Isherwood say that goods may be used as fences or bridges: it is surely the case that items of fashion and clothing may be used as fences and bridges; fashion and clothing delineate one group from another at the same time as they identify common values within a group. In an article in the *Guardian* newspaper, a person describing himself as a 'Trendy Bendy' says that he would probably 'leave the room' if it contained only Raggas and Goths as he says he would 'know we wouldn't get along' (Neustatter 1992: 31). His clothes form bridges with other members of his own group but they form fences between his group and other groups, like Raggas and Goths.

Another way of looking at this matter would be to propose a 'strong' version of Douglas and Isherwood's argument. In this strong version, the

40

metaphors turn military: items of fashion and clothing are no longer seen as fences and bridges but rather as weapons and defences. The process that items of fashion and clothing are part of is not seen as one of differentiation and identification but rather as a form of struggle, or even warfare, in which groups fight for domination and supremacy. It was noted above that culture is constitutive of a social order; on this account, culture represents the various different areas of struggle where positions of relative power in that social order are constantly fought and re-fought. It was also noted above that culture could be seen as a signifying system through which that social order was communicated and reproduced; on this account, positions of relative power within that social order are also disputed and challenged. Meanings communicated by means of this signifying system may also be refused or contested and the social order challenged by means of fashion and clothing. Fashion and clothing, then, may be understood as weapons and defences used by the different groups that go to make up a social order, a social hierarchy, in achieving, challenging or sustaining positions of dominance and supremacy.

Reference was made above to 'groups'. Any complex society will, by definition, consist of a number of different groups and, as was seen above, unless such a complex society exists, fashion will not exist. These groups may be class, race, sex or gender groups, for example, and each will occupy a position in the hierarchy of the social order; each will exist in positions of dominance or subservience with regard to other groups within the social order. It is claimed that fashion and clothing are used, not only to constitute and communicate a position in that social order, but also to challenge and contest positions of relative power within it. The ideas, beliefs and values of groups, which are expressed in fashion and clothing, and which are used to challenge the beliefs, values, ideas and experiences of other groups, may be referred to as those groups' ideologies. The concept of ideology is a very complex one and it will be defined more closely later. For our purposes here, however, ideology may be defined as the set of beliefs, values and ideas about the world and the things in it which is characteristic of, or peculiar to, a social group. Fashion and clothing are used as weapons and defences in that they express the ideologies held by social groups which may be opposed to the ideologies of other groups in the social order.

Reference was also made above to social groups being in positions of dominance and subservience relative to one another. The ideologies which are associated with those groups may be said also to be either dominant or subordinate. Marx and Engels wrote in *The German Ideology* that

> the ideas of the ruling class are in every epoch the ruling ideas, i.e. the class which is the ruling *material* force of society is at the same time its ruling *intellectual* force.
>
> (Marx and Engels 1970: 64)

41

By the 'ruling material force' is meant the class which has control over the technologies, materials, machinery and labour power that are involved in the production of fashion and clothing. The social class which has these things at its disposal will be dominant, not only in social and economic terms, in what Marx calls 'material' terms, but also in terms of ideas, in terms of ideology. Similarly, any class that does not have these things at its disposal will be subordinate, not only in social and economic terms, but also in terms of ideas. Fashion and clothing, as cultural phenomena, may now be understood as practices and institutions in which class relations and class differences are made meaningful.

Angela McRobbie explores these aspects of fashion as cultural production in her *British Fashion Design* (1998). She begins from what she sees as the unconvincing equation of designing and designing for capitalism, the proposal that fashion designers, for example, are simply 'working for capitalism' (1998: 1).This is the idea that fashion design is unproblematically and thoughtlessly furthering and reproducing the operations and class identities of the capitalist market, without providing any critical or challenging energy. Fashion and clothing are therefore not only ways in which social groups are constituted as social groups and by means of which they communicate their identity. It is another aspect of ideology that it ensures the functioning of a system of dominant and subservient positions within a social order. Fashion and clothing are ideological, then, in that they are also part of the process in which social groups establish, sustain and reproduce positions of power, relations of dominance and subservience. They are, moreover, part of the process in which those positions of dominance and subservience are made to appear entirely natural, proper and legitimate. The positions of dominance and subservience are made to appear natural and legitimate, not only to those in positions of dominance, but also to those in positions of subservience. If the positions of dominance and subservience appear and are experienced as legitimate and natural, then they can be accepted, or consented to, not only by those in positions of dominance, but also by those in positions of subservience. That is, fashion and clothing are ways in which inequalities of social and economic status are made to appear right and legitimate, and therefore acceptable, not only to those in positions of dominance, but also to those in positions of subservience. The term used to describe this situation is 'hegemony'.

While subsequent chapters, notably those on class and gender, will deal with these issues in much more detail, an example or two may make some of them a little clearer. Forty describes how, in eighteenth-century England, printed cottons were relatively expensive and were worn only by the more affluent middle- and upper-class women. With the development of the cotton industry in Lancashire in the early nineteenth century, however, these printed cottons became cheaper and working-class women could afford to buy the new cotton dress material for themselves. Consequently, by 1818, a draper in London could report that these cotton prints were worn principally by servants and the lower classes. In response, the middle and upper classes abandoned printed cotton dress material in favour of 'plain white dresses . . . inspired, it was said, by the wish to imitate the form of classical figures' (Forty 1986: 73–5). While printed cotton was expensive, the middle and upper classes were happy to use it to differentiate themselves from their social inferiors; they were happy to use it to show how different their experience and understanding of the world was from the lower classes. When printed cotton became cheaper, the lower classes found that they could use it to challenge and subvert the position of superiority enjoyed by the upper classes; they could use it to undermine the difference between the classes. Thus, the upper classes were forced to find something else with which to re-establish their difference and signify their superiority.

What is happening in this example is that fashion and clothing are being used to make the differences in power and status that exist between the lower and the upper classes appear to be legitimate and proper. The differences in power and status between these groups are actually the result of a series of historical accidents, the result of the things that people have done, but fashion and clothing have the function of making them appear to be legitimate, right and almost the work of nature rather than people. Marx even uses fashion and clothing as an example to make just this point. Having lambasted Proudhon as a philosopher for seeing things upside-down, he then takes issue with Proudhon as an economist: he asserts that while Proudhon understands 'that men make cloth, linen, silk-stuffs, in certain determinate relations of production . . . he has not understood . . . that these determinate social relations are just as much produced by men as are cloth, linen etc' (Marx 1975: 102). Fashion and clothing, then, are part of the process in which a social group's experience of the social order is constructed. In this case they are part of the process in which the unequal distribution of power within that social order is experienced as legitimate.

The above example clearly shows how Douglas and Isherwood's ideas of fences and bridges might be applied to fashion and clothing, the lower classes establishing a bridge, by wearing printed cottons like their social superiors, and the upper classes in response building a fence, by wearing plainer cottons, unlike their social inferiors. It also shows quite clearly how the upper classes are keen, if not desperate, to naturalise their higher status by means of fashion and clothing. They have an interest in winning the consent of the lower classes to their own superior status. And one way of achieving this consent is to represent the status difference in terms of fashion and clothing. A difference of social status is made to appear on the level of fashion and clothing and is thus rendered visible, acceptable. What it does not show so clearly is that a group's ideas are expressed in their fashions and clothing, and that these ideas often exist in conflict, that hegemony is a sort of moving battle that must constantly be fought, if necessary, in a number of different places. What it also perhaps does not show so clearly is the challenge made by the lower status group to the social position of the higher status group.

The example of punk may be understood as a more explicitly ideological phenomenon. It is possible to see, in the use of lavatory chains, bin-liners, safety pins, '"cheap" trashy fabrics . . . vulgar designs . . . and "nasty" colours' documented by Hebdige (1979: 107), an ideological assault on the aesthetic values of dominant classes, if not capitalism itself (Figure 5). Chains, bin-liners and safety pins are not used by the dominant classes as decoration, clothing and jewellery, nor are they necessarily worn in the places on the body that the dominant classes would wear decoration and jewellery. The fabrics, colours and designs are only cheap, vulgar and nasty to a particular group of people and, in employing them to construct a series of punk looks, punk may be seen as opposing the values of that particular group of people. Similarly, as Hebdige says, 'conventional ideas of prettiness were jettisoned along with traditional feminine lore of cosmetics' (Hebdige 1979:107). What had been traditional, conventional and dominant ideas and beliefs about prettiness, and feminine prettiness in particular, were abandoned in favour of a completely different set of ideas and beliefs In these ways, fashion and clothing are used as ideological weapons in a struggle between social groups. One set of ideas, an ideology, is set against another set of ideas, another ideology.

What is happening in this example is that different ideas and beliefs about aesthetics, for example, are being expressed by means of fashion and clothing. The dominant classes have one set of ideas and beliefs, the dominant ideology, and, while they might share many of the beliefs of the dominant ideology (otherwise it would not be dominant), the subservient classes may also have a different set of ideas and beliefs: both ideologies can find expression in fashion and clothing. Punk is using fashion and clothing to challenge the dominant ideology and to contest the distribution of power in the social order. The way punk is doing this is by drawing attention to the unnaturalness of the dominant class's conceptions of beauty, to show that these conceptions have been thought up by people by thinking up alternative conceptions. If the dominant ideology can be shown to be a conception operating in the interest of only one class, then its legitimacy and its naturalness may be drawn into question. To do this is to show that what the dominant ideology presents as legitimate and natural is in fact no more legitimate or natural than any other conception.

A more recent example may be found in hip-hop. Alan Light (1999) suggests that in the early 1990s the group Public Enemy 'redefined . . . the very role pop musicians could play in contemporary culture' (1999: 165), articulating 'the sociopolitical frustrations of not just the ghetto but the black middle class as well' (Ibid.: 167). There was a fashionable edge to the challenge hip-hop provided, early Run-D.M.C. being notorious for rejecting the 'rah-rah fashionistas . . . [and] their champagne, diamonds and cocaine' (Wilbekin in Light (ed.) 1999: 277). The use of sports wear (trainers/sneakers, hoodies and

Figure 5 Punks and policemen, early 1980s

tracksuits, for example), of dookie/Dukie ropes of gold chain and of intri-
cately razor-cut hair (the effect of which is difficult to reproduce for whites),
may be seen as a challenge to mainstream white middle-class styles. Young,
ghetto-based black youth used fashion and music to challenge dominant
white, middle-class ideologies.

There is a further complication to this situation that should be pointed out
here. It is that, being a continually moving battle, the working of hegemony
does not stop with punk's or hip-hop's challenge. Punk- and hip-hop-
inspired or related fashions may be found in any high street. Chanel took the

45

gold ropes and incorporated them into catwalk fashion in 1991 and Tommy Hilfiger used Coolio, Raekwon and Sean Combs as models in the mid-1990s. The dominant classes and the dominant ideologies have recuperated the objects and items and the meanings of the objects and items. The trappings of punk and hip-hop have become or been made into commodities and, some would say, if it was ever upset, the balance of power has been truly re-established in the favour of the dominant classes.

This section claims to have shown how fashion and clothing, in addition to being forms of cultural production and communication, are ideological phenomena involved in the establishing and reproduction of positions and relations of power. To see fashion and clothing solely in terms of their being communicative or cultural phenomena is to limit one's perspective to that of structuralism or semiology. It has been pointed out as one of the failings of structuralism, if not semiology, that it does not or cannot deal on its own with matters like the workings of power. Thody recalls the Sorbonne students of 1968, for example, who claimed that *'Le structuralisme ne descend pas dans la rue'*, which he translates as saying that 'structuralism is no street fighter' (Thody 1977: 108). The addition of something like an account of ideology to the analytic tools of semiology is necessary in order to provide anything like a complete account of these phenomena. The account will be developed in more detail in chapter four, where Barthes' account of myth will be used to complement the introductory account of ideology found here and in chapters five and six, where these issues will be looked at from the perspective of social class and gender.

FASHION, CLOTHING AND TRIVIA II

We may now be in a position to shed some more light on the debate concerning the curious status of fashion and clothing in contemporary culture. It was noted in the Introduction that fashion and clothing could be seen or valued in two ways: they could be given a positive value and be seen as attractive and useful, or they could be given a negative value and be seen as trivial and deceptive. The preceding discussion and Williams (1961) in particular may be able to help in explaining the curious cultural profile enjoyed by fashion and clothing noted in the Introduction. The negative view dismisses fashion as inferior, as trivial, as creating false or misguided desires and as perpetuating false and misguided views, as being cosmetic and synthetic.

But on Williams' account, the designing and wearing of fashions and clothing may be seen as versions or forms of creativity. According to Williams, the arts, within which fashion design may be placed, are seen as cultural production. As such, fashion and clothing are productive of the world in which we live. They are in this sense, along with all other creative production, productive of the everyday reality which we experience and pass on. To dismiss fashion and clothing on the grounds that they are or encourage deceitfulness or triviality can only make sense if, beyond fashion and cloth-ing, there is a separate reality against which the deceitful and trivial appear-ances of fashion and clothing could be measured. If it is the case that fashion and clothing, as creativity or cultural production, are part of the ways in which a world is created, experienced and passed on, then there can be no separate reality. As Williams says, 'the contrast between art and reality can be seen, finally, as a false meaning' (Williams 1961: 35).

Much the same argument can be made on the basis of, or in the terms of, the above discussion of power and ideology. The claims that fashion and clothing are trivial and deceptive, and that they create and reproduce false desires and views, for example, may be expressed in terms of ideology. It may be claimed, then, that insofar as the desires and views of and for fashion and clothing are the products of ideology, they are deceptive and misleading. The dominant ideology has been seen to be partial in the sense of only permitting an incomplete understanding of phenomena and also of being the view of only one class. Consequently any views and desires concerning fashion and clothing that are the product of this ideology will by definition be partial, deceptive and misleading. Another way of putting this case would be to say that insofar as the ideas, beliefs and values expressed by items of fashion and clothing are the product of a class position, they are ideological and therefore deceptive.

Much the same response to these arguments can be made as was made above to the arguments concerning creativity. The arguments regarding ideology only make sense on the basis of there being something outside of ideology, against which the charges of deception or triviality could be meas-ured. It makes no sense to claim that fashion and clothing are deceptive or misleading but then to offer no standards against which to judge the decep-tion. Similarly, it makes no sense to claim that fashion and clothing are trivial and then to offer no standards against which to judge what is and is not trivial. If there is no such 'outside' to ideology then there is nowhere for non-ideological standards to come from. And, insofar as ideology is constitutive of experience, insofar as it gives meaning to objects and events, then there does not seem to be an outside to ideology that would make any sense to us. As Williams might say, the contrast between ideology and reality may be seen as a false meaning.

Finally, then, the curious cultural profile enjoyed by fashion and clothing may be understood as the result of a conflict between the desire for there to be a 'beyond' to ideology, for there to be a place where class divisions, for example, are absent, and the realisation that there can be no such beyond. Those who see fashion and clothing as trivial and deceptive, and who bemoan their shallow and exploitative natures, are those who desire such a beyond. Those who see fashion and clothing as evidence of creativity and cultural production are those who realise that there is no such beyond and who are happy to enjoy the play of cultural difference as it is found in fashion and clothing.

CONCLUSION

This chapter has established fashion and clothing as cultural and communicative phenomena. It has shown how, and in what sense, fashion and clothing are cultural phenomena and it has explained the sense of culture that is being used. Fashion and clothing are cultural in the sense that they are some of the ways in which a group constructs and communicates its identity. They are two of the ways in which the values and identities of groups may be communicated both to other groups and also to members of those groups. It has also been shown how, and in what sense, fashion and clothing are communicative. They are communicative in that they are non-verbal ways in which meanings and values are produced and exchanged. On this account, then, culture and communication are very closely linked; indeed, culture may even be said to be a communicative phenomenon. In this way, culture has been explained in terms of communication. The idea that fashion and clothing, as cultural and communicative phenomena, are intimately bound up with matters of power and status was introduced and explained in terms of ideology. And the ambivalent response of western societies to fashion and clothing, where fashion and clothing are at once both attractive and somehow repugnant, was explained in terms of a relation to the workings of ideology.

FURTHER READING

- Fiske, J. (1990) *Introduction to Communication Studies*, Routledge, contains one of the best accounts of **semiology and communication**. Section one of Corner, J. and Hawthorn, J. (eds) (1980), *Communication Studies*, Edward Arnold, contains a number of different perspectives on what communication might be.
- Williams, R. (1976) *Keywords*, Fontana, and (1981), *Culture*, Fontana/Collins, are the best places to start investigating the matter of **culture**, and Billington, R. *et al.* (1991) *Culture and Society*, Macmillan, is not a bad way of continuing.
- I am reluctant to recommend my own work here, but the **question whether fashion is art or design** may be considered in the light of chapter one of my (1998) *Art, Design and Visual Culture*, Macmillan. Guy Julier discusses the definition of design in his (2000) *The Culture of Design*, Sage. The matter is further discussed by Sung Bok Kim (1998) 'Is Fashion Art?' in *Fashion Theory*, Volume 2, Issue 1, pp. 51–72, who argues that fashion is art because the notions of art and fashion have been widened to include each other.
- Davis, F. (1992), *Fashion, Culture and Identity*, University of Chicago Press, is quite close to some of the concerns of this chapter, especially in the first chapter, 'Do clothes speak? What makes them fashion?'. Davis does not, however, go into nearly as much detail on the matters of either **culture or communication** as the present chapter. Tim Dant's (1999) *Material Culture in the Social World*, Open University Press extends the notion of fashion and clothing as communication and looks at the ways in which they are 'lived', the ways in which the individual and the individual's body changes the clothes whilst they are being worn and washed, for example, and at how this makes them an instance of material culture.
- For more general information on hip-hop, try the following website, and the one recommended at the end of chapter seven: http://rap.about.com/mbody.htm

3

THE FUNCTIONS OF FASHION
AND CLOTHING

INTRODUCTION

The previous chapters have provided a definition of what fashion and clothing might be and of the possible differences between them. Fashion and
clothing were defined or looked at in terms of communication and culture.
The present chapter will concentrate on what fashion and clothing might be
for, on the different functions or jobs that fashion and clothing might have.
Another way of posing these questions would be to ask the reasons why
people adorn their bodies, why people wear and have worn clothes. It will be
noted that, while it makes sense to ask these questions of clothing or dress, it
does not always make sense, or the same sort of sense, to ask them of fashion.
The chapter will provisionally, and for the sake of argument, separate the
material functions of fashion and dress from their cultural functions.
Material functions are those connected with protection and modesty and
cultural functions are to do with communication. As with all such distinctions, there is a flaw here in that the material functions also have a cultural
function: what a culture chooses to protect itself from and the ways in which
it does so with dress are also ways in which that culture communicates its
identity as a culture. It is not the case that the material functions are
unchanging and do not vary between cultures. As will be seen, which parts of
the body need to be covered in the name of modesty and what they should be
covered with will vary from culture to culture. The material functions also
have a cultural function and serve to construct and communicate cultural
identity.

In *Sartor Resartus*, which was originally published periodically between
1833 and 1834, Thomas Carlyle reports how Teufelsdröckh, Professor of
Things in General, imagines that the 'first purpose of Clothes . . . was not
warmth or decency, but ornament' (see Keenan 2001a). 'The first spiritual
want of a barbarous man is Decoration; as indeed we still see among the
barbarous classes in civilised countries' (Carlyle 1987: 30–1). A little later,
however, the Professor seems to be claiming a rhetorical function for clothes.
He describes two individuals, 'one dressed in fine Red, the other in coarse

49

threadbare Blue: Red says to Blue "Be hanged and anatomised"; Blue hears with a shudder and . . . marches sorrowfully to the gallows' (Carlyle 1987: 47–8). Teufelsdröckh then wonders, 'How is this?' How can this happen when Red has no physical hold or threat over Blue? What has happened is that Blue has accepted the necessity of performing an action that is ultimately prejudicial to him, seemingly on the basis of what Red is wearing. What Red is wearing performs what must be among the strongest of rhetorical functions. The Professor provides the answer:

> Thinking reader, the reason seems to me twofold: First that *Man is* a *spirit*, and bound by invisible bonds to *All Men;* Secondly, that *he wears Clothes*, which are the visible emblems of that fact. Has not your Red, hanging individual, a horsehair wig, squirrel skins and a plush gown; whereby all mortals know that he is a JUDGE?
>
> (Carlyle 1987: 48)

Leaving aside for the moment the claim that 'all' mortals would know that Red is a Judge (for, clearly, only those who were members of the society in which it had been agreed that these colours and materials signify 'Judge' would know this), two things are worth extracting from this passage. The first is that clothes here are clearly fulfilling a rhetorical function: they are convincing Blue that he should obey Red who is telling him to be hanged and anatomised. The second is the identification of clothes as the visible emblems of the invisible bonds between all men. Again, on the proviso that the word 'men' in this passage is shorthand for 'humanity' or 'all members of a community', it is clear that Teufelsdröckh considers clothes to have a role in the production and reproduction of society. Indeed, he says 'Society, which the more I think of it astonishes me the more, is founded upon Cloth' (Carlyle 1987: 48).

The claim, that society is founded upon cloth, is quite a claim to make. What it means is that part of the role or function of cloth, of dress or clothing in this context, is to make society possible, to be part of the production and reproduction of positions of relative power within a society. What Red and Blue are wearing in Teufelsdröckh's example produces their positions of relative power and authority. It will be noted that this is a completely different claim to the claim that positions of relative authority or status are merely reflected by clothing, by what people wear. And it can be noted what a powerful counter-argument it provides to popular ideas, considered in the Introduction, concerning the triviality or the relative unimportance of fashion and clothing: it is hardly trivial for society to be founded upon cloth, as Teufelsdröckh suggests. Many of the issues raised here will be returned to in chapters five and six where fashion, clothing, social class and the production and reproduction of society will be investigated.

MATERIAL FUNCTIONS

PROTECTION

With warmth, decency and ornament, however, Carlyle's imaginary Professor has hit upon some of the functions most commonly attributed to clothing. The next three sections will consider each of them in turn. In *The Language of Clothes*, Lurie continues her pursuit of the metaphor of clothing as a language by arguing that 'we put on clothing for some of the same reasons as we speak'; these are to make life easier, to 'proclaim or disguise' our identity and to attract sexual attention. They are also, as she points out, essentially the same reasons as proposed by Laver in his 'Principles of Utility, Hierarchy and Seduction' (Lurie 1992: 27). While other chapters in the book deal with 'fashion and status' and 'fashion and sex', the section on 'why we wear clothes' in *The Language of Clothes* considers the idea of utility solely in terms of protective clothing. Clothing is seen as offering protection from the weather and some anecdotal examples concerning how protective clothing may become fashionable are provided. No attempt is made to account for how clothing communicates or disguises identity.

Like Lurie's, Rouse's account of why people wear clothes in *Understanding Fashion* (1989) refers to protection, modesty and attraction, but Rouse also includes communication as a major function of clothing, offering more detail and more analysis. Rouse's account of protection begins with the Functionalist anthropologist Malinowski, who argued that things like shelter were cultural responses to basic physical needs. In the case of shelter, the basic physical need is that of bodily comfort and as Polhemus and Procter point out, this basic need for bodily comfort 'prompts people throughout the world to create various forms of shelter' (Polhemus and Procter 1978: 9). These various forms of shelter may range from igloos to grass huts to three-bedroom semis and from umbrellas to clothing. According to this view, clothing, although not necessarily fashion, is a response to a physical need for protection and shelter.

Flügel devotes the whole of chapter four of *The Psychology of Clothes* to the notion of protection and clothing, despite arguing in chapter one that, as a motive or reason for clothing, protection 'has few if any advocates' (Flügel 1930: 16). To be fair, however, he does debate more fully whether protection or decoration is the primary motivation for clothing in the course of chapter four. The chapter is nothing if not exhaustive, covering surely all of the things, both material and immaterial, that clothing could possibly be conceived as protecting body and soul from. Clothing protects the body from the cold, the heat, 'accidents incidental to dangerous occupations and sports' (Flügel 1930: 70–1), human or animal enemies, and physical or psychological dangers.

These psychological dangers are manifold, including a whole range of 'magical and spiritual agencies' which may be warded off with the aid of amulets and other magical adornments (Flügel 1930: 71). Moral dangers may also be avoided by the use of thick, dark-coloured and stiff clothing, such as a monk's habit. This may sound implausible, but a Hasidic Jew seems to back Flügel up on this point. He said that 'Hasidic clothing serve [s] as a guard and a shield from sin and obscenity' (Poll 1965: 146; also in Roach-Higgins *et al.* (eds) 1995: 221–35). Finally, there is a more general way in which clothing may be said to offer protection and that is as protection 'against the general unfriendliness of the world as a whole' or 'as a reassurance against the lack of love' (Flügel 1930: 77). Flügel manages to link this function to 'womb fantasies', fantasies of returning to the 'warm, enveloping and protecting home where we spent the first nine months of our existence' (Flügel 1930: 77). It may be that similar feelings are also engendered by 'favourite' items of clothing; of course, one is not actually protected from traffic accidents or the ill will of others, but such items may make one feel protected in this way.

As both Rouse and Flügel realise, however, there are various problems involved in saying that there are basic human needs to which clothing is the cultural response. One problem is that different cultures make different responses to those needs. Some cultures are so different from that of late twentieth-century Europe that it may even be difficult to recognise that they are responding to a basic need for protection at all. Both Rouse and Flügel use the example of the Yaggans or Yahgans of Tierra del Fuego, who were visited by Charles Darwin, to show how tenuous is the connection between clothing and the need for protection. According to Flügel,

> Darwin's often-quoted observation of the snow melting on the skins of these hardy savages seems to have brought home to a somewhat startled nineteenth-century generation that their own snug garments, however cosy and desirable they might appear, were not inexorably required by the necessities of the human constitution.
>
> (Flügel 1930: 16–17)

Wilson is less charitable towards Darwin and the rest of the nineteenth-century generation who, she says, would have seen these 'savages' being naked in the snow only as 'further evidence of their idiocy' (Wilson 1985: 55). The point is made, however, that the link between clothing and protection from inclement weather is not a natural one, even if it was not strictly necessary to go all the way to Tierra del Fuego to find an example; the Ancient Britons, for example, are well known for wearing only woad, and the Picts are so called because they decorated their bodies with tattoos or pictures.

It might also be worth pointing out that it is not only between different societies and cultures that the response to the need for protection from the weather will vary: variation can be found, even within the same culture, in the response to the 'need' for protection. There are groups of young men in the cities of the north-east of England, for example, who display almost 'Fuegian' indifference to the cold, walking the streets in the bitterest cold with only a T-shirt for protection. Rouse refers to girls in the 1960s, who would brave snow drifts and below-freezing temperatures dressed only 'in the briefest of mini skirts and coats' (Rouse 1989: 2–3). Given these arguments, it would certainly be unwise to argue too strongly that protection is the most important function of clothing. This is not to suggest that nobody ever wears an item of dress for protection, that would clearly be absurd, but variation within cultures and between different cultures as to what constitutes protection caution against seeing protection as the prime function of clothing.

MODESTY AND CONCEALMENT

The cases for and against modesty as the prime reason for wearing clothes bear some resemblance to the arguments noted above concerning protection. The argument for modesty revolves around the idea that certain body parts are indecent or shameful and should be covered so that they cannot be seen. Both Flügel and Rouse locate the origin of attitudes such as this within the Judaeo-Christian tradition. Flügel argues that a great increase in modesty occurred after the collapse of the Graeco-Roman civilisation. This increase was the result of the influence of Christianity, which places great emphasis on the soul as opposed to the body. As Flügel points out, Christianity teaches that paying attention to the care and luxury of the body is 'prejudicial to the salvation of the soul', and one of the best ways of diverting attention from the body is to hide it (Flügel 1930: 57). Hiding the body by means of clothes thus becomes associated with the desire to avoid feelings of sin and shamefulness.

Rouse takes a slightly different approach, relating the wearing of clothes to the understanding of the Genesis story in the Bible. Before the Fall, Adam and Eve 'were both naked . . . and they were not ashamed' (Genesis 2: 5, quoted in Rouse 1989: 8). After Adam and Eve had eaten the fruit of the Tree of Knowledge, 'the eyes of both of them were opened and they knew that they were naked; and they sewed fig-leaves together and made themselves aprons' (Rouse 1989: 8). Here it is explicitly the case that humanity's recognition of nakedness as a shameful condition leads to the wearing of clothes. This quote may also be used to introduce the idea that one of the functions of clothing, if not always of fashion, is to distinguish masculine from feminine: Steele quotes Merriam's humorous account of Adam's 'manly, rugged . . . outdoor' style fig-leaf in contrast with Eve's 'dainty, feminine, definitely slimming' fig-leaf (Kidwell and Steele 1989: 6).

Vivienne Westwood's 'fig leaf' body stocking (Figure 6) makes explicit play with notions of modesty and concealment. Indeed, there is a case for discussing it under the next heading for this chapter, immodesty and attraction. The body stocking features a strategically placed representation of a fig leaf, such

Figure 6 Vivienne Westwood 'Fig Leaf' body stocking from 1989 'Voyage to Cythera' collection, courtesy of Vivienne Westwood

that modesty is preserved and the wearer is 'decent'. But the very existence of the fig leaf draws the gaze inevitably to the female vagina, so that the effect is one of display, rather than modesty.

Rouse suggests that for a long time the story of Adam and Eve in the Garden of Eden was believed to be literally true; that this was actually what happened. Hard as this might be to believe, it explains the actions of many Western Europeans, and of many Western European missionaries, in judging new civilisations and cultures on the basis of whether they wore clothes and, if so, how far they approximated to western styles. As Brown points out 'early missionaries often encouraged their converts to adopt western dress' (in Roach and Eicher 1965: 10). Polhemus and Procter recount how, having been introduced to 'snug ... cosy' clothing by Darwin and the others on the *Beagle*, the 'savages' of Tierra del Fuego suffered ill-health and a decline in population. They imply that the clothing and the ill-health were not unconnected (Polhemus and Procter 1978: 10).

The case against modesty as the main function of clothing is succinctly made by Brown: 'There is', she says, '. . . . no essential connection between clothing and modesty since every society has its own conception of modest dress and behaviour' (in Roach and Eicher 1965: 10). This is not to say, of course, that there are no conceptions of shame or modesty, but rather that those conceptions will be different in different cultures. There is no definition of modesty or shame that is natural or essential and therefore found in all cultures. So, while some form of self-adornment may well be a 'necessary sign of full humanity' (Hollander 1993: 83), what counts as proper adornment will vary from culture to culture. It might also be pointed out that, even within the same culture or society, different interpretations of modesty or decency will be found.

Examples of the cultural relativity of notions of modesty or shame abound. Hoebel recounts a 'favoured tale among anthropologists' which concerns the somewhat dubious practices of Baron von Nordenskiold on one of his Amazonian expeditions. The Baron wanted to buy the labrets or facial plugs of a Botocudo woman,

> who stood all unabashed in customary nudity before him. Only irresistible offers of trade goods at long last tempted her to remove and hand over her labrets. When thus stripped of her proper raiment, she fled in shame and confusion into the jungle.
>
> (in Roach and Eicher 1965: 16–17)

Polhemus and Procter tell a similar story concerning Masai women, 'whose genitals are covered only by an absurdly brief leather skirt' but who would be 'overcome with shame' if anyone, even their husbands, should see them without their brass earrings (Polhemus and Procter 1978:10).

Examples of the relativity of notions of modesty or shame within a culture might include Rouse's example of underwear. She argues that if 'we'

55

(presumably meaning late twentieth-century Europeans, although gender is not clear) were to appear wearing our underwear while sitting on the bus, we would still feel embarrassed and indecent, even though the prohibited parts of our bodies were covered and we were 'theoretically decent' (Rouse 1989: 8). The gender of 'we' is significant in this regard if the offence of appearing in public without any clothes on is considered. Men who appear naked in public can be charged with indecent exposure, but women will be charged with causing a breach of the peace. Indecency is relative here in that only men's nakedness is considered indecent by law.

Hoebel concludes that

> Such circumstances make it perfectly clear that the use of clothing does not rise out of any innate sense of modesty, but that modesty results from customary habits of clothing or ornamentation of the body and its parts.
>
> (in Roach and Eicher 1965: 17)

This sounds counter-intuitive, that modesty is a result of wearing clothes rather than a reason for wearing them, but it is a point with which Rouse also agrees. Using the example of young children, who are 'conspicuously lacking in a sense of modesty', often to the intense embarrassment of their parents, Rouse points out that children have to be taught which parts of their bodies are shameful and therefore need to be covered (Rouse 1989: 9). Learnt behaviour is cultural behaviour and cannot possibly be the result of nature or essence. This point may be used to add a further gloss to Carlyle's point, about society being founded on cloth (see pp.49–50); society is founded upon cloth insofar as socialisation into the standards of modesty through adornment is required in order that an individual becomes a member of a society, and thus that society continues or is reproduced.

There would appear to be one or two forms of concealment that are not necessarily to do with modesty. As Holman points out, some dress or clothing performs the function of camouflage (Holman 1980: 8). It is not only military dress or uniform that performs this function; Holman suggests that cosmetics which hide blemishes on the skin, 'deodorants whose smell masks body odours' and clothing which obscures the shape of body parts may all be considered to be camouflaging something in some way. All are making something, a blemish, a smell or a feature, either not appear at all or appear smaller or less obtrusive, by means of covering or masking. It may be worth speculating that more clothing and fashion than one might originally suspect performs this function. It was, after all, Beau Brummell, the leader of early nineteenth-century fashion and personification of fashionable clothing, who suggested that if John Bull turns to observe your clothing then you are not well dressed. Some fashion and clothing have the function of camouflaging the wearer in order that they do not draw attention to themselves. The suggestion is, then, that more fashion and clothing than might be suspected are worn simply to 'fit in' with those around one, and in such cases the name for that clothing might as well be 'camouflage'. In these instances, garments are being worn in order that attention is *not* drawn to the wearer.

IMMODESTY AND ATTRACTION

It should come as no surprise to learn that exactly the opposite theory of the function of clothing to that based upon modesty has also been proposed. On this account, the motivation for wearing clothes is precisely that of immodesty or exhibitionism. People have argued that it is the job of clothing to attract attention to the body rather than to deflect or repel that attention. The body, then, is more openly on display according to the immodesty argument, rather than being hidden or disguised, as it is according to the modesty argument. It may be of interest to note that, where the modesty argument stressed that a move towards full or proper humanity was accomplished with the wearing of clothes, the arguments concerning immodesty stress the move towards a more animal-like status that is accomplished by wearing clothes. Arguments that stressed modesty as a function of fashion and clothing emphasised the humanity of the wearer; arguments that stress immodesty tend to emphasize the animality of the wearer.

Rudofsky, for example, is explicit on this matter; he argues that 'man's and animal's clothes serve much the same purpose sexual selection' (in Rouse 1989:11). The equation of man with animal is unproblematic for Rudofsky, even to the point where he feels happy referring to the stuff that animals are covered with (fur, hair and feathers) as 'clothes'. The only difference, it seems, is that roles are reversed between the animal and human worlds. In what Rudofsky calls the 'animal kingdom', it is the male who appears in great finery, and uses it to attract a mate. In human society, however, he thinks that it is the female 'who has to track and ensnare the male by looking seductive' (in Rouse 1989: 11). Clothing as well as fashion are explained by reference to the need for women to attract a mate. According to Rudofsky the woman has to keep her mate 'perpetually excited by changing her shape and colours' (in Rouse 1989: 11). This is one of the few occasions thus far that fashion, as opposed to dress or clothing, has been made available to analysis in terms of function.

Rouse also reports Laver's attempts to explain clothing in terms of immodesty or display. Laver employs what he calls the Seduction Principle, the Utility Principle and the Hierarchical Principle in these attempts (see p.51). The first and last of these principles are used to explain the differences in the sorts of display that are achieved by men's and women's dress. Women's clothes, he says, are 'governed' by the Seduction Principle and men's clothes are 'governed' by the Hierarchical Principle (in Rouse 1989: 12). That is, women's clothes are intended to make the wearer more attractive to the opposite sex because, throughout history and prehistory, men have selected 'partners in life' on the basis of the woman's attractiveness. Men's clothes, however, are intended to display and 'enhance social status' because women, 'for the greater part of human history', have selected their life partners on the basis of their ability to 'maintain and protect a family' (in Rouse 1989: 12). So, women's clothes display the woman's sexual attractiveness and men's clothes display the man's social status.

Rudofsky's and Laver's positions have also been associated with what has become known as the 'theory of the shifting erogenous zone'. This is the idea that clothing, and in some cases fashion, is the result of the ways in which different areas of the body are seen as attractive at different times in history. Flügel, for example, claims that a culture's sexual interest in the female anatomy continually shifts from one part to another, now the bust, now the behind, now the legs and so on. He claims that these shifts are reflected in the ways in which fashions change (Flügel 1930: 160; cf. Laver 1969b: 241). Vivienne Westwood's mid-1990s experiments with bustles might be seen as an attempt to shift attention to women's bottoms, as opposed to their breasts or legs, in the interests of accentuating a 'new' erogenous zone.

There are various problems with this type of account, not the least of which is demonstrated by the example of the 'fig leaf' body stocking, discussed above, where notions of modesty and immodesty seem to collapse into each other and make themselves present at the same time in the same garment. (This example raises the possibility of garments being ambivalent, or, as will be argued in chapter seven, undecidable.) It is also often unclear whether reference is being made to all clothing or only women's clothing. And, if it is said to be fashion that is explained by the theory, then it is often difficult to see where the definition of fashion as change ends and the shifting erogenous zone begins. As Steele argues, 'in the past, men wore clothing that was at least as erotic and extravagant as women's clothing' and 'yet no one has suggested that changes in men's fashions reflected . . . shifting sexual interests on the part of women' (Steele 1985: 35). She might also have pointed out that, as men wear or wore erotic dress, so women wear and have worn dress that has marked their social or political status. Steele herself seems to be unsure here whether it is clothing or fashion that is to be explained by these shifting erogenous zones, but the point is made that there seems to be some asymmetry between the treatment afforded to men and women with regard to their clothes. The argument here is that, if it is men's clothes and fashions that are to be explained, then why have the fluctuations in women's interests in the male anatomy not been chronicled?

Steele also argues that, while it is 'perfectly plausible that different fashions could emphasize different parts of the body', it is not to say that the changes reflect 'society's shifting interest in these various parts of the body' (Steele 1985: 36). She says that fashion has more to do with the way in which one style comes after another, as some kind of almost 'natural' progression which adheres to the particular rules of modesty in vogue at the time, than it does

58

with the perceived attractiveness of a part of the body. If it is indeed fashion that is to be explained, as opposed to dress or clothing, then it is very easy to make the mistake of identifying changes in women's fashion as a culture's changing interest in different parts of women's anatomy.

Finally, Rouse is surely correct to suggest that explanations of either clothing or fashion of this type 'show a considerable disregard for historical accuracy' (Rouse 1989: 12). There have been many periods in history when men have worn extremely elaborate and attractive clothing. And, as noted above, it is hardly unknown for women to dress in such a way that their social status is displayed and enhanced, whether that status is high or low. One might also point out that, in the same way as modesty and concealment vary from culture to culture, so too do immodesty and display. While not wishing to deny that a lot of clothing, and fashion, is intended to display and enhance the sexual or social attractiveness of both men and women, it cannot be denied that many non-European cultures set little or no store by such displays. Nor can it be denied that there is variation as to what counts as sexual or social attractiveness between those cultures that do.

But it is probably the set of assumptions regarding the natural or essential behaviour of men and women that is most offensive in both of these accounts. Both assume that there are modes or patterns of behaviour that are natural to men and women, and that they are natural to them in the same way as behaviour is natural to animals. Thus they assume that it is natural for women to be decorative and seductive. They both assume that it is the natural role for men to be seduced by female beauty and then to want only to look after these seductive creatures. As Rouse says, 'clothing cannot be reduced to a mere trigger for a biological mating instinct' (Rouse 1989: 15). It might be worth pointing out that these types of accounts also seem to be firmly heterosexualist, in the sense that none of them conceives of the possibility that men and women might wear some clothing to attract sexual partners of the same sex.

CULTURAL FUNCTIONS

COMMUNICATION

In the previous chapter, fashion, clothing and dress were said to be cultural phenomena insofar as they were signifying practices. They were, that is, some of the ways in which a social order was experienced and communicated. So, by means of fashion, dress and clothing, an individual's position in that social order was experienced and communicated. And there is a sense in which all of the examples used so far have presupposed a communicative function. Roach and Eicher point out, for example, that fashion and clothing symbolically tie a community together (Roach and Eicher 1979: 18). It is suggested that social agreement on what will be worn is itself a social bond which in turn reinforces other social bonds. The unifying function of fashion and clothing serves to communicate membership of a cultural group both to those who are members of it and to those who are not.

In terms of protection against the elements, the Yaggans, with snow melting on their skins, are experiencing and communicating their place in a particular social order just as much, and in much the same way, as the Europeans with their snug and cosy garments. The Masai women, with their seemingly absurdly brief skirts and brass earrings (see p.55), are also communicating their membership of a cultural group and in much the same way as European women, who will also take certain precautions against immodesty while wearing absurdly brief skirts. Protection, camouflage, modesty and immodesty are all ways of communicating a position in a cultural and social order, both to the other members of those orders and to those outside them. This section will look at fashion, dress and clothing in terms of their communicative functions.

Holman's essay 'Apparel as communication' (Holman 1980) is fairly comprehensive on these matters. It provides an exhaustive, although not very detailed, taxonomy of the functions of apparel and is written from a social-psychological standpoint. Roach and Eicher's essay, 'The language of personal adornment' (Roach and Eicher 1979) is both comprehensive and detailed. It covers the matter of communication and clothing from an anthropological standpoint. The following account is heavily indebted to Roach and Eicher, who identify ten kinds of information which clothing may be used to communicate.

INDIVIDUALISTIC EXPRESSION

The relation between clothing, or fashion, and the idea of individual expression is more complex than may at first appear, and is dealt with in more detail in chapter four. This section is not concerned with explaining how clothes express, but with the different types of thing which they may be said to express. It was noted in the introduction to chapter two that one kind of popular prejudice concerning fashion, clothing and communication involved beliefs concerning the link between colours and moods. It cannot be denied that clothing and fashion may be used to 'reflect . . . reinforce, disguise or create mood' (Roach and Eicher 1979: 8). Bright, contrasting colours may reflect light-heartedness, at least in parts of the West. Linear contrast, where lines change direction or intersect, may also be used to reflect inner dynamism. As Roach and Eicher say, 'thus, at least for Americans, contrasting line and colour can express exuberant mood to others and also reinforce the same mood in the wearer' (Roach and Eicher 1979: 8).

The wearing of what are perceived as happy, joyous lines and colours may be used in the attempt to change a person's mood, from down-hearted and melancholic, for example. The purchasing and wearing of new clothes is an increasingly well-documented way in which some people attempt to alter their mood. It is increasingly well documented as it seems that more and more people are becoming 'addicted' to the feelings they get when they do wear something new. Those feelings may be of increased or reinforced uniqueness or of pleasure in presenting a different appearance to the world, and it is not difficult to understand the appeal of those feelings to certain people. Individuals may also derive aesthetic pleasure from either 'creating personal display' or from appreciating that of others (Roach and Eicher 1979: 7), although these aesthetic qualities will inevitably be given non-aesthetic meanings. They will be interpreted or used to stand for things that are not simply to do with aesthetics: these will be dealt with in chapter four.

Simmel's argument that fashion depends upon the conflict between 'adaptation to society and individual departure from its demands' (Simmel 1971: 295) is also relevant at this point (see p.13). Roach and Eicher suggest that the emotional survival of humans somehow depends upon their ability to strike a balance between conforming to society and preserving a sense of self-identity. Fashion and clothing are ways in which individuals can differentiate themselves as individuals and declare some form of uniqueness. Clothes that are rare, either because they are very old or very new, for example, may be used to create and express an individual's uniqueness. Clothes that are neither very old nor very new, and which are moreover mass-produced, may also be used to create this effect. By combining different items and different types of items, individual and, indeed, unique dress may be effected. The ways in which these types of difference and combinations work to produce meaning will be introduced and fully explained as 'syntagmatic' and 'paradigmatic' differences and combinations in chapter four. They may also be seen and followed up in the account of bricolage, the use of odds and ends to create new and original works, in chapter seven.

SOCIAL WORTH OR STATUS

Clothing and fashion are often used to indicate social worth or status, and people often make judgements concerning other people's social worth or status on the basis of what those people are wearing. Status may result or accrue from various sources, from occupation, the family, sex, gender, age or race, for example. It may be fixed or it may be changeable; the former case is known as 'ascribed' status and the latter as 'achieved'. So, one's occupational status may be that of a refuse collector, a local government officer or a university lecturer. Family status is a result of being a brother, or a mother, or a second cousin, for example. Status that is the result of one's age may be gauged by whether one is over or under the age of eighteen in Great Britain, or whether one is an old age pensioner, for example. Clearly, status that is the result of one's sex, race or family position cannot be changed easily and is fixed or 'ascribed'. Occupational or marital status is more easily changed and therefore 'achieved', at least in most western societies.

All cultures take great care to mark different statuses clearly. They probably take even greater care to mark those who are undergoing changes in status. Anthropological accounts of clothing and fashion will, consequently, be extremely interested in studying these phenomena as well as those examples where status is deliberately blurred or made unclear (see Leach 1976: 55–60). The advertisement for Levi jeans which appeared in the mid-1990s featuring a New York transvestite being leered at by a lascivious cabbie until 'she' notices some facial stubble and begins to shave, plays upon such ambiguous status. All cultures will use clothing, if not fashion, to distinguish male from female, most will use it to mark the difference between secular and religious classes, and some will use it to mark membership of different families. Major changes in status, such as going from being single to being married, or going from being married to being a widow/er, will be marked by all cultures and are often accompanied by the most elaborate and costly changes in clothing. In many western societies, the transition from being single to being married typically involves the bride wearing white, and being marked by something like a honeymoon. In those same societies, the transition from being married to being a widow typically involves the woman wearing black and being marked by a period of mourning.

Various sumptuary laws, enacted throughout the world at different times, may be seen as examples of dress being tied to status. Roach and Eicher refer to an ordinance passed in late fourteenth-century Nuremburg which declared that 'no burgher, young or old, shall wear his hair parted; they shall wear the hair in tufts, as it has been worn of old' (Roach and Eicher 1979: 12). This is interesting in that it is social status that is singled out here; status as it relates to age is deemed irrelevant. They also refer to a highly detailed set of laws from the Tokugawa period in Japan (1600–1867) which specified the exact fibres out of which each social class could make their sandals (Roach and Eicher 1979: 13). Because it involves the possibility and desirability of moving between classes, it may be said that this example concerns fashion, as well as clothing or dress. It was noted in the Introduction how fashion seemed to require the possibility of moving between classes in order to exist.

The use of clothing to indicate status as it relates to age may be seen in some of Lurie's chapter on youth and age. She touches on the example of long and short trousers (Lurie 1992: 45–6). There may no longer be many young boys who undergo the experience of fighting for the right to wear long trousers at school when their mothers insist that they wear demeaning and childish short trousers. But those who do will not forget the satisfaction that accompanies wearing long trousers. Lurie also refers to the way in which very young girls wear 'completely non-functional' AA and AAA 'training bras' as 'a sign' that they will eventually become women (Lurie 1992: 45–6). In the cases of both boys and girls it is the status, the feeling that one is a grown-up man or woman, that is indicated by the various garments and which is so desired. It might be worth speculating that the so-called 'Young Fogey' look of the 1990s, in which relatively young men dress in the manner of an older, or old-fashioned model of masculinity, with tweeds, sensible brogues and twill trousers, for example, is another version of this phenomenon.

DEFINITION OF SOCIAL ROLE

The different types of status noted above, regarding class, occupation, sex and so on, are all accompanied or surrounded by a number of expectations. These expectations define or express how individuals occupying those positions of status are to behave, and may be referred to as roles. A person's social role, then, is produced by their status and refers to the sorts of ways in which they are expected to behave. For example, the status of a wife is accompanied by the role of wife, and the status of local government officer is accompanied by the role of local government officer. In all societies, wives are expected to behave in certain ways and not in others. In societies that have them, local government officers are also expected to behave in certain ways but not in others.

Clothing and fashion may also be used to indicate or define the social roles that people have. They may be taken as signs that a certain person occupies a certain role and may therefore be expected to behave in a particular way. It has been claimed that the different clothes, and the different types of clothes, worn by different people enables social interaction to take place more smoothly than it otherwise might. The fashions and clothes worn by doctors, nurses, visitors and patients in a hospital, for example, indicate the role of the people wearing them. Knowledge of the person's role is necessary in order that one behaves appropriately towards them. This sort of knowledge could be seen as helping to avoid embarrassment; as a visitor to a hospital, one already has a good idea as to how to behave towards the doctor and what sort of behaviour to expect from him or her. The Hollywood film *Working Girl* shows how fashion and clothing signal social roles, and also how they may be used to disguise social position. The secretary (Melanie Griffith) abandons her cheap, working-class clothes (along with her cheap, working-class boyfriend), and literally steals her nasty, 'bony-assed', female boss's clothes in order to appear, and be taken seriously, as a businesswoman (as well as attracting the romantic interest of serious businessman Harrison Ford).

Clearly, another way of looking at the relation between social role and fashion or clothing is to see the latter as making inequalities in the former appear to be natural or proper. For example, the differences in clothing between doctor and nurse may be understood as legitimating differences of power and status between the two to the extent that it is thought proper for the doctor to be patronising and impatient to the nurse, and for the nurse to suffer such indignities without complaint. The difference in status, and the different expectations with regard to behaviour, are made to appear natural and proper when they are given concrete form in clothing and fashions. The difference in what the individuals are wearing seems to justify treating them differently. The way that fashion and clothing may be used to be critical of the ways that inequalities have been made to appear natural and proper is touched on by Roach and Eicher. They refer to the ways in which, in the late 1960s and early 1970s,

> racial roles, the roles of rich and poor, the roles of male and female were questioned and efforts made, particularly by the young, to articulate new roles within all these categories and to wear dress that reflected these new roles.
>
> (Roach and Eicher 1979: 11)

These points will come up again in chapters five and six, where they will be treated in more detail and in relation to the reproduction and critique of gender and class identities and positions.

ECONOMIC WORTH OR STATUS

While it is obviously closely related to social worth and also to social role, economic status is slightly different to both. Economic status is concerned with position within an economy. This section will look at the ways in which fashion and clothing may indicate productive or occupational roles within an economy. As Roach and Eicher point out, 'adorning oneself can reflect connections with the system of production characteristic of the particular economy within which one lives' (Roach and Eicher 1979: 13). Fashion and clothing may reflect, that is, the sort of economic organisation that one lives in, as well as one's status within that economy.

Roach and Eicher suggest that the uniform of policemen (Figure 5), predominantly dark blue, with a helmet and badges, indicates what sort of services may be expected from them. They suggest that a nurse's uniform does the same thing, also giving an indication of the sorts of services which may be expected from someone wearing it. Uniforms here give an indication of economic worth or status insofar as they indicate the services, as opposed to the roles, to be expected from an individual. This aspect of clothing and fashion may be described as signifying the economic, or contractual side of adornment, as opposed to the social or the cultural side. And it may be found on a number of levels.

In addition to giving some idea of the sorts of services to be expected of people, clothing may indicate what sort of job they have. Fashion and clothing may suggest at which level in an economy people operate or work. The well-known descriptions of people and their jobs as either white-collar or blue-collar indicate what sort of jobs those people do. White-collar means that the person's job requires wearing a suit or smart jacket with a shirt and tie, or that it is not a job that involves using one's hands. Blue-collar means that the job involves manual labour. The use of the phrase 'pink-collar', to indicate a white-collar worker who is a woman, does not seem to have taken off in quite the same way as the others. This may be as a result of confusion with other uses, in similar contexts, of the word 'pink', which indicates that homosexuality is intended. However, white and blue, in the context of collars, indicate economic status; white-collar workers are generally perceived as being of higher status than blue-collar workers. It may be, of course, that this perception is only made by the white-collar workers whose job it is to write about such matters.

Roach and Eicher suggest that, in America, 'women's dress is generally more ambiguous in its symbolism of occupational role than is men's' (Roach and Eicher 1979: 13). They are writing about the large numbers of women 'who are exclusively homemakers' here. They argue that it is partly because industrial societies recognise only occupations which produce income in the form of money that women's dress is ambiguous. As such societies do not recognise homemaking as a proper occupation, the women who are home-makers have no clearly defined or perceived status in the economic structure. There is, therefore, no form of dress that could 'correspond' to that status. And women's dress and fashions are, therefore, for the most part ambiguous with regard to economic or occupational status.

They argue that nineteenth-century traditions are also partly responsible for this ambiguity. Nineteenth-century expectations that women would per-form a more decorative role and indulge in more personal display than men persisted into the twentieth century. This means that women's dress and fashion, even when women are working alongside men in white-collar occupations, still tend not to indicate occupational or economic status. There are 'occasional' attempts to indicate women's occupational status by means of clothing and fashion, such as the adoption in turn-of-the-century America of something approaching the dominant white-collar male worker's dress. But, as Roach and Eicher say, it may be that the comparative novelty of white-collar work for women has meant that fashion and clothing have yet to catch up (Roach and Eicher 1979: 14).

POLITICAL SYMBOL

The workings of power are also clearly very closely connected to economic and social status. And it is clear that fashion and clothing are just as closely connected to the workings of power. However, it is as well at least to try to keep the analytical issues separate in these matters. This section revisits some of the issues that were introduced above, in the discussion of the definitions of fashion and non- or anti-fashion. Roach and Eicher suggest that 'adorn-ment has long had a place in the house of power' (Roach and Eicher 1979: 15), and it must be emphasised that both fashion and non- or anti-fashion may be analysed in terms of their political function. What has been referred to as fashion and what has been referred to as adornment, which is not necessarily fashion, may be used to illustrate the workings of power.

65

While the definition of power will be dealt with in more detail in chapters five and six, it is worth indicating that fashion and clothing are implicated in the workings of two different conceptions or kinds of power. These may be characterised as 'Power' and 'power'. The first refers to the power of the state, of government or party-political power; 'power' refers to the workings of power between people, on a much smaller scale. The latter, 'power', refers to the ways in which power works between parents and children, for example, or between lecturers and students, and the former refers to the ways in which power is exercised by the state or representatives of the state. Professor Teufelsdröckh's Hanging Judge (see pp.49–50) would be an example of someone exercising 'Power'.

Roach and Eicher suggest that Napoleon 'reintroduced types of dress that were symbols of state from the old regime to support the legitimacy of his empire' (Roach and Eicher 1979: 15). Modes of dress from a previous state regime are being used here to attempt to give a new regime legitimacy by hijacking some of the grandeur of that previous regime. This would be an example of the relation between clothing and 'Power'; here power is to do with the operation and legitimation of the state, and clothing is being used as a way of helping to achieve that operation and legitimation. Tina Mai Chen's (2001) essay investigates the use of dress in Maoist China. While the Mao suit was the Communist Party uniform, encouraging certain forms of social behaviour and demonstrating the wearer's position as part of the 'vanguard' of 'revolutionary proletarian struggle' (2001: 155), Chen shows that other textiles and prints were demanded by and made available to the population (Ibid.: 148). The example of anti-fashion that was used above in chapter one, Queen Elizabeth's coronation gown, may also be seen as an example of the relation between clothing and 'Power'. The 'traditional' and 'fixed' nature of the gown is a sign of continuity, a way of making the House of Windsor appear legitimate and proper. An example of fashion being put to the service of political power may be seen in the use of beauty spots in eighteenth-century England. Apparently, political preference could be indicated at this time by wearing one's beauty spot on either the right or the left cheek. Whig women wore their spot on the right cheek and Tory women wore it on the left; those claiming political neutrality wore two spots, one on each cheek (Roach and Eicher 1979: 16).

Examples of the relation between fashion, clothing and 'power' include the late 1960s' and early 1970s' youth, mentioned above. These people adapted their fashions and clothing to try to reflect the new roles between different social groups. Thus, attempted changes in power relations between different races and different sexes were expressed or reflected in terms of fashion and dress. Many workers in professions like social work are wary of wearing anything that will mark them out as an obvious figure of power to their clients and will tend to avoid a show of opulence. Consequently fashions and clothing that will mark them out as establishment or authority figures will be avoided and some sort of attempt made to dress on a level with the client. Doing this, of course, they run the risk of falling into the 'sandals and oatmeal-coloured hand-knits' stereotype. In the 1970s and 1980s, various American police forces abandoned their uniforms and adopted civilian clothes in order to appear more friendly and approachable. This may also be explained as an attempt to transform, or at least camouflage, the perceived power relations between the state and its citizens.

MAGICO-RELIGIOUS CONDITION

It seems plausible to suggest that this section will be dealing with dress and clothing, rather than with fashion. This is because magical and religious practices rely for their effects on elements like the fixed or god-given status of officials, and the high value placed upon tradition and the maintenance of order. Teachings and practices that alter with the fashion are not religious or magical practices. Reference to the magical or religious use of clothing has been made above, in the section on protection (see p.51). Flügel, for example, refers to the use of amulets and other magical adornments to ward off malevolent magical and spiritual agencies (Flügel 1930: 71). He suggests, less convincingly, that the thick, dark, stiff cloth of monks' habits may help to avoid or escape moral dangers. This section, however, is more concerned with the use of clothing to indicate such things as belief and strength of belief.

So, whether worn permanently or as a temporary measure, dress and clothing may indicate membership of, or affiliation to, a particular religious group or denomination. They may also signify status or position within that group or denomination, and they may indicate strength or depth of belief or participation. Crawley cites numerous cases of dress being worn temporarily for religious or magical purposes. He refers, for example, to the Muslim practice of wearing only the *ihram* when undertaking the *hajj* or pilgrimage to Mecca. The *ihram* consists of 'two seamless wrappers, one passed around the loins, the other over the shoulders'. And he notes the Zulu practice, reported in 1857, of tearing up and trampling into the fields the mantle worn by the king. At the festival of new fruits the king would dance in this mantle, made of grass or herbs and corn leaves (Crawley 1965b: 138–41).

Among the clearest and most well-known examples of religious dress are those of the Roman Catholic clergy and the Hasidic Jews. Roach and Eicher (1965), as well as Rouse (1989) and Poll (1965) may be consulted on the latter. Poll provides the most detailed account, describing the dress codes of each of the six classes making up the Hasidic community of New York. For example, the *Rebbes* constitute the highest class in this particular social order; they are the most religious and their observance and behaviour are entirely ruled by their religion. The *Sheine Yiden* are the third group; they are known as religious professionals, teaching the Talmud, performing ritual slaughter and circumcisions. The *Yiden* are the lowest class in this order; their behaviour and observance is neither intensive nor frequent.

Each of these ranks and levels of observance has a corresponding dress code. The *Rebbes* wear all of the regalia, *shich* and *zocken* (shoes and socks), *shtreimel* and *bekecher* (sable fur hat and long silk coat), *kapote* (long overcoat worn as a jacket), *biber hat* (hat made out of beaver) and *bord* and *payes* (beard and side-locks). In the middle, the *Sheine Yiden* do not wear the *shich* and *zocken* or the *shtreimel* and *bekecher*, but they do wear the other things that the *Rebbes* wear. The *Yiden*, however, wear only the minimum of regalia, the 'dark, double-breasted suits that button from right to left' (Poll 1965: 142–57; also in Roach-Higgins *et al.* (eds) 1995).

It is clear that dress is being used here to indicate strength and depth of religious belief and observance in a number of very intricate ways. The different forms of dress indicate first, and most obviously, that one is a particular type of Jew and second, but less clearly (at least to the *Goyim*), which level or grade of observance one practises.

SOCIAL RITUALS

Social rituals, such as weddings and funerals, have been mentioned above with regard to the use of fashion and clothing to indicate different positions of social worth or status. In this brief section, fashion and clothing will be considered simply in terms of the way in which they may be used to mark the beginning and end of rituals, and to differentiate between ritual and non-ritual. In many western rituals it is expected that, while the ritual is taking place, those involved in it will wear something different from their usual attire. One does not normally wear the things one wears every day to a wedding or a funeral. In the former case, one usually wears something smarter, newer or better than everyday wear. In the latter case, what one wears is to a great extent prescribed by the rules of the ritual.

RECREATION

Recreation may be seen as the obverse, or other side, of ritual. Where ritual is formal and rule-governed, recreation is supposed to be more informal, even if it is not necessarily less rule-governed. Fashion and clothing may be used as recreation or to indicate the beginning or end of periods of recreation. The former requires either time or time and money and, in this respect, may begin to function as an indicator of social class. As Roach and Eicher point out, in societies where 'leisure is a scarce resource monopolised by a social elite', having the time and money to engage in leisure will signify membership of that elite (Roach and Eicher 1979: 19).

In the same way that fashion and clothing were seen above to signal the beginning or end of ritual, they may also be seen to signal whether one is engaging in recreation. Clearly some recreational activities, like cricket or fishing, will demand a change of clothing and permit one to show off the latest fashions in those activities. Others, like drinking in pubs or watching television, will not necessarily demand a change of clothing. Where the latter do involve a change of clothing, it is interesting to note that while members of lower social classes generally dress up to go out, members of higher social classes generally dress down. Members of lower classes will want to look smarter than they do while maybe working manually during the day. Members of higher classes, however, will want to wear something less formal than the relatively smart clothing they have been wearing all day. This is clearly a substantial generalisation, paying no attention to either the age or the sex of those involved, but it may be usefully compared with the account of white- and blue-collar workers in relation to Veblen's account of conspicuous consumption found in chapter five. There it will be seen that Veblen argues that members of the higher social classes will dress in clothes that are expensive, wasteful and both difficult and costly to care for. Here, on the contrary, it is suggested that in certain circumstances the opposite is true.

To point out that fashion and clothing have a recreational aspect is partly to indicate that they may be the occasions of pleasure, that they may simply be fun, ways of deriving pleasure. These are not necessarily aspects that are emphasised by writers on clothing and fashion. This may be because fashion and clothing already have enough problems in being derided as trivial pursuits; writers may be reluctant to add to the idea that they are only a bit of fun that nobody need take very seriously.

There are at least two misconceptions operating here. The first is that fashion and clothing may be seen as merely a bit of fun. This chapter has proposed that fashion and clothing are not only fun, but that they also have social and cultural functions. It has also suggested that these social and cultural functions are not simply appendages to the main business of human life, but that they are essential in a number of ways to that business. The second misconception is that pleasure and fun are simple matters. While they will be discussed in more detail in chapters five and six in relation to gender, it is worth raising here the issues of gendered pleasures and of different kinds of pleasures.

Flügel, for example, spends what will seem to some a suspiciously large part of *The Psychology of Clothes* discussing the somatic pleasure of wearing clothes. Many people derive a great deal of pleasure from the feel of certain fabrics and textiles. But Flügel comments at length and in some detail on the pleasure experienced by fit, young bodies in moving those bodies and in flexing the muscles of the body. He also writes of the pleasures to be gained from feeling clothes moving over the skin. And, of course, he advocates the pleasures to be gained from wearing no clothes at all, from feeling the sun and the breeze upon one's naked skin. Similarly, few will doubt the pleasures to be had in looking at attractive people dressed in lovely clothes; it is hard to explain the appeal of fashion photography and fashion magazines with end-less pictures of pouting models flouncing up and down catwalks otherwise. The pleasure gained from looking, scopophilia, is different to the kind of pleasure gained from touching and feeling. It also seems to work in a different way, depending upon the gender of the person doing the looking. Berger has pointed out that 'men look at women. Women watch themselves being looked at' (Berger 1972: 47). He is suggesting a fundamental difference in the pleas-ures gained by looking and being looked at, and much work has been done in developing the insight into this asymmetry. So, while fashion and clothing may be fun, an opportunity for light-hearted playfulness, they are not only a bit of fun. Moreover, the analysis of what counts as fun, how one might define pleasure, and for whom, are not simple matters.

CONCLUSION

This chapter claims, then, to have outlined the material and cultural functions of fashion and clothing. In doing this, it has added a little more detail to the definitions of fashion and clothing established in the previous two chapters. Various material functions, including protection from the elements, modesty and attraction, were discussed as potential explanations of the function of fashion and clothing, but none alone was able to explain fashion and clothing satisfactorily. What counted as protection from the elements was seen to vary from culture to culture and from one point in time to another. What people understood by modesty also varied between cultures and in time. It was also argued that fashion and clothing could not be reduced to serving the interests of the heterosexual sex drive. The chapter then dealt with the various cul-tural, or communicative, functions of fashion and clothing. These functions are consistent with the definition of fashion and clothing as cultural phenom-ena that was established in chapter two. They are consistent in that culture was itself established as, or defined in terms of, communication. So, culture having been established as a form of communication, this chapter has explained some of the things that are communicated by fashion and clothing as cultural phenomena.

Chapter four will look at how meaning in fashion and clothing is gener-ated. If fashion and clothing have been established as forms of cultural com-munication in the previous chapter, and if the sorts of things that fashion and clothing may be used to communicate have been enumerated in this chapter, then the next chapter must analyse and explain how those meanings are possible, how they are generated or produced.

FURTHER READING

- The classic text on the **material functions of fashion and clothing**, to which this chapter is indebted, is clearly Mary Ellen Roach and Joanne Bubolz Eicher (1979)

'The language of personal adornment', in Cordwell, J. M. and Schwarz, R. A. (eds) *The Fabrics of Culture; the Anthropology of Adornment*, Mouton Publishers. I am not aware of this essay being reprinted anywhere else and suspect that *The Fabrics of Culture* is not the most readily available volume; I thought that these were good reasons for spending so much time simply representing and occasionally updating or augmenting Roach's and Eicher's views.

- Part Two of Eicher, J. B. *et al.* (eds) (2000) *The Visible Self*, Fairchild Publications, provides a selection of readings which deal with **dress and protecting the body** from the environment
- Damhorst, M. L. *et al.* (eds) (1999) *The Meanings of Dress*, Fairchild Publications, also provides a series of readings on topics touched on in this chapter, including the ways in which **religious status, employment status and age** are indicated and communicated.
- And Roach-Higgins *et al.* (eds) (1995) *Dress and Identity*, Fairchild Publications, has sections on the ways in which **economic status, protection from the environment and modesty** are negotiated by means of dress.
- The views of J. C. Flügel, while not receiving as detailed a coverage as Roach's and Eicher's, are just as classic and in many ways are more interesting as they frequently strike one as so odd. This oddness may simply be the product of the 1930s' **psychoanalytic framework** to which Flügel is committed. The first five chapters of *The Psychology of Clothes*, published by the Hogarth Press and the Institute of Psychoanalysis (1950), are well worth a look.

4

FASHION, CLOTHING AND MEANING

INTRODUCTION

As we saw in chapter one, Davis has pointed out that it has become something of a cliché to say that 'the clothes we wear make a statement' (Davis 1992: 3 and in Solomon 1985: 15). Most people are content with the idea that the clothes they wear, and the combinations they wear them in, have or can be given meaning of some sort. Most people will also be happy with the idea that they make choices concerning what to buy and wear on the basis of the meanings that they perceive garments to have. And many people are perfectly happy to let the meanings of other people's clothes influence the way in which they behave towards those other people. It is probably a safe bet, however, that very few people spend much time wondering what sort of thing 'meaning' is, if it is a 'thing', where it might 'come from' and how they or anyone else manages to do anything so sophisticated as interpret it.

As discussed in chapter two, fashion, clothing and dress constitute signifying systems in which a social order is constructed and communicated. They may operate in different ways, but they are similar in that they are some of the ways in which that social order is experienced, understood and passed on. They may be considered as one of the means by which social groups communicate their identity as social groups, to other social groups. They are ways in which those groups communicate their positions with regard to those other social groups. While it should not be assumed that the differences between these terms have been ignored, it is claimed that fashion, clothing and dress are not only ways in which individuals communicate. They are also the means by which social groups communicate and through which communication they are constituted as social groups. However, it is clearly not the case that social groups sit around and explicitly discuss what they will use to communicate and what they will communicate. There seem to be major differences between meanings on the level of individuals and meanings on the level of social groups.

This chapter will consider fashion and clothing in terms of meaning. It will look at various possible sources or origins of meaning before arguing that a semiological account, based on the work of Ferdinand de Saussure and Roland Barthes, is the most helpful and productive. It will suggest that the meanings of clothes may usefully be divided into two types, 'denotation' and 'connotation', each working in its own way on its own level. It will also explain some of the things needed in order to interpret the meanings of clothes. It should be pointed out that the concepts and processes which are explained in this chapter are also applicable to photographs and other images of fashion and clothing. Both denotation and connotation may be used to explain and analyse the production of meaning in drawings, films and photographs, as well as in actual garments. It might be said, then, that these ideas apply to all kinds of images, both two- and three-dimensional, if the popular idea that fashions and clothing are used to construct an image for people is taken at all seriously. Thus, while the ideas considered in this chapter will be explored in most detail in terms of items of fashion and clothing, they may also be used to study various other media, including magazines, television, film and video, in which fashion and clothing are used to create and communicate images, but which this chapter does not deal with explicitly.

There are two kinds of explanation commonly given for the origin or generation of meaning. One locates the origin of meaning outside the garment or ensemble, in some external authority like the designer or the wearer. The other locates the generation of meaning in the garment or ensemble itself, in textures, colours and shapes and the permutations of these colours, shapes and textures. The situation is complicated by the fact that these two kinds of explanation may be found singly (that is, used on their own in a consistent way) or mixed together. This chapter will look at both types of explanation before discussing the semiological approaches to the generation of meanings.

MEANING AS EXTERNAL TO THE GARMENT/ENSEMBLE/IMAGE

There are various candidates for the role of an authority that is external to the garment or ensemble but which claims to be the origin or source of the meaning of that garment/ensemble. The most obvious and most plausible candidate, perhaps, is the designer of the garment/ensemble. Only slightly less plausible, although no less obvious, would be the wearer of the garment/ensemble. Slightly less plausible still, and also slightly less obvious, would be a spectator: a fashion critic, a journalist or even a parent. And, while they should not be discounted entirely, perhaps the least plausible and the least obvious candidates for the role would be religious or political authorities.

The designer

The idea that the designer of the garment or ensemble is the source of the meaning of that garment/ensemble may seem to be the purest and most compelling common sense. it will be asked, rhetorically, 'If the designer does not know what s/he meant by making such a garment, then who does?' This is the idea that meaning is a product of the designer's intentions, where intentions are defined as a person's thoughts, feelings, beliefs and desires about the world and the things in it. Thus those thoughts, feelings, beliefs and desires that the designer has are somehow expressed or reflected in the garment/ensemble that s/he produces. According to this view, then, to enquire about the meaning of a garment or ensemble is to ask about the intentions of the designer and it is to see the garment/ensemble as the expression of the designer's inner thoughts, feelings and beliefs.

This account of the origin of meaning underlies much of the educational practice of fashion and textile design and also much of the spoken and written coverage of the fashion industry. From Foundation Studies to interviews for college places or for *Vogue* magazine, people are interested in what the individual designer is thinking; feelings, thoughts and beliefs are sought, treasured and investigated. From popular television shows to the exclusive pages of glossy magazines, interviews probe what designers think about some issue or other and ask what they are doing in their work. The intentions, thoughts, feelings, beliefs and desires that designers express in their work, are highly prized in education and highly sought after in the media. Clearly, it makes sense to ask about such things only if it is believed that the designer's intentions are the sole source of the meaning of his/her work.

While this account of meaning may appear to be the purest common sense, and while it may even appear to be true, there are various, mainly philosophical, problems with it which mean that it cannot be upheld in any simple form. Firstly, if meaning was what the designer had in his/her head, their intentions, then there could be no disagreement as to the meaning of a garment or collection. If meaning was the product of what the designer was thinking about, then there could be no alternative interpretations of that meaning, and people would not be able to appropriate the meanings of garments and adapt them to their own intentions. Nor would they be able to roar with laughter at the creations of designers, as a Terry Wogan chat-show audience did when confronted with some of Vivienne Westwood's designs. Since there are disagreements about the meaning of garments or collections, and since there are alternative interpretations of works, sometimes from the designers themselves, sometimes coming from the wearers of the garments, meaning cannot simply be a product of the designer's intentions.

There are other problems with this account of where meaning comes from. For example, if meaning really was what was in the designer's head when s/he was designing a garment, the meaning of the garment could not change. It could not vary from place to place and from situation to situation, and it could not differ according to its position in time. It could not do this as the designer's thoughts and intentions at that particular time would not change in time and space. What designer X had in mind yesterday when he/she produced garment Y will remain what he/she had in mind yesterday under all circumstances, even if he/she changes his/her mind about the garment later. Since the meaning of garments does change in time and place, meaning cannot be a product of the designer's intentions in this way. Anyone who has ever felt under- or overdressed will know how time and place can alter the meanings of clothes one thought one knew intimately. The wearing of night garments or underwear outside of bedrooms or bathrooms and at times other than bedtime may also illustrate this phenomenon.

It may also be the case that the designer does not know, or does not know very clearly, what was 'in his/her head' when they designed a particular garment: nobody is going to suggest that the garment so produced does not have a meaning or that it has a vague meaning. This is a long recognised problem. The story from Plato's *Defence of Socrates*, in which Socrates asks the poets what their poems mean, will be recalled. The poets are unable to say what the poems mean, and Socrates remarks that even passers-by in the street often have a better idea of what the poems are about than the poets. There is also the psychoanalytic argument that the designer is not, and cannot be, in total, conscious control of his/her intentions. Psychoanalysis will argue that there are unconscious wishes and desires, which the designer does not know about and over which he/she has no control, that somehow find expression in the designer's garments and other works. Given these problems and objections, it seems plausible to suggest that meaning is not simply a product of the designer's intentions, and cannot only be what the designer says it is.

The wearer or spectator

The cases for and against the wearer or spectator as the source of the meaning of a garment are very similar to those noted above with regard to the designer. In terms of the wearer or spectator (whether the spectator is a parent, a fashion journalist or one's best friend), meaning is again thought of as being the product of what is in people's heads, their intentions. Thus if the wearer gives a garment a particular meaning, the meaning of the garment may be said to be a product of the wearer's intentions. According to this argument, the beliefs, hopes and fears of the wearer are expressed through their use of the garment. There is increasing documentation on the ways in which wearers, or 'consumers' as they are called in the literature, use garments and give them alternative meanings, maybe give them meanings which their designers had not intended.

Partington, for example, investigates how working-class women in the 1950s actively used fashion, in this case the New Look (see Figure 7), 'to articulate class identity in new ways' (Partington 1992: 146). In this case the consumer is not simply a 'passive victim of fashion', being dressed up in a specific version of an appropriate class identity by the fashion and marketing industries. Rather, according to Partington, these women are creating new meanings by using a 'deliberately different appropriation' of the New Look, 'an appropriation that was not the intention' of the fashion and marketing industries. It is clear that whole industries are conceived here as having 'intentions', and that meaning is seen as being a result or a product of those intentions. Similarly, it is the intention of the working-class women that provides or generates the meanings, the new and deliberately different meanings, of the appropriated version of the New Look. Partington's discussion of the issues surrounding passive and active consumption and their relation to the male and female gaze will be dealt with in more detail in chapter six.

If meaning really were a product of the wearer's or the spectator's intentions, however, then different interpretations could not exist; the wearer's intentions would generate the meaning and there would be an end to the matter. Clearly, the wearer's and spectator's intentions often differ. The sexist and selective memories of certain men are full of recollections in which the intentions of wearers were countered and thwarted by those of spectators telling them that they were 'not going out dressed like that'. For those unfortunates without sisters, it should be explained that it is often the case that the meaning which parents see or construct in the clothes worn by their daughters is entirely different to that which the daughters have seen or constructed. Consequently, it cannot simply be the case that meaning is a product of the wearer's or spectator's intentions. If it was, disagreements could not happen.

Authorities

The reference to parents introduces the idea of authority in general as the source or origin of the meaning of fashion or clothing. And the reference to the fashion and marketing industries having intentions suggests that it is not inconceivable that things that are not human individuals should have intentions. It is sometimes suggested, for example, that authorities like schools, the military or governments decide or dictate what the meaning of garments is or should be: in this, they may be treated as analogous to human individuals. And the arguments for and against authority being the source of meanings are also analogous to those noted above.

The activities of schools in deciding on the colours, patterns and cuts to be employed in the construction of school uniform may be described as attempts to decide the meaning of clothing. A school has certain meanings or values that it would like to communicate to the world outside its gates, and one of the ways in which it can do this is by means of the uniform its pupils wear. Consequently one assumes that the colours, patterns and cuts employed in the school uniform are intended by the school to communicate meanings or values like responsibility, smartness, sobriety, scholarliness, orderliness and so on. The school is attempting to say what the uniform, the collection of clothes, means; it is trying to fix the meaning of that collection of clothes as orderly, smart and so on.

Figure 7 Christian Dior's 'New Look', 1947

The case is much the same with regard to the meanings of police and military uniforms (Figure 5). Again, an external authority has decided what a certain set of colours, patterns and cuts will mean. Lurie, in using the extended metaphor on which *The Language of Clothes* is based, writes that to wear uniform is to be partly or wholly censored. It is as if someone else is deciding what the wearer of the uniform can 'say', or as if the people wearing the uniform are 'all shouting the same thing' (Lurie 1992: 18–22). Thus the modern police and military forces may be seen as attempting to decide or decree that a particular set of colours, patterns and cuts will mean discipline, orderliness, uniformity, subordinance and so on.

Although it seems to be rare, it is not unknown for governments to attempt to fix the meaning of fashion and clothing. The most obvious ways in which they attempt to do this is by means of sumptuary laws. The word 'sumptuary' comes from the Latin word *sumptus*, which means 'cost'. Sumptuary laws are laws regulating private expenditure, limiting what people can spend. In 1327 in England, for example, Edward III enacted a law to control 'the outrageous and excessive apparel of divers people against their state and degree' (Freudenberger 1963). In sixteenth-century France, Henry IV passed a law forbidding the bourgeoisie from wearing silk (Braudel 1981: 311). The idea is that authority, here in the form of the monarch, is attempting to decide what fashions and clothing, what kinds of cut and cloth, are appropriate to particular social classes. It is trying to fix the meaning of a particular set of cuts and cloths as being aristocratic', 'bourgeois' and so on.

This kind of legislation appears to have fallen into disuse with the rise and development of capitalism (Freudenberger 1963:144). It is probably not an accident that the only other examples of governments attempting to determine the meaning of clothing and dress that readily spring to mind are from Communist states. The adoption of something approaching a uniform in Mao's China, for example, (see Eicher *et al.* (eds) 2000: 338 for more on this), seems to be a way of fixing the meaning of a particular set of clothes. It may be claimed that certain types or styles of clothing are 'decadent' or 'bourgeois', and that the adoption of the tunic-style uniform is asserting that this uniform means equality, subordinance to the needs of the country rather than the individual and so on.

Interesting as they may be, however, these arguments suffer from much the same flaws as all the others considered so far. If meaning really could be imposed upon a set of colours, patterns and cuts by external authorities like schools, the military and governments, those meanings would not change in time and space. It could be argued that, since they do, meaning cannot simply work in that way. For example, young people have been known to use army surplus uniform to signal their rebellion against the society of which they are supposedly a part. In the 1960s, the Beatles appeared on the cover of their 'Sergeant Pepper' album dressed in something approximating to military uniform, and Jimi Hendrix was known to appear on stage in something very similar. Contemporary young people, who are not pop stars, also use army surplus to indicate rebellion and may sometimes be seen on the news, defending some ancient woodland against rapacious developers. Other people use school uniform for quite different purposes and it is unlikely, although not impossible, that the meanings or the values that the schools hope the uniforms communicate have anything to do with those purposes.

If the meaning of the garments constituting uniform had been fixed by the military, or the school, those garments would not be available to the young, or anyone else, to use to communicate meanings that may in fact be the opposite of what the military or the school had in mind. Given that the garments are available, their meanings cannot have been defined or generated by authority in this way.

MEANING AS INTERNAL TO THE GARMENT/ENSEMBLE/IMAGE

The other potential source for the meaning of a garment or an ensemble is the garment or ensemble itself. Some people will argue that the meaning of the item is somehow 'in' the item, that meaning somehow inheres in the colour, texture or shapes. They will claim that the meaning is a property of the garment or the ensemble, as if it were like a colour – that 'casualness', for example, is the meaning of the garment in the same way as 'red' is its colour. Such people will also claim that the meaning of an image, a drawing or a photograph is somehow 'in' the drawing or photograph. They will assume that meaning somehow resides in the shapes, lines and textures.

It must be said that this is not a very sophisticated position to argue: it is sometimes found in fashion journalism, but it is difficult to find academic instances of it. One often finds, for example, that a white shirt is presented in magazines as being a garment that will 'go with' anything and everything for both men and women. Those same magazines will inevitably describe a little black dress as 'chic' or 'sophisticated' and a little red dress as 'sexy' or 'red-hot'. Silks and satins are always 'slinky', while knitted wool is more often than not 'chunky'. It is as if the qualities are inherent in the garment or the textile; one just has to look at the garment to apprehend its meaning. Academic instances of this position are few and far between, but Professor Lawrence Gowing appears to be one of the exceptions. He is quoted by Berger as referring to the 'visible meaning' of *Mr and Mrs Andrews*, a painting by Gainsborough (Berger 1972: 107). It seems that the meaning of the painting, like that of the garments and textiles noted above, may be understood simply by looking at the painting; meaning inheres in it.

While it may not be a terribly sophisticated position, it is one with much intuitive appeal; it is difficult to resist the idea that some garments are just naff or sexy or casual. The problems involved with this view become apparent if one looks at garments from cultures with which one is not familiar. It is often extremely difficult to say what their meanings are, whether they are sexy or casual or sophisticated or whatever to that other culture. It may be easy to say what they would signify if they were worn in one's own culture, but the possibility that the meaning would be available in one but not another culture is enough to cast doubt on the idea of meaning being a property of the garment. After all, if the meaning was simply in the garment, like redness, then it could be read by people from all sorts of cultures. Similarly, if meaning was simply in the garment or ensemble, that meaning could not change in time; flared trousers would always be cool and medallions would always be sexily sophisticated.

It seems, then, that there are numerous problems involved in the claim that meaning is external to the garment, and there are numerous problems involved in the claim that meaning is internal to the garment. Neither can be upheld in any simple form, and it may be that neither can be consistently upheld in any form at all. It will almost certainly be the case that these arguments will be encountered again and again, however, and that they will be encountered mixed with each other, in different combinations. The rest of this chapter will look at what are known as 'semiological' accounts of meaning, in order to explain the production of meaning in fashion and clothing with greater clarity.

SEMIOLOGICAL ACCOUNTS OF MEANING

'Semiology', from which the word 'semiological' derives, is made from two Greek words, *semeion* and *logos*. *Semeion* means 'sign' and *logos* means 'story', 'account' or 'science'. So 'semiology' will be the science or an account of signs, in the same way that 'biology' is the science or account of living things and 'sociology' is the science or account of society. Saussure, from whom many of the ideas to be discussed in this chapter derive, defined semiology as a 'science that studies the life of signs within society', and he suggested that it would be concerned with what 'constitutes signs, what laws govern them' (Saussure 1974:16). The idea that it is the life of signs in society which is to be studied by semiology is one to be emphasised; too many people leave the definition of semiology at the stage of 'science of signs'. So the following few sections will be concerned with the nature of the sign and with the laws that govern them. They will explain the nature of the sign, they will describe two types or levels of meaning and explain how those levels of meaning are produced. These concepts will then be applied to fashion and clothing in an attempt to explain the social and cultural production of meanings in fashion and clothing in terms of them. Finally the role of signs in social life, as they relate to power and ideology, will be discussed. In this way, the chapter hopes to take into account both Saussure's original proposal for semiology, that it study the life of signs in society and not apart from the society in which they are found, and Dant's description of material culture, that fashion and clothing are not to be studied only as codes (or systems of signs), but in relation to material culture, as a mixture of social and cultural values and sign systems (Dant 1999: 107).

The sign

Semiology points out that humans do not communicate directly, as if by means of telepathy. It is not the case that one can merely think something and have someone else understand it immediately and perfectly. There may be times when such a capacity would be useful but, one suspects, there would be many more when it would be inconvenient or downright embarrassing. Instead, human communication involves the use of one thing to stand for or represent something else. I have to use printed words to represent my thoughts in order to communicate those thoughts to you, the reader. And you will have to use spoken words in order to tell all your friends what a wonderful book you have just been reading. In both cases one type of thing, the written or spoken word, is being used to represent another type of thing, thoughts and opinions. Human communication, then, involves the use of 'signs'.

For Saussure, the sign is made up of two parts. Those parts are called the 'signifier' and the 'signified'. Saussure is concerned with language and for him 'signifiers' are the physical part of signs, they are the sounds or the shapes of words. The 'signified' is the mental concept to which that signifier refers. It is the meaning of the signifier. Together, they form the 'sign' (Saussure 1974: 65–7). The sound that is made speaking the word 'shirt' is a signifier. It stands for or represents the item of male clothing. The item of male clothing is the signified. The shapes that form the written word 'shirt' also constitute a signifier. The written form 'shirt' also stands for or represents the item of male clothing. And, again, the item of male clothing is the signified. Neither the spoken nor the written forms are the shirt, they do not look like or sound like the shirt, but they are used to signify, to stand for or represent, the shirt.

However, this chapter is not only concerned with spoken and written signs. It is also interested in objects and images, and it must begin to account for the meanings of those objects and images. What is needed is a definition of the sign that will apply to the objects and images that go to make up fashion and clothing. Saussure's definition of the sign may be generalised in such a way that it applies to more than the linguistic sign. So, while the sign is still made up of two parts according to the more general definition, the signifier is anything that stands for or represents something else, and the signified is the something else that is being represented. Following this more general account, fabrics and textiles as well as garments and parts of garments can be signs. Ensembles, collections and images may also be considered as signs.

To be more precise, they can be considered and analysed as signifiers, as standing for or representing something else. For example, a man's collar, worn open and without a tie, may be explained as a signifier. It may signify informality or casualness; it is not itself either of these things, but it stands for or represents them. Casualness, then, is the signified here. The same collar, worn closed and with a tie, may also be analysed as a signifier. It stands for or represents formality or smartness, and formality and smartness would be the signified. A coarse, hairy, woollen tweed may signify rusticity and the countryside whereas a fine, smooth, woollen worsted may signify urban sophistication. Neither the tweed nor the worsted is any of these things, but they are used to signify them. It is because one knows the code regarding open and closed collars that one understands whether smartness or casualness is signified. A code is a set of shared rules that connects signifiers with signifieds; if the code is unknown, then there is likely to be uncertainty as to what a particular signifier is signifying. Thus, if someone does not know the code that connects hairy tweeds with rusticity and smooth worsteds with the city, they may be said not to know the meaning of these textiles; they do not know where they are conventionally worn.

Pink bootees will usually signify that the baby wearing them is a girl, while blue bootees will signify that the wearer is a boy; the colours themselves are not any sex at all, but are used to signify or stand for one or other sex. The shapes, tones and colours that are found in fashion drawings and photographs may be explained as signifiers of what the drawings and photographs are drawings and photographs of. In a photograph of Yves Saint Laurent, for example, the shapes and tones or colours are the signifiers and Yves Saint Laurent is the signified. Again, the shapes and tones or colours are not the man but they represent him.

Now, while it seems plausible to suggest that the objects and images that go to make fashion and clothing may be considered as signs that are themselves made up of signifier and signified, it also seems plausible to suggest that the examples above work on different levels and in different ways. For example, pink and blue appear to signify girl and boy babies in a different way and on a different level to the way and level in which shape, tone and colour signify Yves Saint Laurent, and both appear to be different to the way and level in which urban sophistication is signified. The next section will attempt to explain those different levels in terms of different types of meaning.

Denotation and connotation I

Figure 8 is a picture of a gentleman wearing a jacket and some form of short trousers. While it may be analysed and explained in terms of signifiers and signifieds, it should also be pointed out that the signifiers and signifieds work on a number of different levels. Those levels will be explained in terms of different types of meaning. First, various lines, shapes and patterns may be recognised as representing parts of a jacket. Some shapes are recognised as standing for lapels, pockets, buttons, pleats and a belt, for example. They are

Figure 8 Norfolk jacket, 1905

not those parts of a jacket but they represent them. Second, the lines, shapes and patterns which go to form lapels, pockets, buttons, pleats and belt may be recognised as representing a particular style of jacket and trouser. In this case, the signified of those particular lines, shapes and patterns is a Norfolk jacket, worn with knickerbockers. Third, the jacket, or indeed the whole ensemble, may be considered as a signifier. The outfit itself may be understood as standing for a whole way of life. The signified here would be a gentlemanly, if not aristocratic, leisured, patriarchal, late-Victorian way of life.

Now, some semiologists disagree as to whether the first and second levels of meaning referred to above really are different. Panofsky, for example, would argue that they are different, and he calls the sort of meaning to be found on the first level 'formal' meaning. Barthes may well have considered them to be different levels at one stage of his career but not at another. Knowing, for example, that something is a cuff is certainly different to knowing that something is a barrel cuff or a French cuff. That is not to say, however, that these are different types of knowledge, merely that it is possible to know different types of things. This chapter, then, will argue that the first and second levels are both versions of what is known as 'denotational' meaning and that the third level is 'connotational' meaning. It will argue that the sort of meaning found on the first two levels noted above is denotational, and that which is found on the third is connotational.

Denotation is sometimes called a first order of signification or meaning. It is the literal meaning of a word or image, what Fiske suggests is the 'common-sense, obvious meaning' (Fiske 1990: 85–6). The dictionary definition of a word provides denotational meaning. The denotational meaning of an image, a drawing, painting or photograph, is what the image is an image of. Thus, the denotation of the word 'tweed', as it is found in *The Cambridge Encyclopedia*, is 'a coarse, heavy, wool, outerwear fabric, first made in S. Scotland, manufactured in several distinctive weave patterns'. The definition goes on to mention that the fabric is mistakenly associated with the River Tweed and that 'its manufacture in the I. of Harris was developed c.1850 by Lady Dunmore' (Crystal (ed.) 1990:1240). The denotation is factual, it concerns what the fabric is made of; where it is made, when it was made and so on. The denotation of the Norfolk jacket (Figure 8), as it appears in *The Encylopaedia of Fashion*, is

> originally worn by men in the second half of the nineteenth century, the Norfolk jacket, named after the Duke of Norfolk, was a hip-length garment made of wool tweed, with large patch pockets, box pleats front and back and a self-material belt.
>
> (O'Hara 1986: 180)

Again, the denotation is factual, concerning what the jacket is made of; when and where it was made, worn and so on.

Figure 8 may also be described in terms of denotational meaning. Some of the denotation has already been referred to in the discussion of levels of meaning above. The denotation would include the following, 'a gentleman, holding a cane in his right hand and with his left hand in his pocket, wearing a Norfolk jacket and knickerbockers. Standing in a field, he is also sporting a moustache, and wearing a cloth cap and what appears to be a turndown collar'. The denotation is the answer to the question 'what is that a picture of?'; it is what the image contains. It would be possible to supply more of the denotational meaning of the image if it were known who the man is, what his name is, whether he is one of the guns or one of the beaters, for example. Although it is not strictly part of what the image contains, one might perhaps add that the image first appeared in the April 1905 issue of *The Tailor and Cutter* magazine.

It will be noted that, given the factual or literal nature of denotative meaning, it is possible to be incomplete and/or mistaken on this level of meaning. For example, the above account is not specific with regard to the man's social status and it makes no mention of his footwear; it may well not be a turndown collar and the cane may well have a proper name. Because of this, denotation will tend not to vary from person to person; the literal meaning of tweed or the literal content of an image is not likely to differ significantly between people. At least, it must be said that the denotational meaning of words and images is not likely to differ significantly between people who are members of the same culture or who use the same language.

Connotation is sometimes called a second order of signification or meaning. It may be described as the things that the word or the image makes a person think or feel, or as the associations that a word or an image has for someone. Technically, or semiologically speaking, it is the denotative sign (the unity of signifier and signified), considered as a signifier. The signified of this signifier will vary from person to person, as the word or image will have more or less different associations for different people. Words and images will have different associations, or connotations, for different people because those people are different. They may be different sexes, genders, ages, classes, nationalities and races, for example. They may also have different jobs, or no job at all. All of these differences can produce or generate different associations of words and images for people. They will all produce or generate different connotational meanings for words or images.

This is probably to over-emphasise the differences, for it is remarkable that people from roughly the same age, class and cultural group will come up with almost identical connotations for a given word or image. The word 'tweedy', for example, has entered the language, presumably on the strength of the connotations of the cloth, meaning something along the lines of 'slightly old-fashioned and upper-class'. The connotations of silk are so well known that it is almost impossible to advertise haircare and other cosmetic products without them. One series of advertisements for a brand of chocolate even

85

manages to play off the connotations of cotton and silk against one another while showing the viewer a chocolate-coloured Dior dress. Similarly, while Austin Reed endeavour to play on the connotations of grey flannel for their gentleman's perfume, Estèe Lauder hope that their female customers will fall for the connotations of white linen. These connotational meanings are so strong that it is impossible to imagine a perfume called 'Brown Wool' or 'Red Nylon' appealing to anyone at all. The workings of ideology and power in creating and reproducing these dominant readings of words and images will be dealt with later.

It will be noted that, given the associative and subjective nature of connotative meaning, it is almost impossible to be either incomplete or mistaken in giving an account of that meaning. What one person associates with a word or an image can hardly be said to be incorrect or incomplete; nobody is ever taken to task because their connotations are incorrect. As a result of this, connotation may differ widely from person to person, as noted above. It is also the case, however, that connotative meaning cannot simply be found in dictionaries; one cannot understand connotation simply by looking in a dictionary. This is not to say that dictionaries will not occasionally provide connotative meaning. But, as connotative meaning is the product of a person's sex, age, class and so on, in seeking to understand another person's connotative meanings, one must either be the same sex, age, class and so on as that other person, or one must try to imagine what it would be like to be those things. The understanding of connotation is an intersubjective and hermeneutic affair.

Figure 8 may also be analysed and explained in terms of connotational meanings. Some of those connotations, of late-Victorian, aristocratic patriarchy, have already been mentioned. None of these things is literally present in the image and they may differ from person to person, depending on that person's social and cultural situation. Some may not associate the man with patriarchy, with a version of masculine dominance, although others would claim that the upright, stiff and rather phallic connotations of the pose and the cane are hard to miss. Some, who are rather more familiar with the period, may argue that the connotations are of Edwardian, rather than late-Victorian, England. Moreover, there are those who would read connotations of class and status into the image, arguing either that the man is a beater and has been dressed, like a slave, in the livery of his aristocratic master, or that he is one of the guns and is using the associations with the Duke of Norfolk to reinforce his own aristocratic status.

Other examples can be thought of. The Principles advertisement used in chapter six (Figure 16), may be analysed and explained in terms of denotation and connotation. The denotation is straightforward: indeed, the ad provides some of the denotation for us. Although the reproduction is too small to see it, the bottom left hand corner of the ad tells the reader that her dress is navy, knitted and costs £50. Other elements of denotation can be seen for themselves and one is either correct or incorrect in identifying them. There is a young woman sitting, shoeless, with her legs crossed on a cream/white sofa. There are three or four cushions visible and a man with his hand in his pocket is walking past; his blurred bottom half may be made out. All this is part of the denotational meaning of the image. Although they will vary more or less slightly from person to person, according to age, sexuality, gender, social class and so on, and there are, therefore, no incorrect connotations, there will often be a consensus as to the connotations. Fashion students with whom I have discussed this image in class have agreed that the woman has a job in the media and drives a BMW 3 series or a Volkswagen Golf. She has plain carpets, or stripped pine floors in her flat and her boyfriend's name is Richard. Clearly none of this, surprisingly detailed, information is 'in' the image in the same way that the denotational meaning is. Yet these and other connotational meanings were read from the image and generally agreed upon: the associations of the image and the things it made people think were largely shared by the members of the different groups with whom it was discussed.

Denotation and connotation, then, are two levels of meaning. They may also be considered as two types of meaning. The pink and blue bootees mentioned above may, therefore, be said to connote the sex of the baby wearing them. It should also be pointed out that, so strongly is this pair of opposed colours, or dichotomy, rooted in this culture that pink and blue now have connotations of gender, of masculinity or femininity, and may even be used to denote sex and gender. Tickner suggests, for example, that it may be possible for trousers to imply masculinity so strongly that 'they can be used to stand for it because they have become exclusively identified with it' (Tickner 1977: 56). The open collar, worn without a tie, may be said to denote that one is not at work, that one is in an informal setting. But an open collar, worn without a tie, may in turn have connotations of scruffiness and untidiness and even suggest that one is unfit for work. The trickiness of these concepts does mean that they may be made to work on a number of different levels and in all sorts of places.

Finally, it must be pointed out that denotation and connotation are analytic concepts. They are to be used in the analysis and explanation of experience, rather than to be found in it. For example, it is never the case that one receives denotative meaning and then, later, the connotative meaning. The two types of meaning are understood at the same time. Nor does one ever think, 'I wonder what connotations I have of that'. Denotative and connotative meaning cannot generally be separated in this way in everyday life, although they must be separated in this way in order to carry out the analysis and explanation of fashion and clothing. Denotation and connotation are different types or levels of meaning; the next section will consider the different ways in which meanings are produced or generated.

The arbitrary nature of the sign

It has been argued above that meaning is not simply a product or expression of the designer's, wearer's or spectator's intention, of what is in their heads. It has also been argued that meaning is not simply a product of the garment or ensemble, that garments or ensembles are not meaningful by themselves. Saussure's version of this argument is to say that the relation or bond between the signifier and the signified is arbitrary (Saussure 1974: 67), and he is quite correct when he says that this principle dominates all semiology and that it has innumerable consequences. The idea that the relation between the signifier and the signified is arbitrary means that there is no natural or God-given relation between the two (Saussure 1974: 69). It also means that the relation between signifier and signified is not a matter of individual choice (Saussure 1974: 69, 71).

For example, it is the relation between the written or spoken word 'shirt' and the item of male dress signified that is arbitrary. There is no natural connection between the signifier, the written or spoken form of the word, and the signified. The written or spoken words 'skirt' or 'shift' would do the job of signifying the item of male dress just as well as 'shirt'. Nor is the relation a result of individual choice. One cannot use the signifier 'skirt' or 'shift' to represent the item of male dress without being continually corrected or eventually incarcerated. Similarly, there is no natural relation between the colour pink and the female sex. Blue or red or any other colour could be used to denote femaleness. Nor is the relation a matter of individual choice; many men feel uneasy about wearing pink because they recognise the effeminate or gay connotations of the colour and have no wish to appear to be either. If there is no natural connection between signifier and signified, then meaning cannot be simply a product of the garment or ensemble. And if the relation is not a matter of individual choice, then meaning is not simply an expression of what is in a designer's or a wearer's head.

Saussure's account of the position of the semiological subject may be compared with Marx's account of the historical subject. In *Course in General Linguistics*, Saussure claims that the signifier,

> although to all appearances freely chosen with respect to the idea that it represents, is fixed, not free, with respect to the linguistic community that uses it . . . language always appears as a heritage of the preceding period.
>
> (Saussure 1974: 71)

Meaning cannot be simply a product of what is in a designer's head because the signifiers with which s/he would construct and communicate it are always part of a heritage over which s/he can have had no control. In some ways, this formulation is strikingly similar to Marx's account of the historical position of humanity. He says that,

Men make their own history, but they do not make it just as they
please; they do not make it under circumstances chosen by themselves, but under circumstances directly encountered, given and
transmitted from the past.

(Marx and Engels 1968: 96)

If the word 'meanings' is substituted for 'history' in the quote from Marx, the
result would not look out of place in Saussure's *Course*. The idea is that
meanings are constructed by using signifiers from an already existing
structure over which the individual has no control.

Syntagm and paradigm

The arbitrary nature of the sign means that it can only be the socially sanctioned differences between signs that produce or generate meaning. There is
nothing in pink or blue that is naturally male or female; any other colours
would do, so long as they were different colours. It is not up to the individual
to choose what pink or blue will mean; there has to be social agreement on
the matter. There is nothing in the word 'shirt' that relates it naturally to the
garment; any other word would do, so long as it was sufficiently different to
all other words. Nor is it the individual who decides what the word will mean;
there will be no communication without social agreement. So, meanings are a
product of the difference or the relation between signs: as Saussure says, 'in
language, as in any semiological system, whatever distinguishes one sign from
the others constitutes it', there are only differences 'without positive terms'
(Saussure 1974: 120–1). Moreover, meanings are the product of social agreement, they are the product of negotiation between people. There are two sorts
of difference, two ways in which a sign may differ from another sign. There is
'syntagmatic' difference and there is 'paradigmatic' difference.

Syntagmatic difference is the difference between things that may come
before and after one another, and paradigmatic difference is the difference
between things that may replace one another. Syntagmatic difference is to do
with the signifying sequences or wholes that can be constructed using signs,
while paradigmatic difference is to do with the sets from which signs are
selected in order to form those sequences or wholes. A menu is the usual and
clearest example of how these two types of difference work. Syntagmatic
difference is the difference between courses, while paradigmatic difference is
the difference between items within courses. Thus syntagmatic difference
determines that, for most Western European cultures, the main course is eaten
before the sweet but after the starter. Paradigmatic difference determines that
one eats prawn cocktail *or* soup *or* melon as a starter. Here, the syntagm is
the entire sequence; the sequence and order in which one eats a meal is a
signifying sequence or whole. The paradigm is the set of items from which
one item is chosen as a starter.

These sequences and choices are socially sanctioned ways of organising differences, of making difference meaningful. There is no natural reason why roast chicken should not be eaten as a starter, why it should not exist in paradigmatic difference with other starters, but Western European cultures generally do not do this, and instead place it in a position of syntagmatic difference with regard to other starters. These differences are meaningful and significant within the culture. Indeed, it was argued in the previous chapter that they were constitutive of the culture. That these sequences and choices are significant or meaningful may be judged by imagining the reaction that is likely to meet the person who orders roast chicken *and* roast beef for a main course or who orders ice-cream for a starter. The reason some people perceive foreign cuisines as daunting is often the result of not knowing the syntagmatic and paradigmatic differences between items on the menu and wanting to avoid ordering the equivalent of chips and custard.

It is claimed that these two sorts of difference also account for the production of meaning in fashion and clothing. It will be recalled that syntagmatic difference is the difference between things that form a signifying sequence or whole. Syntagmatic difference, then, is the difference between the constituent parts of a garment. It is the difference between the garments in an outfit or ensemble and between an autumn collection and the following spring collection. It will be recalled that paradigmatic difference is the difference between things that can replace one another. Paradigmatic difference, then, is the difference between the collar styles that can appear on a man's shirt. It is the difference between the different types of jacket that may be chosen for an outfit or ensemble and the difference between the items that go to make up an autumn collection.

Syntagmatic difference is the difference between the collar, cuffs, buttons, sleeves, shoulders, front panels and back panels of a shirt, for example. All are necessary to form the syntagm or signifying whole that is the shirt. It is also the difference between the shirt, tie, jacket, shorts, trousers, socks and shoes of an outfit of gentleman's clothes. In Figure 9, syntagmatic relations or differences run vertically; one would normally wear a collar, a jacket and a pair of trousers. All are necessary to form the signifying whole of the ensemble. The relation between the elements in a syntagm is 'this *and* this *and* this'. Paradigmatic difference is the difference between the different collar styles (e.g. turndown, cutaway, button-down, tab and pin) from which one must be chosen to make the shirt (Figure 9). It is also the difference between the different styles of lapel, either notched or peaked, and the different styles of trousers, with or without pleats for example, that one must choose between. The relationship between elements in a paradigm is 'this *or* this *or* this'. In Figure 9, then, both syntagmatic and paradigmatic difference are illustrated. What need to be added are the kind of rules that determine that a jacket with a peaked collar will also be double-breasted, and that, if a jacket is double-breasted, it should never be worn with a waistcoat, for example. These are also rules concerning syntagmatic and paradigmatic differences.

One example of the way in which these ideas can help us think about fashion design can be found in the example of the Comme des Garçons shirts which were produced in 1988 with two collars and different-sized buttons. What is happening here is that the rules of syntagm and paradigm are being playfully manipulated and 'broken'. The normal rules for shirts would be that, in the syntagm of a shirt, one collar from the paradigm of available choices would be chosen. One paradigmatic set, from which a choice could be made, concerns the types of collar. The paradigm contains turndown, cut-away and button-down, for example (see Figure 9). Another paradigmatic set, from which a choice could be made concerns the number of collars a shirt can have. Usually, shirt-makers choose to have one collar per shirt: whichever collar was chosen, the rule would be that a shirt contains only one collar of a particular type. By having two collars, the Comme des Garçons shirts are breaking the syntagmatic and paradigmatic rules. The different-sized buttons may be explained in a similar way. From the paradigm of buttons (which would include different materials, shapes and sizes, for example), the rule would be that, customarily, one shape, size and material would be chosen. In selecting different-sized buttons and combining them in one shirt, the rules are being broken. One of the functions of such an analysis is that it provides another perspective on the myth of creativity and inspiration that is so often found in connection with fashion design. What is perceived as idiosyncrasy, or artistic originality, is revealed as the manipulation of a number of relatively simple rules. Such a perspective will not be welcome everywhere, however, and as Gillian Dyer points out, there is always the danger that such semiological analysis becomes 'excessively formalistic and inward-looking, mystifying more than it clarifies' (1982: 182).

Colours and textures may also be explained in terms of syntagmatic and paradigmatic difference. Clearly, the colours exist as a paradigmatic set. One colour may replace another. A blue shirt may replace or be replaced by a white shirt. A combination of colours, selected from the paradigm of colours, may also be considered syntagmatically, as in an outfit. Here the possibility exists of judging whether or not a colour goes with another, judging it in terms of the syntagm of which it is a part. Textures, likewise, exist as a paradigmatic set. One texture, one sort of fabric or textile, may replace or be replaced by another. The velvet jacket may replace the linen jacket which in turn replaced the tweed in the search for the right look in an outfit. Having selected the texture, having inserted it into the ensemble, it becomes part of the syntagm, part of the signifying whole, and may be judged as part of that syntagm.

If meaning is a product of these differential relations between elements, then meaning may be changed by altering those differential relations. By changing the ways in which elements relate to each other syntagmatically and

91

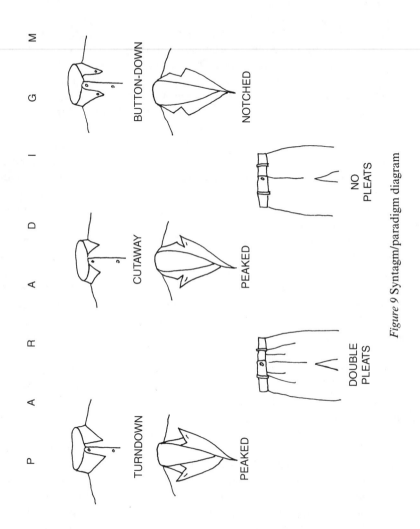

Figure 9 Syntagm/paradigm diagram

Figure 10 Tattersall check shirt 2001, courtesy of Morrison McConnell and Coats plc

paradigmatically, the meaning of garments and ensembles may be changed. Supposing that the analogy has not already been stretched too far: it is claimed that in the same way that changing the choices made at the various stages on a menu changes the culinary experience, and alters the meaning of the meal, changing the choice of garment changes the sartorial experience, and alters the meaning of the ensemble. The meaning of fashion and clothing, from the smallest cuff detail to the seasonal flux of international shows, may be explained in terms of syntagmatic and paradigmatic relations of difference.

Leach asserts that 'taken out of context, items of clothing have no "meaning"' (Leach 1976: 55). A Tattersall check shirt (Figure 10), for example, means nothing on its own. Placed in the context of a pair of beach shorts and sandals, it would be judged 'not right' or 'too smart'. Placed in the context of a city suit, it would again be judged 'not right' or 'not smart enough'. In both of these cases, the shirt does not 'go with' the other items; the syntagmatic and paradigmatic rules that govern these differences determine that the shirt is 'wrong' in both of these examples. However, placed in the context of a tweed jacket and corduroy trousers, for example, the shirt is 'just right', suggesting the appropriate level of countryside informality. It is context, then, the place of the item as defined by syntagmatic and paradigmatic differences, that generates the meaning of the item. Semiology may be thought of as a theory of contexts, a theory which describes how the contexts in which items of clothing exist actually work. Syntagmatic and paradigmatic relations, then, are the contexts in which things exist and from which their meanings derive. It is argued here that syntagmatic and paradigmatic relations can explain all the contexts that a garment, an ensemble or an entire seasonal collection may inhabit. This involves the claim that, no matter what the larger context that was suggested as the real source of meaning, that context would have to be describable in terms either of syntagmatic or paradigmatic difference. That is, whatever larger context was proposed as the real source of meaning, that larger context would have to be either syntagmatically or paradigmatically related to the element that was being discussed.

Denotation and connotation II: myth and ideology

The account of denotation and connotation found in Barthes' work is also relevant to the understanding of the workings of ideology. As Volosinov writes, 'the domain of ideology coincides with the domain of signs . . . Whenever a sign is present, ideology is present too' (Volosinov 1973:10). It was noted in chapter one that communication is not an 'innocent' or 'neutral' activity; that it is one of the ways in which positions of inequality, dominance and subservience are produced and reproduced in society. It is, moreover, one of the ways in which those positions of dominance and subservience, which are the product of human behaviour, are made to appear to be natural, a

94

product of nature, and therefore unquestionable. This was referred to as hegemony (see p.42). Hegemony refers to the situation that exists when certain social groups, or certain fractions of social groups, in positions of dominance, are able to exert their social authority as a result of their power appearing and being experienced as natural and legitimate. Fashion and clothing, then, as forms of communication, are themselves part of this process. By means of fashion and clothing, positions of dominance and subservience are made to appear and are experienced as natural, not the result of human action. Hegemony, then, may be thought of as a sort of moving battle, which Gramsci refers to as a 'moving equilibrium' (Hall and Jefferson (eds) 1976: 401), which constantly has to be re-won on a series of different battlefields, including those of fashion and clothing.

Barthes' account of denotation and connotation may also be used to explain the ways in which the products of human, historically located actions are made to appear to be natural. It may be used, that is, to further our understanding of how ideology works. The two main sources for Barthes' account of denotation, connotation and ideology are the essays 'Myth today' (in Barthes 1972) and 'Rhetoric of the image' (in Barthes 1977). In the former, Barthes writes that myth performs the same function as ideology: myth, he says, 'has the task of giving an historical intention a natural justification and making contingency appear eternal' (Barthes 1972: 142). It will be recalled from chapter one that this was one of the definitions of ideology. Myth, then, is Barthes' version of ideology. It has the task of legitimating existing power relations by making them appear to be the work of nature, rather than of historical and contingent human actions. In 'Myth today', then, ideology is called myth. In 'Rhetoric of the image', however, ideology is called rhetoric; rhetoric is said to be the signifying aspect of ideology (Barthes 1977: 49). Rhetoric has the same function in this essay as myth has in 'Myth today', that of naturalising the historical and humanly contingent.

Barthes explains all of this in terms of denotation and connotation. Ideology (or myth, or rhetoric, as Barthes calls it) operates for the most part at the level of connotation. As Barthes has it, the 'common domain of the signifiers of connotation is that of ideology' (Barthes 1977: 49). Connotation was seen above to be a second order level of meaning, based upon denotation. Denotation was something like the literal meaning of a term or an image, and connotation was the feelings, associations and impressions that the image or term caused to come to mind. Connotations were the result of one's class, sex, age, nationality and so on, and consequently changed from person to person as class, age and so on changed. It is on the level of connotation, then, that ideology is to be found. The feelings, associations and impressions that come to mind are the result of a person's class, sex, age and so on. They are the source, in a sense, of ideology.

So, ideology, or myth, operates mainly on the level of connotation. It is the function of denotation to naturalise connotation, or ideology, to make it appear as if it has always been this way. As Barthes says, 'it is . . . the denoted message which "naturalises" the system of the connoted message' (Barthes 1977: 51). That is, denotation appears to be a level of meaning that is not a product of class, age, sex and so on. Denotation appears to be a literal level of meaning, one that is free of variables and the same everywhere it is found. It may appear, therefore, not to be ideological, to be almost a product of nature and not the result of contingent things like class, age and sex. Because denotation appears to be a natural kind of meaning, one believes that the connotations are also natural. Of course, this is the effect of the rhetoric of the image; ideology is the process in which the work of culture is presented to be understood as the work of nature (Barthes 1977: 45–6).

WRITING ABOUT FASHION AND CLOTHING

So far, this chapter has been concerned with what might be termed 'visual fashion', with the appearance of fashion and clothing. It has explained how the meaning and images of garments may be accounted for in visual terms. Fashion and clothing, however, are also written about; magazines and articles in the popular press also deal with fashion and clothing. As was noted in the Introduction, there are numerous glossy magazines for sale which offer advice on what to look like and how to achieve a certain look. One way of viewing these magazines is to see them as offering advice on what to communicate and how to communicate it. These magazines and articles construct garments, ensembles and collections as meaningful and communicative by writing about them. The exhortations to buy or wear a certain colour or texture and the captions accompanying a photograph are ways in which garments are made meaningful in terms of, or by means of, the written word. There is also some work to be done on written fashion and clothing, with fashion and clothing as they have been written about. Barthes has probably done the most in this area and it is his work that this section will be looking at.

Anyone who has been tempted to look into *The Fashion System* (Barthes 1983) will be aware that it is not the easiest reading. Moreover, it must be admitted at the outset that the work has been almost universally written off, even by Barthes himself, as a semiological disaster. Barthes attempted to claim that there were extenuating circumstances for the work, when he suggested in an interview that he had been misled by a 'euphoric dream of scientificity' (reported in Thody 1977:107 and Culler 1975: 38). It would perhaps be more accurate to say, however, that while the first part of *The Fashion System* is correctly described as 'two hundred pages of head-splitting analysis', the last seventy pages have been lauded as both witty and accessible (Thody 1977: 100). The first part, entitled 'The vestimentary code', contains the head-splitting analysis which is Barthes' *echt*-structuralist attempt to be scientific, and the last seventy pages, entitled 'The rhetorical system', are indeed both witty and accessible, more akin to Barthes' earlier work

Mythologies (1972). So, while the opinion of most critics is probably that *The Fashion System* is more of a nightmare than a dream, they also seem to agree that it is possible to be misled in interesting ways.

In this work, Barthes distinguishes what he calls the 'vestimentary code' from the rhetorical system. The vestimentary code operates in terms of denotation and the rhetorical system operates in terms of connotation. It is the function of the latter to make the arbitrary status or character of the former appear natural. The analysis of the vestimentary code is an attempt to discover a 'constant form' in order to understand how 'vestimentary meaning is produced'. That is, Barthes must first define signifier and signified on this vestimentary or denotative level: he must, as he has it, 'determine which are the syntagmatic (or spatial) units of the written garment and which . . . are the systemic (or virtual) oppositions' (Barthes 1983: 59–60). In this attempt to define the signifier, Barthes comes up with the basic syntagmatic unit, which he calls the 'matrix'. The matrix is a structure or an economy; it is a relationship between object, support and variant, which are involved in signification.

Barthes' example may make the meanings of these terms clearer. Barthes uses the sentence, or 'utterance', 'A cardigan sporty or dressy, if the collar is open or closed' as his example. As he points out, it is, in fact, two utterances:

cardigan • collar • open = sporty
cardigan • collar • closed = dressy.

Since the sentence contains a double signification, denoted by the 'if X or Y' structure, there are strictly two utterances here. The idea is that this is a typical sentence, or utterance, which one might find in a fashion magazine. It may, like all other such sentences or utterances, be reduced or analysed into its constituent parts. The constituent parts are object, variant and support. In this example, 'cardigan' is the object, which 'receives' the signification, 'open/closed' is the variant, which 'constitutes' the signification, and 'collar' is the support, which supports or bears the signification (Barthes 1983: 62–3). More exciting examples can be imagined and explained in terms of these ideas. When Run-D.M.C chose to leave their Adidas unlaced in the late 1980s and early 1990s, the result could be analysed thus:

Trainers • laces • present = cool
Trainers • laces • absent = uncool.

The trainers, or sneakers, are the object, 'laces' are the support and 'present/absent' are the variant.

Barthes must then explain what are the types of things that can fit into these categories, what may and may not be object, support or variant. For example, 'a skirt, a blouse, a collar, a pair of gloves, or a pleat can sometimes be the object, sometimes the support, and at still other times both at once' (Barthes 1983: 87). These are called 'species', and Barthes claims that there

97

are sixty different kinds (or genera) of these species (Barthes 1983: 105–10). The system begins to get very complicated very quickly and the head-splitting nature of it all becomes quite apparent. A flavour of the complexity may be seen in the example of knots. Barthes says that 'a knot, for instance, is a species of the genus "fasteners", but it can have sub-species of its own: hatter's knot, cabbage-knot, butterfly knot' (Barthes 1983: 100). As Culler points out, 'garments or parts of garments which are syntagmatically incompatible – which cannot be combined as elements of a single outfit – are placed within paradigmatic contrast within a single kind' (Culler 1975: 36). The idea is to specify the rules which determine, for example, that 'if a member of the kind "collar" is the support, then the object must belong to one of a limited set of kinds: roughly, garments which have collars' (Culler 1975: 36). The species and genera are also important to Barthes' account as they form the basis for the connotative meanings of the fashion system. They mark, he says, the 'threshold of the intelligible' in that they define the significant differences between objects and supports (Barthes 1983: 98).

The variants are treated similarly. In total there are thirty variants of existence and relation. Variants of existence include form, which is relatively 'rich' and concerns the workings of terms like 'straight, rounded, pointed' and so on, weight, which is not so 'rich' being limited to terms like 'tight' and 'heavy' and length (Barthes 1983:119, 125, 132). Variants of relation include variants of position, which are to do with the ways in which orientation in space, horizontal, vertical and transversal, is signified (Barthes 1983: 144). The variants of relation also include degree, which deals with the ways in which terms like 'little', 'very', or 'halfway' function (Barthes 1983:158). The idea is that the variants are things which cannot be found on or in the same support and so form a paradigmatic group. Thus a garment may be described as light and straight but not as light and dark.

This analysis is supposed to account for the production of denotative meaning, what Barthes calls vestimentary meaning. Culler is not unrepresentative when he argues that the account of the vestimentary code is unsatisfactory insofar as it is 'confused, incomplete and unverifiable' (Culler 1975: 37). However, whereas in 'Rhetoric of the image' it is the function of denotation to naturalise the workings of connotation (ideology), in *The Fashion System* the opposite is the case. Here it is the function of the rhetorical level, connotation, to naturalise the denotative or vestimentary meaning. As Larrain points out, 'a most important feature of this rhetorical level is that it tries to naturalise the arbitrary character of the vestimentary signs, disguising the tyrannical decisions about fashions as if they were facts in a natural process' (Larrain 1979: 135).

As Barthes says, 'fashion is both too serious and too frivolous at the same time' (Barthes 1983: 242). That is, it is at once completely dictatorial ('Every woman will shorten her skirt to just above the knee, wear pastel checks and walk in two-tone pumps'), and completely trivial ('gingham, for the

98

weekend', irrespective of the properties of the fabric) (Barthes 1983: 263, 207). It is both of these things at the same time, and Barthes argues that it is 'because fashion is tyrannical and its sign arbitrary that it must convert its sign into a natural fact or a rational law' (Barthes 1983: 263). It is, then, completely arbitrary when it specifies 'gingham for the weekend', for example. Any other fabric would be fine for the weekend, after all. At the same time it is completely mandatory, it takes the imperative voice. 'Every woman will shorten her skirt . . . ' has the same sort of tone to it as 'Leaves will fall from the trees in autumn', as if it is describing a natural process rather than the tyrannical and arbitrary process of fashion. It is in this way that the rhetorical level, connotation, naturalises the vestimentary level.

A different form of writing about fashion is analysed in Fiske (1990). Here, he looks at the ideological operations of magazines for young women. Echoing Wilson's point, noted in chapter one above, that fashion is 'primarily associated with Woman' (Wilson 1990: 209), Fiske demonstrates how these magazines introduce young women to a particular prevailing ideology of femininity by means of fashion. The implication of the articles on fashion in such magazines is that 'fashion (or appearance) is women's work'; young women are led to believe that they need to look stylish for men (Fiske 1990: 180). Magazines such as *Seventeen*, an edition of which Fiske analyses in some detail, exist to disseminate 'a set of meanings of femininity that are made to appear attractive and realistic to young women, yet finally serve the interests of those with power, that is middle-class men' (ibid.). In Fiske's example, the use of pinafores, denim and hair styles is shown to construct a version of femininity in such a way that the model is engaging to young women yet ultimately in the interests of men. The edition of *Seventeen* also illustrates the way in which young women's resistance to some of the ideology the articles are pushing is incorporated, or rendered harmless. As Fiske says, the 'no make-up look', which the article proposes is 'a strategy to incorporate the resistance of many young women to the ideological practice of painting their faces' (1990: 184). The magazine must contain some of the oppositional feelings of its audience if it is successfully to appeal to that audience (Fiske 1990: 185). Editions of *Cosmo Girl*, *Sugar*, *19* and *More* for November and December 2001 contained no evidence of such opposition. Without exception, the articles in these magazines which related to fashion and make-up were concerned with the ways in which readers could make themselves look like Victoria Beckham, Jennifer Lopez and Christina Aguilera, for example. There was no alternative presented and, to this middle-class male's eyes, not a trace of irony. The ideological function of the magazines, as described by Fiske, was prevalent and evidently so sure of itself that there was no need to incorporate the oppositional feelings of its audience.

CONCLUSION

This chapter has tried to explain the main problems involved with some accounts of meaning, and has presented what is claimed as a more satisfactory account. Semiology was used to account for two types or levels of meaning, denotation and connotation, and how those types or levels were generated by means of syntagmatic and paradigmatic difference. It was then argued that communication also involved relations and positions of power, and that fashion and clothing were ideological phenomena, implicated in the creation and reproduction of those relations and positions. Finally, Barthes' account of written fashion was introduced and attempts made to make sense of it. Chapter five will begin to apply some of these ideas to the question of how class and gender are signified in fashion and clothing. The ways in which class and gender identities are constructed and communicated will be explained by using ideas like paradigmatic difference, denotation and connotation.

FURTHER READING

Part of the motivation for writing the present volume was the lack of suitable material on semiology and fashion. The problem was, and some will no doubt say still is, that while there are some very good general introductions to semiology there is very little that deals sympathetically with the semiology of fashion and clothing. The analytical rigour and precise terminology of semiological approaches remain unpopular and are often mistaken for bloodless academic exercises (cf. Dyer 1982: 182).

- One of the very good general **introductions to semiology** is Fiske, J. (1990) *Introduction to Communication Studies*, Routledge. References to fashion and clothing, however, are few. The first few sections of the second chapter of Rouse, E. (1989) *Understanding Fashion*, BSP Professional Books, are less concerned with the full spread of semiological analysis but more relevant to clothing and fashion, drawing on Edmund Leach's excellent, but very anthropological (1976) *Culture and Communication*, Cambridge University Press.
- The **primary texts**, perhaps surprisingly, are among the best places to look. Saussure's (1974) *Course in General Linguistics*, Fontana/Collins, is perfectly clear, so long as one does not stray too far from the sections on the nature of the sign, linguistic value and syntagmatic and paradigmatic (which latter Saussure calls associative) relations, for example. Barthes' essay 'Myth today', in his (1972) *Mythologies*, Paladin, starts off clearly and gets more difficult, as indeed does his essay 'Rhetoric of the image', in (1977) *Image, Music, Text*, Fontana/Collins, the second half of the last sentence of which defies interpretation to the present day for this author.
- It was suggested that these ideas could be used to analyse and explain the workings of all kinds of media images, not just fashion and clothing garments. For a treatment of **fashion photography** Susan Sontag's essay on Richard Avedon in UK *Vogue* for December 1978 would be worth looking at and there is a tantalising chapter in Barthes' (1983) *The Fashion System*, University of California Press. There are a number of interesting references to follow up. Craik, J. (1994) *The Face of Fashion: Cultural Studies in Fashion*, Routledge, devotes an essential chapter to fashion photography. Ash, J. and Wilson, F. (eds) (1992) *Chic Thrills: A Fashion*

Reader, Pandora, contains a number of analytic essays from various feminist perspectives concerning such photographers as Della Grace, Deborah Turbeville, Herb Ritts, Bruce Weber, Helmut Newton. For more historical perspectives, Clark, R. (1982) 'Norman Parkinson: fifty years of portraits and fashion' in the *British Journal of Photography Annual* and Harrison, M. (1991) *Appearances: Fashion Photography since 1945*, Jonathan Cape, might be considered. Hilary Radner's essay 'On the Move: Fashion Photography and the Single Girl in the 1960s' and Elliot Smedley's essay, 'Escaping to Reality: Fashion Photography in the 1990s' are both collected in Bruzzi, S. and Church-Gibson, P. (eds) (2000) *Fashion Cultures: Theories, Explorations and Analysis*, London, Routledge.

- There are a few essays on **fashion journalism and fashion writing**. Laird O'Shea Borrelli's (1997) essay, 'Dressing Up and Talking about It: Fashion Writing in *Vogue* from 1968 to 1993', appears in *Fashion Theory*, Volume 1, Issue 3, pp. 247–60. It considers the effects of the different editor's styles on the writing and the tone of the writing. Agnès Rocamora's (2001) essay, 'High Fashion and Pop fashion: The Symbolic Production of Fashion in *Le Monde* and *The Guardian*' (in *Fashion Theory*, Volume 5, Issue 2, pp. 123–42), uses the work of Bourdieu to analyse the cultural significances of the different types of fashion writing found in these newspapers.
- For website offering an introduction to semiology, try *www.langc.tohoku.ac.jp/ ~holden/Work_in_Progress/Semieon.htm*

5

FASHION, CLOTHING
AND THE REPRODUCTION
OF SOCIETY

INTRODUCTION

So far, this book has attempted to define fashion and clothing and has tried to explain the different functions of fashion and clothing. Fashion and clothing have been explained as cultural phenomena, and as communicative phenomena and the ways in which different types or levels of meanings are generated and communicated by means of fashion and clothing have been examined. The next two chapters will consider fashion and clothing from the perspective of or in terms of class and gender. Beginning from the Marxist schema employed by Larrain (Larrain 1979: 44), and the examples of jeans and men's suits, the present chapter will consider fashion and clothing as reproductive practice, as activities which construct and reproduce existing class and gender identities. It will consider them as ways of constructing and reproducing people's circumstances. Chapter six will consider fashion and clothing as revolutionary practice, as activities which contest or critique those identities. It will consider fashion and clothing as ways of transforming people's circumstances, as activities which aim at transforming those circumstances.

In many ways, the conceptual distinction between reproduction and revolution is an illegitimate one. In many ways, therefore, the strategy of dividing the chapters in this way is misguided. It is an illegitimate distinction because, for many topics (and class and gender are two such topics), even to bring the reproductive nature of the activities to light is already a revolutionary practice. To consider class and gender as being the sort of things that are constructed, signalled and reproduced is already to have begun the process of contesting the prevailing or dominant ideology, which says, for example, that they are natural activities and positions. To consider them in this way is to neglect or ignore the fact that fashion and clothing are the scene of the various moving battles in which meanings and identities are fought over. With this warning in mind, however, the present chapter will look at the ways in which fashion and clothing constitute, signal and reproduce class, sex and gender relations. Chapter six will look at the ways in which fashion and

102

clothing may be used to challenge or to contest those class, sex and gender relations. Chapter seven, on post-modernity, will examine the ways in which fashion and clothing may be considered to be both reproductive and revolutionary at the same time, the ways in which they may be seen as undecidable.

REPRODUCTION

The use of the word 'reproduction' in this chapter cannot go unremarked or unexamined; it is not being used in its most common or everyday sense and must be defined, especially as it will be used later in relation to concepts like sex and gender. Joanne Entwistle introduces the idea by looking at the notion of change in fashion and society. She refers to the argument that 'fashion responds to social and political changes, reflecting and reproducing these changes' (2000: 80). This is the idea that fashion replicates developments and events in social and political life. It is being used here to refer to the ways in which the continued existence of institutions, practices and products, as well as the relative social positions of people and the ideas and beliefs they hold, are ensured. Institutions, from the local art school to the international fashion industry, survive largely unchanged from generation to generation. Practices, from dressing male babies in blue and female babies in pink to using ecologically dangerous bleaches and dyes, endure from day to day. Products, from shell-suits to Sackville Street suits, continue to be bought and sold. Positions of relative dominance and subservience, with regard to both class and gender, persist. And, more often than not, ideas and beliefs outlast the people who hold and believe them. The word 'reproduction' is being used here to refer to the ways in which elements of culture (practices, products, institutions, ideas, beliefs and status) are sustained, the ways in which the continued existence of these things is ensured.

In her (1994) book *Sex and Suits*, Anne Hollander points out that the male suit has 'stayed virtually the same for two hundred years' (1994: 4). This 'staying power' (ibid.) is part of the sense of reproduction as it is used in this chapter. The ideas (such concepts as masculinity and respectability, for example), and practices (tailoring and men's clothes stores, for example), surrounding men's wearing the suit, along with the basic form of the suit itself have not changed very much in two hundred years. The suit, practices and ideas have been reproduced: as Hollander has it, the suit has its own 'self-perpetuating symbolic and emotional force' (ibid.). John Fiske explains the idea of reproduction in terms of jeans. In his book *Understanding Popular Culture* (1989), he shows how jeans reproduce the ideas and practices of the economic system in which they are made, bought and sold (ibid: 14). The economic system he has in mind is capitalism and he shows how jeans reproduce ideas concerning freedom, individuality and the natural. These ideas have become part of the meaning of jeans (partly through advertising), and they help to make the product attractive so that people will want to keep on buying them. Everyone wants to think of themselves as an individual and if jeans are seen as individual then they will provide an opportunity for people to construct themselves as individual by buying the jeans. This, of course stimulates a market for the product. As he says, 'jeans are so deeply imbued with the ideology of white capitalism that no one wearing them can avoid participating in it and therefore extending it' (ibid.). It is this self-perpetuating, or reproduction, that is of concern to this chapter.

There are, as Williams points out, two main senses of the word 'reproduction' (Williams 1981: 185). There is a mechanical or electronic sense, in which one speaks of printed, photographic or digital reproduction, for example. This sense includes the idea of a copy, or of an exact copy; mechanical or electronic reproduction may reproduce something identically many thousands of times. And there is a biological sense, in which one speaks of sexual or genetic reproduction. This sense does not include the idea of a copy, still less of an exact copy; sexual or genetic reproduction may reproduce the species but there are characteristic differences or variations between the individuals that make up the species. Some cultural phenomena might be best described or understood using the sense of mechanical/electronic reproduction, and not only those involving printing techniques, the use of mechanical sewing machines or computeraided design and production. Others might be best described or understood using the sexual/genetic sense of reproduction, and not only the ways in which garments sometimes seem to develop almost organically, as if they were living things (for example, the way in which lapels or flares widen or narrow with time).

As Williams also points out, however, since the uses of the word are always going to be metaphorical, it will never be straightforward to speak of reproduction in either sense (Williams 1981: 185). Having said this, the metaphor that is the biological or sexual sense of reproduction does seem more appropriate to the metaphor that is culture, especially when it is remembered that cultural production originally applied to agriculture, selecting and developing species of plants.

FASHION, CLOTHING AND CLASS I

With these reservations regarding the use of the word 'reproduction' in mind, this chapter must explain the relations between fashion, clothing and class. The relations between fashion, clothing and class were introduced in chapter two, where they were related to power and ideology. This section will look again at these issues, in a little more detail and from a slightly different perspective. It was argued in chapter one that the existence of fashion, if not clothing, was conditional upon there being different classes in society and upon upward movement between classes being both possible and desirable. It would not be possible to signal one's membership of a particular class by means of fashion and clothing if there were not different classes of which to be a member. Just as obviously, it would be completely pointless to indicate one's desire to be, or to be considered as, a member of a particular class by means of fashion and clothing if such movement were not possible. It is, then, a very simple society that has no fashion.

Indeed, on Marx's account, it is unlikely that there has ever been a society that has not, at least potentially, been a society that had fashion. This is because, for Marx, 'the history of all hitherto existing society is the history of class struggles' (Marx and Engels 1992: 3). This is a very complex sentence, referring to many different issues and debates, but one of the things it says is that all societies have always been societies consisting of different classes. All must, therefore, have been potentially fashionable societies, societies which used changes in clothing to construct and communicate class identities. How, then, should we define class? According to Marx, class is largely defined in terms of economics:

> Insofar as millions of families live under economic conditions of existence that separate their mode of life, their interests and their culture from those of the other classes, and put them in hostile opposition to the latter, they form a class.
>
> (Marx and Engels 1968: 170–1).

In this quote there is again the reference to struggle and opposition, but it is economic conditions that divide the way of life, interests and culture of different classes. What this means is that class is a product of different economic conditions.

In order to understand what is meant by these economic conditions, it may be helpful to take a few steps back and look generally at the Marxist account of society. (Having said 'the Marxist account', it must be said that there are many different Marxisms, all offering different interpretations and accounts, and that the following is partial in all senses.) Marxism says that people need food, shelter and clothing in order to survive. While individuals might, just, be able to provide all these things for themselves on their own, it is much easier for people to enter into social relationships in order to provide food, shelter and clothing. So people form society because they have to; a single individual is unlikely to be able to provide food, shelter and clothing all on his/her own and must enter into social relationships in order to survive. Now, Marxism claims that different classes may be formed only when a society is so well organised that it produces more than the minimum needed just to survive. The claim that was made above, that a very simple society has no fashion, may now be understood in Marxist terms as saying that fashion will only appear once the minimum subsistence levels have been exceeded.

The transformation of nature in the provision of food, shelter and clothing is called 'production' in Marxism. Production may be analysed into two elements, the forces of production and the social relations of production. The forces of production, also referred to as the means of production, include things like the technology, knowledge and machinery involved in production. The forces or means of production also include raw materials, land and the labour power of men and women. The social relations of production are the social relations that people enter into in production. In providing food, shelter and clothing, then, people may form groups of hunters, they may be farmers, or factory owners and workers. These terms refer to social relationships. According to Marxism, the forces of production and the social relations of production change in time; different periods of time, what Marx refers to as 'historical epochs', are characterised by different modes of production. As Marx says, 'social relations are intimately connected with the forces of production. In acquiring new forces of production, men change their mode of production' (Marx 1975:102).

For example, in ancient civilisations the forces or means of production were actually slaves, and the mode of production is called slavery. The social relations that existed would have been between owner and slave. In feudalism, alongside technology and knowledge, the main force or means of production was land. One of the social relationships that people could enter into would have been that between lord and serf and the mode of production agricultural. In capitalism the main mode of production is industrial. The force or means of production characteristic of capitalism is capital, which may take various forms – factories, tools, machinery, knowledge and so on. The social relations of production are essentially those of employer and employee, bourgeoisie and proletariat as Marx has it. The change from feudalism to capitalism involved a change in the forces or means of production, new technologies and new knowledge led to new machinery, and with them came a change in the mode of production.

Social class, however, is defined in terms of a relation to the means of production in each of these different modes; one's relationship to the means or forces of production determines which social class one is a member of. So, for example, in ancient civilisations slave-owners own the means of production, the slaves. In feudalism, the aristocracy owns the forces or means of production, the lands and technologies, and the serfs do not, they only work on the land. In capitalism, the capitalist owns the plant, the factory and the technology while the worker merely works in the factory, with the plant and technology. The classes, then, are freeman/slave, lord/serf and bourgeoisie/proletariat, and they are the result of different relations to the means of production.

Another way of expressing this would be to say that each class has a different interest in the forces or means of production and, in Marxism, these interests give rise to conflict or contradiction; they are the occasion of the struggle referred to in the quote above (see p.105). For example, put very simply, the bourgeoisie has an interest in profiting from the labour of the working class and the working class has an interest in profiting from its own

and reproduce social class, to reproduce a social order in which different and unequal social classes existed.

Indeed, the sumptuary laws of this period may be explained as attempts to regulate precisely what the different classes could wear. They may also be seen as attempts to naturalise the differences between classes by specifying what the different classes were and were not permitted to wear. They may be seen as evidence of the awareness of those in positions of dominance that their dominance was not necessarily either legitimate or proper, and that it needed supporting or shoring up by means of sumptuary legislation. As Hurlock says,

> sumptuary laws were used primarily to preserve class distinctions. When members of the nobility found their position of supremacy encroached upon by the lower classes who had attained wealth, they passed laws to restore the respect for the inequality of ranks which had previously existed.
>
> (Hurlock 1965: 296)

While begging the question as to how the lower classes had attained their wealth, the quote makes it clear that these laws were intended to play a part in the legitimation of inequalities of social rank. They were intended to make the inequalities of wealth and power, and therefore the exploitation of one class by another from which those inequalities resulted, appear to be natural and proper. Hurlock reports how, in England, Edward III, who reigned from 1327 to 1377, passed sumptuary laws decreeing that ermine and pearls were to be worn only by royalty and 'those nobles whose income exceeded one thousand pounds' (Hurlock 1965: 298). Around the same time in France, Philippe le Bet was also reserving the use of ermine for members of the royal household (Hurlock 1965: 298).

The Bayeux Tapestry, dating either from around 1080 or from the middle of the twelfth century, according to which authority one consults, is not necessarily a good source of accurate information concerning who was wearing what in the Middle Ages (Figure 11). It may be used, however, to provide visual evidence of the part that clothing plays in the legitimation of a social order. What is generally to be found in the Tapestry is that William and Harold, the members of the aristocracy who are fighting over the possession of land, are the ones doing all the pointing and commanding. The soldiers, who by and large would have been serfs working on the lands of lords loyal to either William or Harold, are the ones doing all the fighting and all the obeying. The two classes are always distinguished by what they are wearing; clothing is used to construct different visual identities for the different classes and thus to naturalise the inequalities of wealth and power. The kings and the aristocracy appear dressed in grander or more elaborate clothing than either the serfs or the soldiers. The argument, at its simplest, seems to be that it is right for one group to obey another, as that other group is wearing something

Figure 11 Bayeux Tapestry, eleventh/twelfth century

different; the difference in clothing is experienced and explained as the source of that other class's authority, rather than a reflection of it or of economic position.

Clearly, there is no natural connection between serfdom and short tunics on the one hand, or between aristocracy and long robes on the other. The length of tunic or robe is not a natural or God-given signifier of social position insofar as one could quite easily imagine a situation in which long robes signified serfs and short tunics signified aristocracy. The forms of dress, long robe or short tunic, form a paradigmatic set, as do the social classes, aristocracy or serf. As one cannot wear both a long robe and a short tunic, so one cannot be both a serf and an aristocrat. The wearing of either a long robe or a short tunic has been codified in such a way that to wear one signifies that one is a serf, and to wear the other signifies that one is a member of the aristocracy.

Capitalism

Capitalism is the fourth form of property, the fourth way in which people may be related socially in the production of goods necessary for everyday life. Marx writes that the great commercial revolutions which took place in the sixteenth and seventeenth centuries, along with geographical discoveries of places like America and parts of Asia, were among the 'principal elements in furthering the transition from feudal to capitalist mode of production' (Marx 1959: 332). In this transition, according to Marx's account, the serfs are robbed of the means of production. They are separated from all property on which they might work and be productive, so that the only thing they have left to exchange is their own labour power. They are also removed from the various guarantees of existence that were afforded by the old feudal system (Marx 1954: 668–9). Ostensibly, capitalism is a set of reciprocal rights and obligations between capitalist and proletarian, or worker. In exchange for labour, in exchange for work performed in the capitalist's factory, for example, the worker receives a wage.

The class structure of capitalist societies is a good deal more complex than the schema pictured so far has suggested: intermediate and transitional classes obscure the simple capitalist-worker structure, for example, and working class and bourgeoisie are each capable of being subdivided a number of times (Marx 1959: 885). The working class may be subdivided into categories such as unskilled, semi-skilled and skilled labour, and Marx refers to such subdivisions of the bourgeoisie as the 'petit bourgeoisie', referring to the owners of small businesses, shopkeepers and the like. He also refers to 'the middle classes . . . situated midway between the workers on one side and the capitalists and landowners on the other' (in Bottomore and Rubel (eds) 1961: 198). So, neither the bourgeoisie, the class which owns the means of production, nor the proletariat, the class which does not, should be conceived as homogeneous or monolithic structures; each may be divided into class fractions. According to the ideology of capitalism, upward movement between these classes is both possible and desirable. Downward movement is also, of course, possible and, according to the ideology of capitalism, deeply undesirable. Indeed, Marx argues that the process in which someone from the lower layers of society becomes a successful capitalist, through 'energy and strength of character', is greatly admired by supporters of capitalism. Recruiting, and thereby assimilating, members of the lower classes is also one of the ways in which the bourgeoisie makes its position of dominance more secure (Marx 1959: 600–1). Within capitalism, therefore, it becomes possible for both fashion and clothing to be used to construct, signal and reproduce the desire for social mobility between classes as well as class identity itself (Figure 12).

One of the most obvious ways in which clothing, as opposed to fashion, may be made to construct, signal and reproduce class identity can be seen in the use of uniform or livery for domestic servants. This is not so very different to the phenomenon encountered above in relation to feudalism, where serfs pressed into battle would have worn the colours of their lords or kings. Moreover, the problem that the sumptuary laws of the Middle Ages were intended to overcome, that of social inferiors aping their superiors, does not seem to have disappeared either. There are, for example, numerous cartoons from the early nineteenth century in which the indignant and crinoline-clad lady of the house orders her identically dressed maid to go and change her

111

Figure 12 Harrow schoolboys, 1951

clothes. Forty claims that the recurrence of cartoons like these was indicative of an anxiety that existed in the minds of the upper classes and which was not relieved until the 1860s, when the uniform of black dress with white cap and apron was widely adopted for use by domestic staff (Forty 1986: 82).

It is argued, then, that the uniform is used to construct the servant's class identity just as much as the crinoline is used to construct the lady's class identity. The lady, who is in a position of dominance, is using her power to construct the visual identity of her domestic staff, people who exchange their labour for her money. Clothing or uniform, then, are not to be understood as reflections, or epiphenomena, of already existing class relations but as the ways in which those class relations are constituted. Clothing or uniform is clearly being seen as signalling class identity in that it is the servant's wearing of the crinoline that the lady interprets as aping her class position and which she finds so objectionable. It is also argued that clothing and uniform reproduce the institutions, practices, products and class positions of capitalist everyday life. The institution and practices of domesticity, in which servants are a feature, are reproduced in that the staff submit to wearing the uniform; by taking the position and wearing the uniform, the institution and its accompanying practices are continued. The products of capitalist everyday life are reproduced, for example, in that someone has to make the garments that go to make up the uniform. In continuing the institution, lady and servant are ensuring that more such garments will continue to be made. The relative class positions are reproduced in that they are precisely positions and roles of dominance and subservience into which the lady and the servant are entering.

In addition to constructing and signalling the differences between classes, clothing may also be used to construct and signal differences within classes. Again it is clothing, in the form of uniform, that is of concern here, rather than fashion. The railway company uniforms explained by Forty may be used to illustrate this point (Forty 1986: 80–1). There are four men pictured: a station master, a passenger guard, a goods guard and a porter. The relative status of each is constructed by the use of different materials out of which their uniforms are made. Thus, for example, the station master's buttons are made of mohair, the passenger guard's made of pressed gilt, the goods guard's of horn, and the porter's of white metal. Maybe the exact significance of these materials for the employees of the time is lost to us now, but it is tempting to see the station master's status as being much higher than that of the porter simply by virtue of his superior buttons. Similarly with regard to the textiles from which the uniforms are made: the station master wears twill (at least in summer), while the guards wear pilot cloth and the porter wears corduroy.

It should be understood by now that there is no natural or God-given reason as to why crinolines should signify bourgeois but not working-class status, nor why corduroy should signify porter but not passenger guard, for example. Each of these garments or materials would do the job just as well as any other. Indeed, corduroy has been used to signify relatively high status from the beginning, used as it was by French kings for their hunting livery. The materials used to make the uniforms form what was explained in chapter four as a paradigmatic set. The ranks through which a worker may rise in the company also form a paradigmatic set. One is either a guard or a porter and so on. And one wears either pilot cloth or corduroy and so on. The paradigmatic set of materials is used to construct the set of ranks or levels in the railway company and the different materials legitimate or naturalise the differences in rank, just as they did with regard to class as discussed above. The hats in Figure 12, for example, form a paradigmatic set. There is no natural or God-given reason why a flat cap should signify lower class rather than the top-hat. Nor is there any such reason why a bow tie should signify higher class than either a four-in-hand type tie or no tie at all. Again they form paradigmatic sets from which a choice is made; the signifier is arbitrary to that extent.

While not wishing to suggest that fashions cannot be uniform nor that uniforms are not subject to or influenced by changes in fashion (see Young 1992, for example), the use of fashion, as opposed to clothing or uniform, to construct and signal social class must now be considered. It has, of course, been argued above that it is only within class-based societies, in which social mobility is both desirable and possible, that fashion is to be found. The idea of social mobility being possible and desirable makes sense in capitalist society only on the basis that it is upward mobility that is both possible and desired. It is meaningful, that is, only on the assumption that different classes have different statuses and that it is better and more desirable to be of high status than it is to be of low status. It may seem too obvious to bother saying, but according to such an explanation, it is the desire for status that drives fashion in capitalist societies. Braudel quotes a commentator from the early eighteenth century as saying that 'nothing makes noble persons despise the gilded costume so much as to see it on the bodies of the lowest men in the world' (Braudel 1981: 324). Even in early capitalist periods, it is the desire to distinguish oneself from, and to set oneself above, the lower orders that encourages fashionable change. Nicholas Barbon, a trader from the late seventeenth century, approved whole-heartedly of fashion. Fashion, he says, 'is the spirit and life of trade': thanks to fashion, trade remains in movement and man lives a perpetual springtime, 'without ever seeing the autumn of his clothes' (Braudel 1981: 324).

Barbon thus introduces an idea that Veblen was to develop two hundred years later as three related ideas: conspicuous leisure, conspicuous consumption and conspicuous waste (Veblen 1992). Barbon's idea is that, as a result of fashion or, the repeated alteration of dress, one never sees one's clothes grow old, they are always new, in the 'springtime' of their lives. Veblen's ideas of conspicuous leisure, consumption and waste are a sophisticated version of this idea, one which has been used to try to explain the idea of fashion. As Veblen says, while the requirement to dress fashionably and the fact that what is fashionable changes every season are both entirely familiar to everyone, 'no explanation at all satisfactory has hitherto been offered of the phenomenon of changing fashions' (Veblen 1992:122). As C. Wright Mills points out in his introduction to Veblen's work, Veblen offers the ideas of conspicuous leisure, consumption and waste as an explanation of a 'particular element of the upper classes in one period of the history of one nation' (Veblen 1992: xiv). As Veblen says, however, 'no line of consumption affords a more apt illustration than expenditure on dress' (Veblen 1992: 118). These ideas may be applied particularly to fashion; they may be applied to any class-based society in which a class feels a need to set itself apart from the other, socially inferior classes, by means of the things they wear.

Veblen offers three norms or principles with which to explain the changing of fashions. He says that the 'great and dominant norm of dress' is the 'principle of conspicuous waste'. The second norm is the 'principle of conspicuous leisure', and the third is the principle that dress must be 'up to date' (Veblen 1992: 121–2). Veblen is at pains to define the idea of 'waste' accurately. It is not intended in any deprecatory sense and refers generally to expenditure that 'does not serve human life or human wellbeing on the whole' (Veblen 1992: 78). Wasteful expenditure on fashion is greatly increased, he says, if each garment is to be worn only for a short period of time (Veblen 1992:122). This is essentially Barbon's idea, noted above, that one sees one's clothes only in the springtime of their lives. According to this view, fashion consists of a series of imperatives to change one's garments as soon as they are no longer 'up to date'. If the garments worn in one season are discarded before the next season begins, then there will be a lot of garments that are not worn until they are worn out and this may be characterised as waste. Clearly, the ability to replace one's dress in such a way is evidence of one's wealth, or 'pecuniary strength' as Veblen has it. This is one way in which one may conspicuously consume if one has the money.

The principle of conspicuous leisure works in a slightly different way. As Veblen says, if it can be shown that a person is not obliged to work, or is not obliged to work manually, in order to earn a living, then 'the evidence of social worth is enhanced in a very considerable degree' (Veblen 1992: 120). If this can be shown, then the effect of differentiation from those classes that are obliged to earn or work manually for a living is enhanced. He writes, 'no apparel can be considered elegant, or even decent, if it shows the effect of manual labour on the part of the wearer, in the way of soil or wear' (Veblen 1992:120). Consequently, it is not just garments that are expensive to buy and which are discarded at the end of a season that are demanded by the 'leisure classes'; there is also the requirement that they be difficult or expensive to keep clean.

Something of this effect may still be seen today in everyday use of the phrases 'white collar' and 'blue collar' to indicate non-manual and manual labour. A white collar, being more difficult to keep clean and showing the dirt more clearly than a blue collar, would originally have been associated with non-manual work. A blue collar would originally have been associated with manual labour. Manual labour being the province of the working classes and non-manual labour that of the middle classes, 'white collar' signals higher status than 'blue collar'. One interesting exception to this idea may be found in contemporary leisure practices. It is more often the case, for example, that young working-class men will dress up to go out for the evening, wearing something much smarter than they would for work, rather than wearing something casual or scruffy. And it is more often the case that young middle-class men will dress down to go out, wearing something much more casual or scruffy than they would at work, rather than wearing something very smart. These examples seem to indicate the very opposite of Veblen's case. The idea behind the film *The Man in the White Suit*, in which Alec Guinness's character has invented a fabric that does not get dirty, only works because a white suit that does not get dirty, that does not show the effects of everyday life, is presented as a desirable thing. Thus in Veblen's day, it was 'the patent-leather shoe, the stainless linen, the lustrous cylindrical hat and the walking stick' that were used to indicate conspicuous leisure (Veblen 1992: 120–1). The shoe, the linen and the hat being, of course, especially difficult and expensive to keep clean.

There is an asymmetry in the matter of conspicuous leisure, related to gender, that may more usefully be dealt with here than in the section below. It is that, according to Veblen, 'the dress of women goes even further than that of men in the way of demonstrating the wearer's abstinence from productive employment' (Veblen 1992: 122). Women's hats or bonnets, shoes, skirts (along with the 'rest of the drapery'), and their long hair, all hamper women and leave them completely incapable of 'useful exertion'. They all prevent a woman from doing anything remotely like work, and are therefore part of the process of signalling that her class position allows her not to work. Of course, as Veblen is well aware, it is the use of the corset that provides an absolutely guaranteed signal of female uselessness. For him, the corset is 'a mutilation, undergone for the purpose of lowering the subject's vitality and rendering her permanently and obviously unfit for work' (Veblen 1992: 121). The asymmetry in the way women's clothing goes further than men's in signalling leisure is related to the asymmetry in the positions of men and women. Simply, women function as servants in the leisure-class household; they are there to provide evidence of 'their master's ability to pay' (Veblen 1992: 127). Women are economically dependent upon men in this society and are still in some sense the 'chattels' of men; their job is to be the 'chief ornament' of the household. They are living, if not fast walking, proof of the economic strength of their husbands (Veblen 1992: 126-7).

On Veblen's account, then, fashion is essentially a reproductive affair in that it is used by the leisure classes, the superior classes, to construct, signal and reproduce their positions of leisured superiority. Status in Veblen's account is a product of economic wealth, and the possession and use of goods to indicate this status and wealth find expression in fashionable dress. Fashionable dress is used to construct, signal and reproduce positions of economic status. The account given thus far can, without too much difficulty, be used to examine contemporary fashions. Rouse suggests that labels and logos are one way in which the purchasing power of a consumer may be indicated (Rouse 1989: 47). The crocodiles, polo players on three-legged horses, sharks, stylised ticks, hanging sheep and laurel wreaths which adorn the breasts of casual-shirt wearers are one way in which expenditure or purchasing power may be indicated, as are the artfully exposed linings of certain raincoats.

FASHION, CLOTHING, SEX AND GENDER I

In a newspaper article written for the *Guardian* in 1992, Wilson notes the way in which fashion is sometimes the object of 'self-righteous denunciations'. Changing fashions in dress and clothing, she points out, are sometimes the cause of moral outrage in a way that changing fashions in automotive or furniture design, for example, are not. Some people, it seems, feel so self-righteous and so morally outraged that they are compelled to write to the *Guardian*, which at the time had a 'Style' page, and complain either that fashion is demeaning to women or that it is 'irrelevant to serious-minded persons of either sex'. Wilson wonders why this should be, why fashion in clothing and dress attracts such indignant and opprobrious criticism when other forms of fashion do not, and suggests that it may be 'partly because dress is so intimately related to the body'. Because dress is so intimately related to our bodies, because it is thus profoundly connected to our sexual and gender identities, fashion is uniquely able to unsettle and unnerve us. As Wilson says,

> when fashions underline sexuality or when . . . they go in for gender bending, many of us may feel threatened and insecure. For women especially, the exaggerated and often arbitrary standards of 'beauty' . . . can be disempowering and even offensive.
>
> (Wilson 1992a: 34)

This chapter must begin to address these issues. Drawing on the semiological insights of the previous chapter, the relations of fashion and clothing to sex, gender and the body must be analysed. This chapter will begin to examine how fashion and clothing construct, signal and reproduce sex and gender. To paraphrase Rouse, fashion and clothing are instrumental in the process of socialisation into sexual and gender roles; they help shape people's ideas of how men and women should look. It is not the case that fashion and clothing simply reflect an already existing sex and gender identity, but that they are 'part of the process by which attitudes to and images of both men and women are created and reproduced' (Rouse 1989: 108).

There may well be a world where it is possible to say something like 'sex is to gender as nature is to culture' and not get into any trouble. This is not that world. The sex/gender distinction is useful, then, but not without its attendant problems. It is useful insofar as sex can be described as a natural phenomenon; sex may be described as being a collection of biological or physiological differences. It is a fact of nature, then, that men have one set of reproductive equipment and women have a different set; sex is determined by the presence or absence of the bodily parts necessary for reproduction. It is also useful insofar as gender can be described as a cultural phenomenon; gender differences may be described as cultural differences. It is a cultural fact, then, that masculinity consists in one set of appropriate characteristics and femininity consists in a different set; in some cultures, for example, to be properly feminine is to be modest, caring and nurturing while to be properly masculine is to be aggressive, domineering and employed outside the home.

The main problem that arises in relation to the ideas of sex and gender consists in trying to define which aspects of male and female behaviour are natural, or biological, and which aspects are cultural. People's actual behaviour cannot always easily be analysed into two separate and distinct categories, 'the natural' and 'the cultural'. The problem arises very quickly as to exactly where sex ends and gender begins. Some argue that it is not clear whether or to what extent men are naturally different from women. They will argue, for example, that it is unclear whether the supposedly masculine characteristic of 'competitiveness', or the supposedly feminine characteristic of 'passivity', are natural or biological, the results of some hormonal overload, or whether they are cultural, the products of a response to specific social situations.

Another way of presenting this problem would be to show that what one culture presents as masculine characteristics, another culture understands as feminine characteristics. For example, where most contemporary Western European cultures regard the preparation of food for the family to be one of the more obviously feminine tasks, involving as it does the domestic care and nurture of family members, the Wahiba of Oman consider it a traditionally masculine task. There is a further confusion here in that western chefs, who are in charge of food preparation in restaurants, are predominantly male. The preparation of food outside the domestic environment, in exchange for money, becomes a masculine thing to do. So, while for the most part it would be fair to say that gender is the way in which a culture makes sense of biological difference, the ways in which it makes sex meaningful, there are points, like these, where the distinction between nature and culture seems to be in danger of breaking down. It may be worth remembering that the distinction between nature and culture is not itself found in nature, but is a product of culture; consequently, it is the source of rather more questions than answers.

A similar pattern is found when fashion and clothing are considered in terms of sex and gender. It is tempting to suggest that sex difference in dress is signalled by the presence or absence of a certain characteristic, while gender difference in dress is found in the meaning ascribed by the members of a culture to the presence or absence of that characteristic. This will not do, however. As Tickner has pointed out, 'although some kind of sex distinction in dress is virtually universal, the particular attributes emphasised as masculine and feminine have varied widely according to time and place' (Tickner 1977: 56). Gaultier may persist with his idea of skirts and dresses for men, for example, even though the majority of men find it perhaps a little too camp, preferring, when they do wear a skirt, the more obviously manly attractions of the kilt. They may also claim, with Steele, that the kilt is acceptable in that it is '*not* a female skirt' but some sort of national dress (Steele 1989a: 9). So, while what a culture considers as masculine or feminine dress may change, sex and gender distinctions may be made by means of the wearing or not wearing of a particular garment, colour, texture, size or style of garment.

For example, sex may be signalled by wearing trousers or not, as has been conventional in the West, or by wearing an apron or not, as was conventional with various peoples in Africa (Crawley 1965a: 75). In the West, since around the nineteenth century, men have worn trousers while women have not, and the men referred to by Crawley have traditionally worn an apron while the

Clothing helps disting uish sexes. Fashion is different for both, often accentuating the sexual aspects of the body women have not. In these cases the presence or absence of a garment is used to signal sexual difference, but the particular garment used varies from culture to culture. The meaning ascribed to the presence or absence of either trousers or apron may be described as gender, a product of cultural difference. It is probably unusual, however, to be able to suggest that, in both these cases, something like the same meaning may be communicated by the presence or the absence of the garment in these different cultures. The phrase 'she wears the trousers' is used metaphorically to refer to a dominant woman in a relationship in the West. And the Dinka call the men of various other neighbouring tribes 'women' as an insult because they wear an apron.

Colour, likewise, has been used to signal sex difference. It is not unusual for people in the West today to associate pink with girls and blue with boys. Nor is it unusual for people to feel distinctly uneasy when wearing the 'wrong' colour. But, as Steele points out, 'in the eighteenth century, a pink silk suit was regarded as appropriate attire for a gentleman' (Steele 1989a: 6): the association of pink with femininity and blue with masculinity was made in nineteenth-century France and it is only since about the 1920s that this latter association has become common in the West. In these cases, the garment and the colour exist in what was explained in chapter four as paradigmatic differences. It is completely arbitrary which garment or colour is deemed by a culture to be masculine or feminine, but once the decision has been made, the colours or garments form a paradigmatic set and meanings are determined or generated by means of the choices made from that paradigmatic set.

Men look, women appear

'Men act, women appear' is Berger's famous formulation or description of the situation that exists between men and women (Berger 1972: 47). He is claiming that there exists a fundamental asymmetry in the relation between men and women. It is not quite a straightforward version of a distinction between active and passive, as shall be seen, but it is closely related to that distinction. Berger is claiming that in Western European cultures, it is characteristically the role of men to be active, to be the gender that observes, that surveys, the opposite sex. He is also claiming that it is the role of women to be more or less passive, to be observed or surveyed by the opposite sex. Women's roles are complicated insofar as they have also to observe themselves being observed. Berger writes that 'men look at women. Women watch themselves being looked at' (Berger 1972: 47); in that women watch themselves being looked at, they are not entirely passive on this account. If men 'survey women before treating them' (Berger 1972: 46), if men decide how to behave towards a woman on the basis of her appearance, then women have to keep an eye on how they are appearing to men. As Berger says, a woman

119

has to survey everything she is and everything she does because how she appears to others, and ultimately how she appears to men, is of crucial importance for what is normally thought of as the success of her life.

(Berger 1972: 46)

This formulation introduces two important ideas. The first is the idea of the gaze and in particular the male gaze. These ideas are taken from psycho-analytic theory and are usually found in connection with the ideas of pleasure and desire. Freud asserts that 'visual impressions remain the most frequent pathway along which libidinal excitation is aroused'. 'Most normal people', he says, desire to look at and derive pleasure from looking at things they find sexually attractive (Freud 1977: 69). This pleasure in looking is commonly called scopophilia; extreme or perverse forms of scopophilia are referred to as voyeurism and exhibitionism. While Freud's position on these matters developed through time, it seems reasonable to claim that people do gain pleasure from looking and that it is, initially at least, on the basis of visual impressions that libidinal interest is aroused. In Freud's account it is when looking or being looked at become the sole source of sexual pleasure that they become fixations and thus perverse. In this society, people who do gain inordinate amounts of sexual pleasure from such perversions are called 'peeping toms' and 'flashers'.

Mulvey's account of scopophilia is developed in terms of Hollywood film; she is concerned with the ways in which heterosexual men look at heterosexual women and the sorts of pleasures that are thus generated. The ideas may be taken out of this context, however, and applied to fashion and clothing. According to Mulvey, scopophilia becomes gendered and it is linked to gendered versions of power and desire. It becomes gendered in that 'pleasure in looking has been split between active/male and passive/female' (Mulvey 1989: 19). Her version of scopophilia also includes reference not only to 'taking other people as objects, subjecting them to a controlling and curious gaze', but also to 'using another person as an object of sexual stimulation through sight' (Mulvey 1989: 16, 18). While Mulvey's account might seem simplistic in that it reduces Berger's slightly more complex scheme to a straightforward active/male–passive/female dichotomy, she introduces the ideas of it being a specifically male gaze which is used to control and gain sexual pleasure from women. It is a masculine desire that is satisfied and a masculine pleasure that is gained from a gaze which, again, is essentially masculine. On this account, women are simply to be looked at; they play what is referred to as a 'traditional exhibitionist role', to men's voyeuristic role (Mulvey 1989: 19).

While this is, unfortunately, of necessity a much simplified account of both Freud's and Mulvey's explanations of scopophilia, it does introduce the idea of there being a gender imbalance in the structures of looking, of gaining pleasure from looking and of satisfying desire in looking. One problem with this kind of account is that it is difficult to explain how women are exhibitionistic and men voyeuristic in societies where there is less, or even no, gender distinction by means of fashion and clothing. It was not until the eighteenth or nineteenth century that gender distinctions became strongly marked in Europe. Steele, for example, notes how, up to this time, 'men often wore silk stockings, cosmetics, long curled and perfumed hair . . . petticoat breeches', just like women (Steele 1989a: 15). Wearing things like this would seem to mark men out as pre-eminently objects for a female gaze: men seem to be cast here in the role of exhibitionist, at least as much as women. If this is the case, then, the active/male and passive/female distinctions must also come into question, and one must ask how 'traditional' these roles are. The matter of when and where they become traditional must be settled; Freud's claims are intended to apply to all cultures, whereas Mulvey is not concerned with other cultures and hence these criticisms are not applicable to Mulvey. The questions regarding female spectatorship, of women looking and gaining pleasure from looking, of specifically feminine looks, pleasures and desires, will be considered in chapter six.

The second idea introduced by Berger's formulation is that women are reduced to their appearance in this sort of account. The creation and maintenance of a look, or an appearance, becomes something like a defining feature of femininity. This may be a part of the sense behind the popular or traditional belief that fashion and clothing are somehow especially or properly the concern of women rather than of men. The gender identity of women, then, may be said to be constructed, signalled and reproduced by means of fashion and clothing insofar as women wear the sorts of things that a society deems appropriate for them and insofar as they continue to be 'obsessed' (Oakley 1981: 82) with their appearances.

Clearly, what a society deems appropriate may change. Oakley points out how, in the 1830s and 1840s, femininity consisted in 'frivolity, delicacy, inactivity and submissiveness' (Oakley 1981: 83). As noted in the account given above of Veblen (see pp.114–16), women were considered to be the property of their husbands, and were subservient to men. They were also supposed to be too delicate to be particularly active, something practically guaranteed by the use of the corset. Femininity here, then, was a matter of being frail and unsuited to almost any sort of exertion. It meant being frivolous, essentially 'not serious', and being given over to trifling concerns. Presumably, one of those non-serious matters would have been fashion and clothing: such women would have been encouraged to reflect their frivolity in their dress. The fashions of the time constructed, signalled and reproduced these values. The very opulence of the fashions and clothing was a sign of the husband's financial standing and of his wife's subservience to him, as his possession. Quoting Roberts, Oakley claims that the sleeves of this period were so constructed that 'it was virtually impossible to raise the arm to

Societies differ in how much one is allowed to show. Different levels/views on sexuality.

shoulder height or make an aggressive or threatening gesture' (Oakley 1981: 83). This would also have had the effect of emphasising the delicacy and submissiveness of women. The effect of delicacy achieved by the corset would, as suggested above, also have had the effect of rendering the wearer all but inactive, passive.

Other periods and other places have had different versions of femininity. Other periods and places may define the characteristic features of what it is to be a woman more or less differently. It could be argued, however, that those other versions are still based around appearance. Fashion and clothing, the way a woman appears, will still be the major way in which that femininity is constructed, signalled and reproduced. It might be argued, for example, that in the 1980s and 1990s in Europe and America it became increasingly acceptable for women to be concerned with creating and sustaining a career. Not necessarily for the first time, a model of femininity became available that included being outside of a domestic environment, being in positions of authority, doing a serious job and earning serious amounts of money.

One may idly speculate whether Cosmo-Girl grew up to become Career-Woman, but there does seem to have been something approaching a stereotype created at around this time. Fashion and clothing were used to construct, signal and reproduce the identity of Career-Woman in a number of ways. Davis reports how writers like Molloy, in *The Woman's Dress for Success Book* published in 1977, advocated something like a 'dark-hued, comparatively severe, man-styled jacket, lowered hemline skirt accompanied by attaché case' (Davis 1992: 48). Fraser simplifies and sums up the vision of 'executive womanhood' by referring to a 'fairly strictly tailored suit . . . straightish skirt . . . hemline ending around the knees . . . [and] shoulders that are padded or otherwise enlarged' (quoted in Davis 1992: 50). Fashion and clothing are used here to construct, signal and reproduce the version of femininity that includes doing a job so serious that one is an executive, in a career, and for which one receives a large salary.

Now, clearly, there is no natural connection between delicacy and frivolity on the one hand, and tight sleeves, crinolines and corsets on the other. The latter are not natural or God-given signifiers of the former. While corsets may cause a woman to be short of breath, there are plenty of other ways of rendering someone unfit for work, just as there are many other ways of indicating frivolity apart from a fashionable sleeve. Similarly, there is no natural connection between a business-like and serious manner, on the one hand, and padded shoulders and hemlines ending around the knee, on the other. Again, the latter are not natural or God-given signifiers of the former. There is no reason why light or pastel shades should not be used to signify executive ability and there are many other ways of indicating that one has a career other than by means of a straight skirt (cf. Steele 1989a: 13). What is happening here is that these arbitrary signs are being used to signify a particular status or position. Once it is agreed, among a community of sign users, that frivolity will be signified by a particular sleeve, or that career level will be signified by a particular style of skirt, then a code has been established. By means of this code, members of the community can construct and communicate gender status to themselves and to others.

Interesting, if somewhat anecdotal, evidence of the asymmetry noted with regard to the gender roles of men and women may be found by looking at the style, fashion and so-called 'life-style' magazines that cater for women. The role of fashion photography in reinforcing these roles should not be overlooked. Fashion photography is undoubtedly a major supplier of images, and one of the most powerful media for creating and communicating images of men and women. Along with Hollywood films, it offers many images of different ways of moving, performing various actions, wearing different garments and so on. Counting the images appearing in both advertising and editorial features, women's style and fashion magazines show many more pictures of women than they do of men. For example, the October 1992 edition of *New Woman* contained two full-page pictures of men and sixteen full-page pictures of women. *Cosmopolitan* for April 1992 contained eight full-page pictures of men and of women. And the March 1992 edition of *Elle* contained five full-page pictures of men and sixty-four of women. Pictures of heterosexual couples were not popular with any of the magazines, and pictures of homosexual couples did not feature at all.

It is tempting to explain this imbalance in the numbers of photographs of men and women in women's style and fashion magazines by saying that the photographs in these magazines offer women a chance to survey themselves in many different situations. They enable women to imagine what they would look like, to men, in this situation or in this outfit, without having to commit themselves in any way to that situation or that outfit. It is tempting to see the function of these magazines as a sort of magical mirror in which a woman may see herself as she might appear at the Yacht Club, in the latest Volkswagen, wearing Versace or lounging around in Laetitia Allen, for example. Bruce Oldfield lends this theory some support when he says that what Mrs Average is doing when she looks at a photograph of an outfit in *Harpers and Queen* is imagining what it will do for her and where she might wear it, as part of the process of deciding whether or not to buy it (Coleridge 1989: 254). If this is the case, then it is hardly surprising that there are relatively few images of men in these magazines. Unfortunately, it is unlikely that this is the case, for if one looks at men's style, fashion and 'life-style' magazines, exactly the same situation is found. Thus, counting both editorial and advertising images again, *GQ* for March 1991 contained some sixty-four full-page pictures of men and three full page pictures of women. *Arena* for Spring 1991 contained forty-four full-page pictures of men and two full-page pictures of women. And the April 1991 edition of *Esquire* contained twenty-seven full-page pictures of men and four full-page pictures of women. Unless one is willing to entertain the proposition that the men's magazines are catering for either hidden and unacknowledged, or manifest and acknowledged, homosexual desires, and supposing that the same argument concerning women's magazines can be discounted, it seems that maybe men, too, are being offered the chance to survey themselves as they might appear to women. These matters, of the male and female gaze and of the pleasures associated with each, for example, will be dealt with in more detail in the next chapter.

Little has been said so far in this chapter about the ways in which men's fashion and clothing construct, signal and reproduce their gender positions. As noted above, gender distinctions in fashion were not strongly marked until about the nineteenth century in Europe. According to Rouse, everyday dress for men and women had been 'quite distinct' since the advent of tailoring techniques in the 1340s but, until the end of the eighteenth century, fashionable men and women alike wore 'ruffs, slashed clothes, furs, jewellery, wigs, lace' and so on (Rouse 1989: 109). Around the end of the nineteenth century, however, the general adoption of simple, plain, drab and sober garments and the wearing of trousers in particular, had effectively established a separate and distinct identity for men. Davis dates this development slightly earlier than Rouse, suggesting that, 'by the time of Victoria's accession in 1837, clear and well-bounded gender distinctions had been established for men's and women's dress' (Davis 1992: 39), but it is clear that the kinds of postures and movements made possible by trousers, for example, were becoming part of the gender identity of men at this time.

With the adoption of simple garments, of trousers that enabled one to walk quickly, run and even jump, a new definition of masculinity was also adopted. The qualities of activity and robustness, of fitness and strength, for example, now became part of the identity of masculinity, something that could not have been possible while men were wearing ruffs, wigs, furs and so on. It could be argued, however, that more important than these changes in clothing in altering the gender identity of men were the social changes brought about by the Industrial Revolution. The men of the new middle classes were involved in industry and commerce; as Rouse points out, qualities like 'discipline, reliability and honesty' were demanded in this world (Rouse 1989:11). What Weber has described as the Protestant Ethic, with its stress on the qualities or virtues of 'hard work, sobriety, frugality and personal economic advancement' (Davis 1992: 38), had an effect, not only on the development of capitalism, but also on the definition of masculinity. In order to survive in the worlds of commerce and industry, a man had to be hardworking, sober, frugal and committed to personal economic advancement. And, clearly, a man's clothing was one way of constructing such a gender identity; men's clothing comes to construct and signal this new gender identity.

According to Davis, such was the 'overweening centrality accorded to work, career, and occupational success for male identity ... that clothing was unavailable as a visual means for men to express other sides of their personalities' (Davis 1992: 39). Clothing, if not necessarily fashion as well, is clearly tied here to constructing and signalling gender identity. It is also tied to reproducing this identity, in that women were not, generally, part of the worlds of industry and commerce in the ways that men were. Women's clothing and fashions were still largely frivolous and decorative, and women were still seen as frivolous and decorative beings, not at all suitable (or indeed able, given their corsets and huge skirts) to partake in the active bustling worlds of commerce and industry. Men's privileged access to the factory, the office and the market-place was reproduced, then, by the fashions and clothing that they wore, which were suited to, or suitable for, such places.

CONCLUSION

It would be too simplistic to make too much of the idea that, as the gender identity of men throughout the nineteenth century becomes more active, what they are wearing becomes less apparent. It does seem to be the case, however, that as male and female fashions among the higher classes become more distinct, so do their gender identities. It also seems that, while the women continue to be just about as decorative as they were, the men become less decorative and less visible. It may be claimed, then, that Berger's point is a fair one and that, when considering fashion and clothing in terms of reproduction, men do indeed act while women appear. This chapter has also indicated, if not explicitly demonstrated, the complex intertwining of the matters of class and gender around the difference between fashion and clothing. It has been noted, for example, that clothing is almost universally used to differentiate different sexes but that, while dress among the lower classes in Europe had been used since the 1340s to differentiate different sexes, fashion among the higher classes had not been used in this way. Fashion was used by the higher classes to distinguish class differences, but not sex or gender differences. The next chapter will look at the ways in which class and gender identities may be contested or challenged.

FURTHER READING

- On the **role of ideology in cultural reproduction**, and on the history and development, both Marxist and non-Marxist, of the concept of ideology, one of the best and clearest treatments is to be found in Larrain, J. (1979) *The Concept of Ideology*, Hutchinson. For Marx's own thoughts, the key texts would be Marx, K. and Engels, F. (1970) *The German Ideology*, Lawrence & Wishart, and Marx and Engels (1992) *The Communist Manifesto*, Oxford University Press.
- On gender, Laura Mulvey's essay 'Visual pleasure and narrative cinema' has become the *locus classicus* for the debate surrounding **the male gaze**: the original source for the essay is *Screen* 16: 3, Autumn 1975, p.618, and it also appears in Mulvey, L. (1989) *Visual and Other Pleasures*, Macmillan. Although the debates are obviously centred around cinema, they are relevant to fashion and clothing. E. Ann Kaplan's essay, 'Is the gaze male?', in Snitow, A., Stansell, C. and Thompson,

S. (eds) (1984) *Desire: The Politics of Sexuality*, Virago, comments on Mulvey's argument. A good collection of essays is to be found in Gamman, L. and Marshment, M. (eds) (1988) *The Female Gaze: Women as Viewers of Popular Culture*, The Women's Press.

- Barbon's reference to the **eternal springtime of one's clothes** may be interestingly compared with Caroline Evan's argument in her (2000) essay 'Yesterday's Emblems and Tomorrow's Commodities'. Here she uses the work of Walter Benjamin and Pierre Bourdieu to investigate and illuminate how designers like Martin Margiela, Hussein Chalayan and Jessie Ogden made their garments look aged. Ogden, for example, stained her fabrics to make them look old, Margiela recycled second-hand clothing and Chalayan has buried garments with iron filings to give them a rusty appearance.
- For more on **fashion, society and change**, which was touched upon above, see the chapter 'Fashion, Dress and Social Change' in Joanne Entwistle's (2000) *The Fashioned Body*, Polity Press.
- Another, comprehensive, introduction to Marxism may be found at the following website: www.marxists.org/glossary/

6

FASHION, CLOTHING AND SOCIAL REVOLUTION

INTRODUCTION

In the previous chapter, fashion and clothing were considered as reproductive practices. They were explained as ways in which class and gender identity were constructed, signalled and reproduced, as ways in which people accepted and reproduced their circumstances and conditions. Fashion and clothing, then, were explained as having a role in ensuring the continued existence of both the specific class and gender identities and the unequal positions of power and status that go with those identities. In the well-known and much quoted introductory section to 'The Eighteenth Brumaire of Louis Bonaparte', Marx comments on the use of clothing in times of revolution. He suggests that, just when people seem to be engaged in 'revolutionising themselves and things', just as they seem about to create something that has never yet existed, they borrow their costumes from the past and dress themselves up in the detritus of world history (Marx and Engels 1968: 96). This chapter will consider fashion and clothing as revolutionary practices. It will explain them as ways in which existing class and gender identities may be challenged or contested, as ways in which people may transform their circumstances and conditions. The ability of fashion to perform such a task is not guaranteed. Nathalie Khan (2000) argues that, if fashion is conceived as a set of momentary and current trends, then 'fashion can reflect, but it cannot renew society' (2000: 116). She says, therefore, that fashion can only be radical when it challenges 'its own systems and structures' (ibid.). Her essay then investigates the ways in which the catwalk shows of people like Alexander McQueen, who has used 'severely disabled' models in his shows, question notions of physical beauty and 'walking beautifully' (ibid.: 119 and see Evans 2000). This chapter will try to look beyond fashion's own structures and it will try to explain how fashion and clothing may indeed question and oppose the continued existence of class and gender identities in society, and show how they may be used to dispute and disrupt the positions of power and status that go with those class and gender identities.

REVOLUTION AND RESISTANCE

In this chapter, it is the use of the word 'revolution' that cannot go unremarked as it is not necessarily being used in an everyday sense. The first everyday sense of the word 'revolution' is that of revolving, of movement around a central point. The second is that of complete change, of turning upside-down and of a reversal of conditions. It is probably the second sense which is more pertinent here, as it introduces two ideas that are highly relevant to the chapter: that of complete change and that of a reversal of conditions. Two questions which will be addressed are, first, whether a complete change in conditions is possible, and second, whether a reversal of conditions is sufficient for the purposes of revolution. It must be asked, then, whether it is possible for there to be a complete revolution, for all conditions and circumstances to be changed once and for all. It must also be asked whether a reversal in conditions is enough to prevent the systems or structures, that one is trying to oppose, from re-establishing themselves and incorporating, that is, appropriating and rendering harmless, all critical energies.

The sense of revolution as complete change, as the changing of all conditions and circumstances once and for all, is unsatisfactory for use in this chapter. It is unsatisfactory for many reasons. First, it is impossible to imagine what such a revolution might mean for fashion; fashion may be seen as consisting in a series of changes, but the idea of any of those changes being a final, once-and-for-all change is surely meaningless. The very idea of fashion involves reference to the idea of constant change and it is therefore incompatible with the idea of revolution as a complete and final change in conditions and circumstances. Second, to conceive of revolutionary clothing in terms of a complete and once-and-for-all change in conditions and circumstances is to misunderstand the nature of the problem. The idea that class and gender inequalities are made acceptable to people by means of those inequalities appearing to be natural and therefore legitimate was introduced in chapter two. This idea, that of hegemony, was further developed in chapter four, where the process in which inequalities of power and status are made to appear natural and legitimate was described as a moving battle. This moving battle has to be won continually, on many different battlefields; no one final battle could settle matters of class or gender power once and for all. Consequently, to conceive of clothing, even revolutionary clothing, as offering a complete change in conditions is misleading.

The idea of revolution as a reversal of conditions is also not entirely appropriate to this chapter. This is because this idea cannot account for how the structures and systems that are being contested or critiqued may recuperate from and may even be strengthened by opposition. The idea of reversal seems to imply the idea that, once the reversal has taken place, it remains in place, with no loss of revolutionary force. This cannot account for the ways in which fashion pre-eminently works. Fashion may be presented as a series of novelties: it may be seen as one shape, colour, texture and so on replacing another, endlessly. These novelties, these new things, are not novel or new for very long, and fashion soon adapts to even the most outrageous designs. As Fox-Genovese suggests, shock is one of fashion's tools of the trade 'what fashion can always co-opt is the outrageous' (Fox-Genovese 1987: 9). Consequently, what was once shocking and outrageous becomes taken for granted. The system that was supposedly being opposed soon recuperates and may even benefit from the shock. Thinking of the way in which punk clothing may now be purchased on any high street in mind, Fox-Genovese points out the 'painful irony in social rebels' having to view the signs of their rebellion sported in exquisite materials by those they thought they were rebelling against' (Fox-Genovese 1987: 9). Something that many have seen as a fundamental critique of mass-produced, high street style has been incorporated by that style and is now for sale on that high street.

For these sorts of reasons, and because the idea of 'revolution' seems to promise more than it can deliver, at least in connection with fashion and dress, many theorists prefer to talk of resistance, opposition and struggle rather than revolution. Chapter nine of Elizabeth Wilson's (1985) *Adorned in Dreams*, for example is entitled 'Oppositional Dress' and she shows how various subcultures, from nineteenth-century dandies to twentieth-century hippies, blacks and gays, resisted and opposed dominant groups by means of fashion and dress. Chapter four of Diana Crane's (2000) *Fashion and Its Social Agendas* considers the ways in which nineteenth-century women wore versions of men's clothes as a form of 'non-verbal resistance' to dominant ideologies. These ideas better express the small-scale, moving battles being continually fought. As Clarke *et al.* say, hegemony 'is not universal and "given" to the continuing rule of a particular class. It has to be won, worked for, reproduced, sustained' (Hall and Jefferson (eds) 1976: 40). Fiske (1989) also uses the idea of opposition to describe the ways in which jeans are bleached, torn and ripped in order to evade or combat the forces of domination. In his account disfiguring jeans in these ways is a means of 'distancing oneself' from the ideologies and shared meanings of America (1989: 4). If the jeans express dominant ideas of freedom, hard work and the American (i.e. capitalist), way, then doing violence to them is also a form of doing violence to the ideology.

This chapter will examine the various ways in which fashion and clothing may be used to contest and challenge class and gender identities, as well as the relations of power and status that attend those identities. It will examine the role of fashion and clothing as resistances. In this chapter, resistance will be explained as taking two basic forms, 'refusal' and 'reversal'. Refusal is the attempt to step outside of the offending structures and reversal is the attempt to reverse the positions of power and privilege that operate within those structures. These two forms of strategy will be looked at with regard to class and gender. Finally, a third strategy will be considered, looking at both class

129

and gender, which may stand more chance of not being appropriated or incorporated by the dominant structure.

PASSIVE AND ACTIVE CONSUMPTION

According to Veblen (1992), the leisure classes continually had to change what they were wearing, the fashion, in order to re-establish the differences between them and the classes below them. Once the classes below the leisure classes had started to wear what the leisure classes were wearing, they had to find something new to redefine their differences. This idea may also be found in the work of Simmel (1971), who agrees with Veblen that 'the real seat of fashion is found among the upper classes'. He continues by claiming that

> [the] very character of fashion demands that it should be exercised at one time only by a portion of the given group . . . as soon as anything that was originally done only by a few has really come to be practiced by all . . . we no longer speak of fashion.
>
> (Simmel 1971: 302)

Strictly speaking, according to Simmel, fashion 'affects only the upper classes', and is something that only the upper classes do. The lower classes are left simply to copy the styles of the upper classes, to adopt the styles and shapes as soon and as best they can. Of course, once the lower classes have copied the styles of the upper classes, the upper classes must find new styles to wear, new fashions. They must do this in order to re-establish the visual markers of social difference; once the lower classes are visually indistinguishable from the upper, by virtue of what they are wearing, the upper classes must find some new visual sign with which to signal their social difference. Thus, as Simmel says, 'the game goes merrily on' (Simmel 1971: 299).

While it is not a phrase that is ever used by Simmel or Veblen, this account of how fashion works, of how fashions spread throughout all levels or strata of society, has been labelled the 'trickle-down theory', because the fashions are supposed to trickle down from the higher classes to the lower classes. As McCracken points out in his attempt to rehabilitate the theory, 'the venerable model has been subject to attacks on all sides' (McCracken 1985: 42). He notes that it has been argued, for example, that the sorts of fashions sported by the leisured classes, elite fashions, have been supplanted by mass fashions and that the latter no longer involve the lower classes imitating or aping the upper classes. It has also been claimed that the popular press and the rise of the fashion magazine have led to a situation in which fashions are seen simultaneously by all levels of society and that they are adopted simultaneously as well. It need hardly be added that photographic and televisual journalism have enabled the very latest fashions from all over the world to be transmitted to the rest of the world almost before the models have reached the end of the catwalk. This description of fashion diffusion has led to a model which, if

130

'trickle' is still appropriate, might more accurately be described, McCracken says, as 'trickle-across' (McCracken 1985: 42). Davis notes Blumer's criticisms of the trickle-down theory. Rather than fashions being adopted in order to demonstrate social prestige, Blumer sees the spread of fashion as being to do with 'collective selection'. Fashion is seen, not as a response to class differentiation and emulation, but in response to 'a wish to be in fashion . . . to express new tastes which are emerging in a changing world', and these wishes may be found in all classes, not only among the elite (Blumer, quoted in Davis 1992: 116). The fashion is followed by the collective, not by lower classes who are imitating the upper classes.

A more serious set of problems with the trickle-down theory has been noted by Davis and Partington. First, as Davis notes, this theory cannot account for 'the fashion pluralism and polycentrism that more and more characterise contemporary dress' (Davis 1992: 112). There is only one place for fashions to come from according to the trickle-down theory and that is the social elite, the upper classes. Consequently, it cannot account for fashions that do not emanate from the elite, upper classes; it cannot account for the ways in which different and various class groups, ethnic groups and gender groups, for example, may be the origins of fashions. Instead of there being one centre from which fashion is produced, the social elite, there are now many centres, each producing their own fashions. Partington gives another, slightly different version of this argument. She says that the trickle-down theory 'reinforces a cultural hierarchy in which class-specific lifestyles are ranked', and that it cannot explain either popular fashion or the 'mass-market fashion system' (Partington 1992: 143). This latter point seems to be essentially the same as Davis' noted above; popular fashion and the mass-market fashion system not being concerned with the upper classes, trickle-down theory cannot explain them. It can have no understanding of the more pluralist and polycentred sites of fashion production.

What is implicit in Davis' arguments here, however, is made explicit in Partington's. It is that trickle-down theory conceives of fashion consumers as essentially passive. Davis points out that one weakness of the trickle-down theory is that it assumes that fashion is concerned only with symbolising social class, whereas it is actually about all sorts of other identities: sexual, gender, age, ethnic, religious and so on (Davis 1992: 112). And Partington opposes the model of fashion and clothing that trickle-down presupposes, in which fashion is a 'reflection of socio-economic distinctions' and in which clothes are a simple 'expression of class identity' (Partington 1992:146). Partington, however, also objects to trickle-down theory on the grounds that it conceives of the consumer 'as a passive victim of fashion' (Partington 1992:146). Certainly, in the works of Simmel and Veblen, there is no sense that the lower classes get any say in interpreting the meanings of the fashions that trickle down to them. Nor do they have any option but to imitate their social superiors by means of those fashions. It is rather as if the fashions simply come down to them and that they are merely obliged to wear them. What McCracken sees as one of the saving virtues of the trickle-down theory, that it has predictive power, that it is possible to predict from the present behaviour of an elite group the future behaviour of other subservient groups (McCracken 1985: 42), may also be seen as evidence of just how passive those subservient groups are conceived to be in the trickle-down theory.

This chapter will be dealing, then, with a more active conception of consumers. It will be looking at consumers, if they may still be referred to as consumers and not as producers in some sense, as actively using fashion and clothing to construct and articulate class and gender identities that are not those that are prevalent in society. In this sense, the chapter will be interested in the use of fashion and clothing as resistance to the dominant identities and values, and it will consider how consumers use fashion and clothing as resistance. This notion of active consumption is necessary in order to explain how fashion and clothing may be used to resist and oppose dominant gender and class identities, as well as the positions of power and status that accompany those positions. So, while the passive consumers of the trickle-down theory, who are found in the works of Veblen and Simmel, for example, reproduce their circumstances and conditions by means of fashion and clothing, active consumers criticise and resist those circumstances and conditions by means of fashion and clothing.

FASHION, CLOTHING AND CLASS II

While not wishing to make too much of a satirical work that is nearly four hundred years old, Thomas More's *Utopia* contains some interesting, if inconsistent, thoughts on the matter of fashion, clothing and class. More describes how there is no private property in Utopia, as everything is communally owned (More 1965: 64). Those who have argued that *Utopia* describes a communist society are, clearly, not entirely wrong and More does explicitly set up capitalist society as one of his targets (More 1965: 66). However, whether the communal ownership of property means that class differences do not exist, or that there are classes but that they are organised differently in Utopia, is difficult to tell from the text but More does refer to men and women 'of all social classes' attending lectures (More 1965: 76) and the society does have slaves. More is also quite explicit that Utopia contains neither tailors nor dressmakers, and that 'the fashion never changes'. The clothes that people wear are 'quite pleasant to look at, they allow free movement of the limbs' and they are 'equally suitable for hot and cold weather' (More 1965: 75). Working clothes are leather overalls, 'which last for at least seven years'; these overalls may be covered by a sort of cloak that is always the same colour, 'the natural colour of wool'. Utopians do not care how coarse or fine their thread is, nor do they worry about whether they are wearing wool or linen (More 1965: 78). Utopians are also content with 'a single piece of clothing every two years'; as More says, there is no reason why anyone should want more, 'they wouldn't make him any warmer – or any better looking' (More 1965: 79).

Clearly, there are number of problems with this account. Indeed, as Ribeiro points out, the nature of the project of Utopian literature necessarily generates certain problems (Ribeiro 1992: 226). So, for example, More appears to propose a class-based society without fashion. It may reasonably be doubted whether this is a possible state of affairs, given the analyses of earlier chapters. The communicative function of fashion and clothing does not seem to have occurred to More (despite the fact that he will have been familiar with medieval sumptuary laws) and he proposes only protection and attraction as functions. Moreover, the idea of clothes that are pleasant to look at but which do not make anyone any more attractive might also be a difficult one to make sense of. It may be objected that it is unreasonable to expect a satirical work such as this to be perfectly consistent and theoretically sophisticated on the matter of fashion and clothing. This is a fair point, but most if not all Utopian literature is keen to legislate for fashion and clothing and to propose some perfect version or vision of them, and it is perhaps surprising that such inconsistencies should exist.

Jeans

If Reich is to believed, however, More might have found it difficult to have disapproved of jeans (Figure 13). Up until relatively recently they were available in one basic colour, they may be described as quite pleasant to look at and they allow free movement of the limbs. Davis quotes Reich as saying that jeans also 'express profoundly democratic values. There are no distinctions of wealth or status; people confront one another shorn of these distinctions' (Davis 1992: 68 and see Fiske 1989 chapter one on the 'jeaning of America'). In this sense, jeans may be explained as an attempt to refuse, or to step outside of, all class identification. They may be seen as an attempt to refuse to enter into class positions. While jeans may be found in any number of discourses and used for all sorts of arguments and debates, this chapter is concerned with them insofar as they either do or do not construct and signal class distinctions, and insofar as they may be used to challenge and contest prevailing class identities. As Polhemus says, jeans constitute the first example of 'dressing down, in which middle-class people adopt working-class style' (Polhemus 1994: 24). Whether Reich's statement is now or was ever true is in a sense beside the point: he understands the garment as contesting undemocratic values, values found in a society that makes and operates according to distinctions based on class, wealth and status. If, as Reich says, jeans carry no distinctions of wealth or status, wearing them may be seen as a challenge to the values of a society in which distinctions of wealth and status are important.

Figure 13 Jeans, 1950s

Davis describes jeans as a 'sartorial symbolic complex at war . . . with class distinctions, elitism and snobbism' that were as common in America as they were in the Old World (Davis 1992: 70). They were, however, not always like this, and it may be suggested that they are no longer so; Davis charts the progress of jeans towards this egalitarian status in the 1960s and then, more recently, away from it. The first people, who were not either miners or cow-boys, to take up wearing jeans on any scale were painters and other artists, located around the south-west United States. In the 1930s and 1940s, creative and artistic types began wearing jeans. Arguably more violent and less cre-ative subcultural groups took them up in the 1950s, when 'hoodlum' motor-cycle gangs or 'bikers' began wearing denim. Activists from the New Left started wearing jeans around the 1960s, as did hippies, introducing a more intellectual, but again, no less marginal market to the product. As Davis says, in their own ways, all of these groups 'stood strongly in opposition to the dominant conservative, middle-class, consumer-oriented culture of America', and jeans offered a 'visible means for announcing such anti-establishment sentiments' (Davis 1992: 70). Jeans, then, were used by those critical of the prevailing, or dominant, ideology of the time to construct a position from which that ideology could be criticised and opposed; they constituted a site of resistance to that dominant ideology.

However, almost at the same time as they were becoming a sign of opposition to class identities and positions, jeans were starting to be appropriated or incorporated by the system that they were being used to criticise. As they were being used to signal a desire to escape or refuse the confines of class identities, they were being used precisely to establish those identities. They were becoming domesticated and being turned to the job of constructing and signalling precisely the sorts of class distinctions they had been thought to escape. Davis reports how, in the late 1950s, only a few 'middle-class boys' were wearing jeans and how it was not until the late 1960s that they were adopted by the rest of the middle classes. Figure 13 is of 1950s America and it is quite difficult to tell whether these three lads are delinquent hoodlums or nice middle-class boys from the suburbs. The problem, apparently, was that jeans had disreputable connotations, resulting from their association with delinquent motorcycle gangs and hippies, and the jeans industry had to work hard to dispel these connotations. This is the process of appropriation, or incorporation, noted above. In this process, what was once a challenge to the dominant system is appropriated or rendered harmless by the dominant system, which adopts or adapts the values represented by that challenge. The dominant system incorporates or appropriates the values that once represented a challenge, it takes in those values and makes them its own. Consequently, the battle must be moved to another site in this kind of account; it is a moving battle that must be constantly re-fought and re-won.

Although Davis does not make this case explicitly, it can be seen in his account that the final point in this process of making jeans ultimately acceptable to all was to introduce precisely the sorts of distinctions between the classes of jeans wearer that they had originally been used to counter. By introducing 'symbolic allusions' and by promoting 'invidious distinctions among classes and coteries of jean wearers' (Davis 1992: 72), jeans could be used to signal just the sorts of distinctions the marginal and sub-cultural groups had used them to oppose. The system of class-based, capitalist consumption with its distinctions of wealth and status had appropriated and rendered profitable a product that had been used to oppose that system. In this way, then, the dominant system takes in the values once represented by jeans and makes them its own. The photograph caption describing Lagerfeld's designs for Chanel's denim collection effectively makes the point for Davis: 'a classic suit from blue and white denim, $960, with denim bustier, $360 . . . and denim hat, $400. All at Chanel Boutique, Beverly Hills' (Davis 1992: 68). Finally, it may be argued that the attempt to escape or to step outside of all class identities and positions is impossible. That it is impossible to escape or step outside of these identities and positions may be seen as an explanation of how it is that jeans were so quickly incorporated by the dominant system. For, if the positions and identities are impossible to escape, then it is not surprising that the dominant system can re-establish class distinctions by means of these garments.

Punk

The punk phenomenon of the 1970s noted in the introduction to this chapter (see Figure 5) may also be described as an attempt to use fashion and clothing to challenge class identities and positions. Rouse suggests that punk appeared to develop 'as a reaction against the massive commercialisation of both music and fashion for the young' (Rouse 1989: 297). Music and fashion having become boring and safe, produced by ever more distant, formulaic and packaged 'stars', punk first developed as a sort of 'do-it-yourself' culture, producing its own music and clothing in opposition to the music and fashion system that had become monolithic, unadventurous and predictable. It may also be understood as an attack on the larger economic system that had produced the dole queue, the inner city wastelands and the absence of any meaningful future. As Hebdige says, 'beneath the clownish make-up there lurked the unaccepted and disfigured face of capitalism . . . a divided and unequal society was being eloquently condemned' (Hebdige 1979: 115). The boring and safe music and fashion of the early 1970s were seen as representing the dominant, mainstream and bourgeois culture, making money from the youth that bought its products. Punk was an attempt to challenge both bourgeois culture and the capitalist system that promoted and sold the insipid products of that culture.

The dominant, mainstream and bourgeois culture of the time offered, among other things, an aesthetic: it defined which materials and objects were either beautiful or valuable, or both, and it defined how and where those materials and objects might be worn. It also offered standards and norms of personal attractiveness: rules for how to look, 'approved' hairstyles, rules concerning cosmetics and their use, and so on. So, for example, precious metals and minerals such as gold, silver and diamonds might be combined and worn on wrists and necks as bracelets and necklaces. Fine, clean cottons and smooth worsteds might be made into plain, white shirts and dark, tailored suits. Women's hair would be flowing and feminine, men's would be short and neat; both would be conservative and unobtrusive. Men would not wear make-up and women would aspire to look like the flawless, silky creations of the fashion magazines. This aesthetic provides for the regulation of practices and institutions, as well as of materials and objects. There are rules for what to wear on certain occasions, or for doing certain things, for example. There is also a whole network of professionals and 'experts', in jewellery shops, tailors, retail associations and so on, to advise, inform and, if necessary, arbitrate for the consumer in matters regarding the genuineness, worth or appropriateness of the items on sale.

Punk may be understood as offering a thoroughgoing critique of this aesthetic. It may be explained as offering a reversal of the valuation given to colours, textures and materials in the dominant system. Conventional practices and institutions of high street or bespoke fashion and clothing were abandoned in favour of a more DIY approach. Materials and objects that had hitherto been deemed either worthless or ugly, or both, were worn on and in parts of the body that had not hitherto been adorned. Hebdige provides a useful catalogue of some of the ways that the rules and norms of conventional attractiveness were generally broken, flouted and ignored. For example, cheap, worthless things like safety pins were plunged through cheeks, ears and lips, toilet chains adorned chests, tampons and razor blades hung from male and female ears. 'Cheap, trashy fabrics (PVC, plastic, lurex, etc.) in vulgar designs (e.g. mock leopard skin) and "nasty" colours', like lime green and pink, became part of punk clothing. Men's and women's hair was cut in a variety of bizarre styles; dyed in such colours as 'hay yellow, jet black or bright orange', it was teased and gelled into 'Mohican', spiked and tufted styles. Make-up, like the clothing, displayed the signs of its own construction. So, while clothes were ripped, and seams were displayed on the outside, cosmetics were 'worn to be seen' by both men and women (Hebdige 1979: 107). Sounding alarmingly like Lurie, Hebdige suggests that punk clothes 'were the sartorial equivalent of swear words' (Hebdige 1979: 114), swear words not being part of the polite conversation of the dominant cultures in the same way that punk clothing was not part of conventional bourgeois clothing.

This account has not included the reference to black youth cultures highlighted by Hebdige. It has not, therefore, dealt with punk as incorporating elements of racial or ethnic opposition to dominant values. Nor has it stressed the challenge to gender identities that punk represented. However, it is claimed that opposition to the dominant bourgeois culture in terms of class is evident. Whether this was ever a genuinely working-class challenge, and if so for how long, or whether it traded in what Hebdige calls 'working classness' (Hebdige 1979: 63), taking over the values of earthiness and authenticity, for example, is not in question here. What is clear is that punk 'claimed to speak for the neglected constituency of white lumpen youth' (Hebdige 1979: 63) and that it represented a considerable challenge to the values of the dominant classes. The materials, objects, practices and institutions with which punk challenged mainstream bourgeois culture are all much closer to some version of 'working classness', if not actually drawn from the working classes. The dirty clothes, tarty styles, and 'tasteless' colours and patterns, for example, may all be seen as using elements that might be thought by the middle classes to characterise working-class styles and tastes. In this sense, then, punk may be seen as an attempt at reversing the privilege accorded to styles, fabrics and colours. What was considered good taste by the dominant classes is opposed by using what was considered as poor taste by those classes.

Given this, it is perhaps surprising that punk was appropriated by the capitalist system and adopted by the dominant classes as quickly as it was. Fox-Genovese's observation that the adoption of punk styles by high street fashion stores is a painful irony is no doubt true (Fox-Genovese 1987: 9), but the situation seems somehow to be made worse if Rouse's claim is correct, that 'no style was taken up more quickly by the fashion business' than punk (Rouse 1989: 298). It may be adding entrepreneurial insult to ironic injury to suggest that, not only were punk styles and fashions incorporated by the capitalist system but, despite their calculated offensiveness, they were appropriated by that system quicker than any other. Albeit much tamed and 'domesticated', versions of punk hair may be found in eminently respectable places today. While tampon earrings could never really be said to have caught on, men's and women's earrings show the influence of punk even now. And, while Vivienne Westwood collects prizes and awards from a grateful, if occasionally puzzled, industry, watered-down versions of her work are to be found in every 'Top Man' and 'Chelsea Girl'.

This is another example of the process of incorporation or appropriation at work. In this process, what was once a challenge to the dominant system is appropriated or rendered harmless. This is achieved by the dominant system adopting or adapting the values represented by that challenge. So, for example, the colours, fabrics and textures used by punk are made into high street fashions, and it becomes possible to buy a ready-made version of punk rebellion. The aesthetic and political values of punk are appropriated by, made the property of, the dominant system and the dominant classes. In this way, what started as a challenge to that system and those classes is rendered harmless to them. Consequently, the battle must be moved to another site on this account; hegemony is a moving battle that must be constantly re-fought and re-won in order that the dominant classes retain their dominance. That Vivienne Westwood is sometimes lionised by the trade, that she is, famously, the recipient of an OBE from the Queen of England and the subject of laudatory essays and articles in both popular and academic journals, and that punk-inspired clothing could be bought so soon after it appeared on the streets are all evidence of how effectively punk was appropriated by the dominant culture. Finally, it may be argued that the strategy of reversal adopted by punk is not sufficient on its own to resist being appropriated by the dominant system. As Fox-Genovese writes, being shocking is one of fashion's tools of the trade and what the fashion system can always appropriate is the outrageous (Fox-Genovese 1987: 9).

Hip-Hop

The case of Hip-Hop adds the matter of ethnicity to that of social class in the question of oppositional fashions. Chuck D's (1997) book *Fight The Power:*

Rap, Race and Reality explicitly charts the social, political, economic and ethnic background to Hip-Hop, considering the relation of Black Rap and Hip-Hop artistes to slavery, unemployment, the music business, American and New York City politics and the Nation of Islam, for example. Rap and Hip-Hop are clearly located in these contexts; as Chuck D says, for example, 'if we don't have control over . . . education, economics and enforcement . . . we're on a plantation . . . we live in plantation systems that are still governed by a legal and subtle apartheid in the United States of America' (1997: 48–9). Hip-Hop is set up here as a way of opposing the legal apartheid found in the United States.

The fashions that early rappers and Hip-Hop artistes wore were often

Figure 14 Snoop Dogg in cuffs 1990s

139

ways of resisting and opposing this system. When Run-D.M.C appeared in their unlaced Adidas sneakers, they were making a reference to the way in which shoelaces were routinely removed from prisoners in American jails, in order to prevent inmates hanging themselves. The fashion for oversized and baggy trousers which displayed the waistband of one's underwear also originated in jails: belts were removed from inmates for the same reason that laces were removed, with the result that prisoner's trousers were worn low and that they sagged, thus revealing the underwear (ibid.: 46). Taking these styles and using them outside of prison may be seen as a way of appropriating and commenting on the practices of what is perceived and suffered as an unjust system, while at the same time expressing solidarity with their incarcerated brothers. The Dukie/dookie ropes, which were gold chains, often fastened by padlocks, were also an expression of black identity. They referred either to the condition and experience of slavery, or as rapper Treach explained, to 'the brothers who are locked down' (Wilbekin, in Light (ed.) 1999: 280). The strategy is the same: a symbol of the dominant, unjust and offensive system (slavery or prison), is taken over and ironically and ostentatiously displayed. Run-D.M.C also rejected the world of high fashion in their 1984 'Rock Box', saying that 'Calvin Klein's no friend of mine, don't want nobody's name on my behind' (ibid.: 277). Wilbekin interprets this dismissal of 'the rah-rah fashionistas' as 'neo-Black power . . . creating its own urban street style' (ibid.).

As with punk, however, the distancing and resistant gestures that were involved in black Hip-Hop fashions were almost immediately incorporated into the dominant culture. According to Wilbekin, almost as soon as the fashions appeared on the street, they were in turn appropriated by the world of white, middle-class fashion. In the mid-1980s, Isaac Mizrahi saw the chains on his elevator operator and included them in his 'Homeboy Chic' collection. Lagerfeld draped the female models in gold chains in the 1991 Chanel show. In 1992 Marky Mark, the 'acceptable' face of rap, was to be found on Calvin Klein posters. And by the mid 1990s, Ralph Lauren and Tommy Hilfiger had signed up the likes of Tyson Beckford, Sean Combs and Coolio for their catwalk shows (Wilbekin in Light (ed.) 1999: 279–82). Nor did the appropriation stop there. Sean Combs launched his own fashion line, Sean John, in 1998. Tommy Boy Records produced Tommy Boy Gear. And various members of the Wu-Tang Clan created Wu-Wear (ibid.: 283). Chuck D himself, the voice of Public Enemy, one of the least compromising Hip-Hop groups, got into trouble with the black community in 1991 when he provided the vocals for a Nike commercial, having argued in 'Shut 'Em Down' that Nike should invest in the neighbourhoods whose inhabitants spent so much money on their products (Chuck D 1997: 43–4).

Like Fox-Genovese above, Wilbekin notes the 'irony' involved in the situation. He says it is ironic that the Hip-Hop nation, once so proudly self-sufficient . . . became obsessed with the finer things in life: designer clothing . . . all the things that prove how successful you are by American Dream standards.

(1999: 278)

Specifically and peculiarly black, working-class, ghetto-based styles, styles that originated in slavery and an exceptional experience of the American prison system were turned into the so-called 'ghetto-fabulous' fashions of elite, white and middle-class America.

FASHION, CLOTHING, SEX AND GENDER II

In the previous chapter, Berger's formulation of the situation that exists between men and women was used to explain how fashion and clothing reproduce sex and gender identities and positions. Berger's account of this situation is based on the idea that 'men act and women appear' (Berger 1972: 47). If Flügel is to be believed, what he calls 'The Great Masculine Renunciation' led to men's fashions and clothing becoming more sober. The GMR, the renunciation of elaborate, sumptuous and decorative clothing, has the effect of inhibiting men's narcissistic and exhibitionistic desires. More sober and simpler clothing also enables them to move more freely. While this process is taking place, women's fashions and clothing are becoming more elaborate, more decorative and more restrictive, preventing them from moving freely at all. Thus masculinity becomes defined as the spectator or voyeur of femininity, and femininity becomes reduced to appearance or spectacle.

This section will examine the ways in which gender identities and the positions of relative power in which they exist have been challenged and contested by fashion and clothing. It will examine the ways in which fashion and clothing have been used either to escape from the system of fashion altogether or to reverse the identities and positions accorded to men and women. First, 'early' feminist attempts to oppose and challenge gender identities and positions by refusing or escaping the gendered system of fashion and clothing will be examined. And second, the ways in which gender identities and positions have been reversed, redefining masculinity as a series of appearances and making women more active spectators, for example, will be examined.

'Bra-burners'

Before the hysteria that the phrase 'bra-burners' inevitably causes gets out of hand, it should be explained that the expression is being used as a shorthand way of referring to a feminist position rather than as a description of historical fact. As Evans and Thornton point out, the burning of bras at early Women's Liberation Movement meetings in America began as a rumour; the story became a legend, then a cliché, before finally assuming the status of myth (Evans and Thornton 1989: 4). Whether these garments were ever actually burned is beside the point. What is significant about the phrase is that it indicates a position to be taken on the matter of fashion and clothing. This position is, basically, that fashion and clothing which reproduce existing gender identities and positions are to be refused or escaped from. It is the position that argues that such fashion and clothing are to be opposed or challenged by destroying them on the grounds that they construct, signify and reproduce oppressive gender identities and relations.

According to Evans and Thornton, in the late 1960s and early 1970s 'the entire package of fashion was condemned by feminists' (Evans and Thornton 1989: 1). Fashion and clothing were seen as constructing and reproducing a version of femininity that was false and constricting and that had to be escaped from or got out of. One way of getting out of the gender identity was to get out of, or to refuse to wear, the fashion and clothing that were constructing that identity. The early Women's Liberation Movement, then, saw fashion as articulating an ideology of femininity. These women saw fashion as defining what women were or might become and as conforming to various stereotypes, all of which were perceived as objectionable. Consequently, the Women's Liberation Movement 'rejected' or refused fashion; the aim of the early Women's Liberation Movement was 'to "get out" of fashion' and thereby get out of the imposed gender identities and positions. (Evans and Thornton 1989: 3). Attempting to refuse or escape from fashion by not wearing clothes that were thought to articulate the ideology of femininity, was seen as refusing or escaping from gender identities and positions. Clearly, whether it actually happened or not, the burning of certain garments, bras for example, would have been the logical extreme to have taken this strategy to.

Oakley quotes Cassell in order to describe this strategy. Cassell may be understood as describing how, in the late 1960s and early 1970s, feminists refused fashions and clothes which they believed conformed to stereotypes. Lesbian feminists, for example, did not wear bras, their hair was not styled, they wore no cosmetics and they did not wear jewellery. Many of the things that women had worn under the prevailing ideology of gender, things that were supposed or intended to enhance their appearance, were refused. Such things simply were not worn by these feminists (Oakley 1981: 83). Evans and Thornton add that these women also never wore high heels (Evans and Thornton 1989: 7). It can be argued that this strategy is anti-fashion, in the sense of being 'against fashion', and Sawchuk goes so far as to claim that Oakley assumes an anti-fashion discourse to be 'inherently feminist' (Sawchuk 1988: 67). To be anti-fashion in this sense, then, is to be feminist in that in refusing fashion, one is refusing the gender identities and positions constructed, signalled and reproduced by the fashion.

Evans and Thornton also claim that with the rejection or refusal of fashion came a refusal of narcissism (Evans and Thornton 1989: 6). In refusing the fashion, these early feminists are understood as attempting to refuse the positions of narcissism and exhibitionism that were part of the dominant ideological definition of femininity. These terms, which are part of the discourse of psychoanalysis, where they have certain specialised meanings and are connected with personality disorders, should perhaps be used with more care than they commonly are. As Steele points out, 'the psychoanalytic theory of narcissism is highly complex' and, while it may be true to say that women were and still are permitted by society to take more interest in their appearance than men, this is not evidence that women are 'narcissistic' or 'exhibitionistic' in any psychoanalytic sense (Steele 1985: 29). However, Evans and Thornton claim that 'narcissism is traditionally a female prerogative, a characteristic imputed to women within patriarchy to confirm their inferiority' (Evans and Thornton 1989: 6). Women's interest in or preoccupation with their own dress and appearance is conceived as a trap from which they must be freed; again, exhibitionism and narcissism are conceived as things to be refused or escaped from by refusing or escaping from the constructions of fashion and clothing.

There are various problems with the strategy of refusal. First, it is doubtful whether it is possible to step outside of or to escape gender identities by refusing to wear fashionable garments in this way. For example, some of the tactics adopted by the feminists of the 1960s and 1970s have now become gender-specific and highly eroticised ways in which women may appear. Cosmetic companies fall over themselves to sell women cosmetics which look 'natural', as if the women are not wearing make-up. And heterosexual women, at least, who go bra-less today do not usually have feminist solidarity in mind; they are more likely to know precisely the effect their visible nipples will have on the men they meet. Both of these tactics have been appropriated by the structure they were intended to challenge, and both are now ways in which women's appearances are constructed. Both are now options for how women may appear and thus ways in which those appearances may be enjoyed by men.

Second, even if it is possible not to indicate gender identity in fashion and clothing, there is the risk of those fashions and clothes being used to construct an image of the people wearing them as misguided or even mad. Not only would women wearing those fashions and clothes still be judged on the basis of their appearance, but that appearance may be used by the dominant structure to condemn them to positions of even greater marginality. This would seem to be what happened to the women of the early Women's Liberation Movement. Evans and Thornton describe how the popular press used the rumour of the burned bras to ridicule feminism; as far as the press was concerned, the concern of these women with such garments was simply evidence of their 'craziness' (Evans and Thornton 1989: 4).

'Trouser-wearers'

Davis points out that 'some feminists enjoin women to spurn fashion and its associated habits and attitudes altogether'. He suggests that 'advocates of this position often urge women to dress essentially as men' (Davis 1992: 176). Both of these statements are true and Oakley provides evidence of how feminism has proposed refusing fashion and dressing as men (Oakley 1981: 83). This chapter will argue, however, that spurning or refusing fashion and dressing as men are two different positions or two different strategies. Spurning fashion is a form of refusing fashion, of attempting to step outside of it, and was discussed in the previous section. Dressing as men is a form of reversal, it aims at allowing women to demonstrate that they possess what have hitherto been seen as masculine qualities and abilities, but which have been denied expression by male-dominated codes of fashion and clothing. So, where men have been understood as active/spectator and women as more or less passive/ spectacle, reversalist strategies will advocate fashions and clothing that reverse this structure by encouraging women to be more active spectators and by placing men in more passive roles in which they are the objects to be looked at.

Perhaps the most obvious example of one aspect of this strategy is the wearing of trousers by women in the second half of the nineteenth century. Amelia Bloomer was the owner and the editor of *The Lily*, a reforming newspaper. In 1851, she used *The Lily* to present the Bloomer Costume, which consisted of a skirt that came to just below the knee worn over Turkish trousers, to the public for the first time. The first point to be made here is that the Bloomer Costume, or bloomers, as it became known, simply enabled women to be more active. Foote refers to Mary C. Vaughn of New York who claimed that she did not become out of breath walking in her bloomers, and notes the *Boston Herald* correspondent who described the fifteen to twenty women in bloomers skating gracefully on the Back Bay entirely without accident or injury (Foote 1989: 147). Tickner contrasts the restrictive dress of Victorian women with the activities enjoyed by women in bloomers. Where crinolines 'hampered movement and slowed her gait', low set sleeves prevented her from raising her arms and corsets caused her to faint in 'warm or tiring circumstances', bloomers allowed the Victorian woman to partake in 'innumerable new polkas, waltzes and quadrilles' and ride bicycles, for example (Tickner 1977: 57). These are some very simple ways in which the Bloomer Costume enabled women to be more physically active.

The costume was also bound up, if that is the right metaphor, with women becoming more politically active. Foote writes, 'most women who advocated the bloomer participated in the women's rights movement'. People at the time saw the acceptance of the bloomer as the acceptance of women's rights; they understood that gender relationships were being contested by this item of clothing (Foote 1989: 148). The wearing of what were essentially a pair of trousers by women represents a reversal: where men had been active and women largely passive, bloomers enabled women to be more active, both physically and politically. This reversal was noted in cartoons of the time: both Tickner and Foote refer to Leech's cartoon in which 'a Bloomer' (in what one assumes is the American version of 1852), or a 'Superior Creature' (in the British *Punch* magazine of 1851), pops the question to her blushing and demure gentleman friend.

The main problem with, or the main weakness of, the strategy of reversal is that it assumes that the underlying structure, within which places are being reversed, is innocent. It assumes that the values and meanings that are to be reversed are values and meanings to which one would want to subscribe. For example, it may be the case that there are feminists who do not necessarily want to take over, wholesale, the values of activity. They may argue that there is something objectionable about the notion of masculine activity, that it is unreasonably aggressive, for example, and that there is a properly feminine notion or conception of activity. As Davis says, reversal can tacitly subscribe 'to the notion that men's construction of social reality, as symbolised in their dress code, is the only viable one' (Davis 1992: 176). The objection, then, is that reversal can leave the original structure or oppositions untouched and uncontested and that, if the original structure is left uncontested, it will appropriate any reversal.

'Kinderwhores'

The phenomenon of the 'kinderwhore' represents another form of reversal. It consists in taking an already existing identity or look, or in this case a mixture of already existing identities, which has hitherto been devalued in the offending economy, and celebrating the resulting combination. Most famously associated with the name of Courtney Love, lead singer with the band 'Hole' (see Figure 15), the model Naomi Campbell and the singer-guitarist Polly Harvey have also worn versions of the look. There is some debate as to the origins of the look, Love and Kat Bjelland, singer with Babes in Toyland, being touted as possible sources (see *http://www.weakervessel.com/dolly_style.htm* for example). It consists in wearing a short, frilled and bowed 'little-girl' or 'baby-doll' dress, in pink or white, often with some form of sash or waistband and may be accessorised with a toy doll. The eyes are heavily mascara-ed and the lips are bright red. The hair is untidy and often held in place by girlish slides (Arnold 1999: 289). In a famous *Elle* photograph from 1994, Love was pictured with 'witch' and 'slut' written in lipstick on her forearms. The two looks or identities that are being mixed here, as indicated in the term 'kinderwhore' (which combines the German word for child and the word 'whore'), are those of the little girl, and the slut; Joan Smith (1999: 35) characterised the look as a mixture of jailbait and whore. None of these identities is of high status in western society, yet in the 'kinderwhore' look the

Figure 15 Courtney Love, 'Kinderwhore' look 1994

resulting combination is proposed as a radical and challenging model of femininity.

Arnold suggests that the look is 'unnerving and aggressive . . . fracturing the expected neatness of femininity' (Arnold 1999: 289). In much the same way as that in which Punk disrupted conventional notions of female beauty the 'kinderwhore' disrupts traditional or ideological versions of female decorum. Where conventional models of femininity involve demureness, sexual continence, restraint and tasteful make-up, the ironic take on them performed by kinderwhore replaces these values with 'madness, loss of control' and raises fears of women 'as dangerous and sexual' (ibid.). This represents a clear challenge to those gender identities and Smith goes so far as to suggest that the look created a '*fin de siècle* sexual panic' (Smith 1999: 34). At least two things are happening here. First, the image of the slut or the whore is being paraded and celebrated, where conventional society would rather hide and deprecate it. This is a clear reversal of the status normally accorded such a look. Second, the image of the little girl is being at once elevated and corrupted. Apart from being seen and not heard, little girls are not expected to dress or behave as depraved and predatory sex-monsters in western society: the look elevates the status of the identity and flaunts it. The reversals are designed to 'shock and unbalance' the wider society (Arnold 1999).

The strategy is not unproblematic. The possibility that reversing the status of existing identities and celebrating the result might prove to be a successful form of resistance to dominant ideas is not guaranteed. Clearly, the looks, the identities that are being combined and promoted are only the ones that the original, offensive ideology was supporting. It is not at all certain that the original and conventional ideology will be harmed by such a move because the look merely reproduces a look that is demeaned and tries to promote it. Smith has no doubts that the 'kinderwhore' look merely re-introduces and reproduces another, equally abhorrent, model of female (and male) behaviour, that of the 'nymphet'. Her model is found in Vladimir Nabokov's novel *Lolita*, in which Humbert, the narrator, is seduced by his thirteen-year-old step-daughter Lolita (Smith 1999: 34). The role of fashion and clothing does not play a large part in the novel, although Humbert does confess to a 'predilection . . . for check weaves, bright cottons, frills, puffed-out short sleeves, soft pleats, snug fitting bodices and generously full skirts' and wonders 'what little girl would not like to twirl in a circular skirt and scanties?' (Nabokov 1991: 107). It will be noted that only some of these details feature in the 'kinderwhore' look. Smith's objection is that, so far from being threatening or challenging, it simply 'defuses male fears' and allows men to maintain the pretence that 'adult women are little girls at heart' (Smith 1999: 34). A consequence of this is that 'kinderwhore' introduces the 'tiredest trick in the paedophile book, that of absolving the partner of responsibility either for his desire or its satisfaction' (ibid.).

Thus, the intention may be 'ironic' (Smith 1999: 35) but the supposedly resistant gesture ends up as self-abusing and self-mocking, with no real power to escape the values that were originally found in conventional and limiting ideas of femininity.

'Good lookers'

In her essay 'Is the gaze male?', E. Ann Kaplan raises a number of very important and relevant questions. To the question of the title, she adds 'would it be possible to structure things so that women own the gaze? . . . would women want to own the gaze, if it were possible? . . . what does it mean to be a female spectator?' (Kaplan 1984: 324). It was seen in chapter five that there was a desire to look and that pleasure was derived from looking. Kaplan also raises questions concerning the possibility of specifically female desires and specifically female pleasures. Part of her complex conclusion is the idea that the gaze is not necessarily male, but that 'to own and activate the gaze . . . is to be in the masculine position' (Kaplan 1984: 331). She proposes that if this dominant structure, in which people adopt masculine and feminine positions, is to be successfully challenged, the oppositions in terms of which culture and language operate (male/female, active/passive, dominant/subordinate, and so on) must be transcended (Kaplan 1984: 336). Kaplan's essay, like Mulvey's, is concerned with Hollywood cinema and not with fashion and clothing. There are certain differences between these two areas; responding to a film is different to responding to a person or a picture of a person, for example. However, the questions and issues that are raised by these essays about looking, about the desire to look and the pleasures derived from looking, may be applied to fashion and clothing. This section will consider the reversal in which women actively look at men, who are reduced to being objects to be viewed.

In 1994 Levi jeans were promoted in a television advertisement entitled 'Creek'. In this advertisement, which appears to be set in late nineteenth-century rural America, two young women leave the picnic they are enjoying with their parents and run down towards the river, where they find a discarded pair of Levi jeans. Hiding behind a tree, they watch as the young, male, well-muscled and attractive owner of the jeans rises up from out of the water. The young women seem almost to vibrate and quiver with mounting excitement; Stiltskin's crashing chords crescendo as the camera appears to move down his torso towards where his jeans would be if he were wearing them . . . This ad reprises a theme that was introduced in the 1980s. In the 1980s Levis' ads, models like Nick Kamen and James Mardle pouted gorgeously as they unbuttoned their flies in the launderette or slipped slowly into a bath while still wearing their jeans. As Moore points out, the male body as an object of desire has a long history, going back, she suggests, to the stars of silent films (Moore 1988: 47). But what was new and different about these ads was the idea that here, on prime-time television, was a male body that was there to be looked at. And, in the case of 'Creek', here were two young women who were not only doing the looking, but also clearly getting a great deal of pleasure from that looking.

In the 1980s and early 1990s, the image of what became known as the 'New Man' was everywhere (see Craik 1994: pp. 197ff and chapter three of Edwards 1997 for more on the theme of the New Man). Caring, crying, cosmetic-buying, but not in a wimpy or a girly sort of way, the naked torso of New Man was to be found in Calvin Klein (Eternity), Austin Reed (Grey Flannel), and Yves Saint Laurent (Kouros), perfume ads, in Dormeuil cloth ads, in Jockey Y-front ads, and on the cover of Mothercare catalogues. Magazines, such as *GQ, Arena, For Him* and *The Face*, were published to cater specifically for the self-conscious New Man. Moore quotes Tony Hodges, managing director of the agency that produce the Grey Flannel ads, as saying that for this man, the mirror is perhaps more important than the other person (Moore 1988: 58). There are a number of things going on here. First, as Moore suggests, these images seem to offer the possibility of an active female gaze (Moore 1988: 45). Second, some of these images of men deal in and 'embrace a passivity' that was once completely prohibited, 'symbolically outlawed', as Moore has it (Moore 1988: 54). And third, they seem to testify to what was referred to above as narcissism and exhibitionism, but on the part of men this time, rather than of women. They seem, that is, to offer the possibility of a reversal of the structure noted above, in which men act and women appear: here it is more the men who appear and the women who are active spectators.

It might be objected at this point that men have been in this position before. Hollander, for example, points out that the Dandies of the eighteenth and nineteenth centuries exhibited a 'carefully schooled, detached narcissism' and that they spent 'exacting hours before the mirror (Hollander 1993: 228–9). Wilson agrees that the Dandy was a narcissist but emphasises that it is the understated, 'cool' look that they epitomised, rather than an ostentatious or exhibitionistic display. As Beau Brummell put it, 'if John Bull turns round to look after you, you are not well dressed' (Wilson 1985: 180). Clearly, the Dandies were men who were intensely interested in their own appearance and they spent a lot of time defining and refining the codes of dress, determining, for example, exactly how many waistcoat buttons the most stylish man left undone. There is some doubt as to whether Dandyism was to do with gender. Bayley, for example, argues that Dandyism was an episode in the development of middle-class taste rather than being explicitly concerned with gender identities (Bayley 1991: 159). Hollander, however, is of the opinion that Dandyism was something like a mimicking or an impersonation of female sexual display codes. She says that, while the Dandies were never in love, they were loved by women, and that the Dandies' display of sexual attraction was a direct challenge to the female, 'an exercise, like its traditional feminine analogue, in looking at once irresistible and unattainable'

(Hollander 1993: 228–9). Dandyism, then, would seem to be one occasion in the past when men have been as narcissistic as women are usually held to be, even if they were not as exhibitionistic.

However, the Levi advertisements in particular and the plethora of images of men and New Men generally, allow modern women to look 'actively and powerfully' at them (Moore 1988: 54). In the Levi ads, for example, it is often the case that the men do not know that they are being observed, placing women squarely in the role of voyeur which, in the structure noted above, was the province of the male observer. In the face of such images, women are 'responsible for their own voyeurism and their own desire' (Moore 1988: 55). Moreover, the men in the ads are more often than not entirely absorbed in themselves; when they are not gazing manfully out of the frame they are often taken up with what they are doing or, as in the case of the 'Principles' advertisement (Figure 16), they have been fragmented and reduced to appearance, a nice bottom for example. They are often wrapped up in attending to their own appearance. These magazines are full of ads for clothes and cosmetics, and it could be argued that they create an atmosphere in which it is possible for proper masculine behaviour to consist in taking a much greater interest in appearance. It could be argued that they are one way in which it is made acceptable for men to be concerned with their appearance. The magazines themselves do all they can to encourage this narcissistic approach, and they encourage men to think of themselves in terms of appearances, to become more and more exhibitionistic.

As noted above, there are a few problems associated with the strategy of

Figure 16 Principles advertisement, 1994

decorative and siren-like was called for, and that Utility styles should be worn for performing more practical, functional and housewifely tasks.

The strategy of working-class women at this time according to Partington, was to sample and re-mix these styles in ways that enabled them to 'articulate their own specific tastes and preferences' (Partington 1992: 160). Popular versions of the 'New Look', such as were worn by working-class women, differed 'from both couture and "accurate" (department store) mass-produced versions': the jacket was much looser and the fabric less stiff than in the Dior version, and the neckline was less revealing than the mass-produced copy, for example (Partington 1992:158). Popular versions worn by women at this time were a 'combination of shirtwaist bodies and "New Look" skirt in the same dress' (Partington 1992: 158). These popular versions were also worn in ways different to those envisaged by the fashion industry and design professions. Being a mixture of the glamorous and the utilitarian, these popular versions of the 'New Look' could be worn 'in an "everyday" way rather than for special occasions' (Partington 1992: 159). So the 'New Look' was sampled and re-mixed with the comfortable and serviceable elements of Utility styles rather than the two styles being kept separate and used for different occasions, 'as advised by fashion experts' (Partington 1992: 158). By redefining the meanings of these styles, Partington argues that working-class women 'used fashion to resist the dominant ideologies of femininity' (Partington 1992: 158); by mixing the identities of the styles, they could challenge the dominant dichotomous paradigms of femininity, siren or housewife. The clear distinctions between the styles, insisted upon by designers and reflecting the clear distinctions between models of femininity, were confused by women who articulated their new class and gender identities by means of their 'improper appropriation' of the 'New Look'.

This type of account of how working-class women appropriated the 'New Look' demands a reinterpretation of the structure of the gaze; it demands another kind of new look. In this account, one may see an attempt being made to describe a new look that is not a male gaze. In the account of the way in which men act and women appear in chapter five, men were placed in the role of voyeur and women were placed in the role of narcissist and exhibitionist. Men looked and women were preoccupied with the way they looked, with what sort of a show they were putting on for men. According to Partington's account of how women used the 'New Look', those women had to be both voyeur and exhibitionist/narcissist. They had to be voyeuristic in that they had to be able to 'discriminate between other objects with which to adorn themselves'. This required an active gaze. Women had to be narcissistic and exhibitionistic in order to be able to construct a 'self-image which is dependent on the gaze of the other' (Partington 1992: 156). This strategy may be understood as questioning the oppositions, rather than simply attempting to escape those oppositions or reversing the privilege accorded to one of the two terms. As Partington says,

Rather than seeing narcissism and exhibitionism as inevitably feminine, and fetishism and voyeurism as inevitably masculine, as many
theorists have tended to do, it has to be recognised that these tendencies are interdependent, albeit differently, for men and women.

(Partington 1992: 156)

This strategy is quite different from those of refusal and reversal noted above.
The examples of jeans, punk, bra-burning and trouser-wearing involved
refusal and reversal but the women referred to in Partington's essay are
not trying simply to escape or refuse all class and gender identities. Nor
are they trying simply to reverse the valuations accorded class or gender
identities. Rather, they are subverting the existing dominant system by preventing it from functioning in the ways it had functioned hitherto. They are
doing this by appropriating, making their own, apparently incompatible
elements from that system and combining them in what had been considered
improper ways. The 'New Look' has been prevented from working as a glamorous, decorative look that turned women into a 'tempting siren' by the
insertion into it of elements from Utility styles. And, in the same move, the
dominant dichotomy of 'housewife/siren' has been prevented from functioning in the ways it had hitherto, by the use of the two styles to articulate a new
set of class and gender identities in a new version of the 'New Look'. It is
argued that the 'improper appropriation' of the 'New Look', the making
proper or making one's own of a specific style or look in such an improper
and unapproved way, is what prevented the challenge of these women from
being itself appropriated again by the dominant system.

CONCLUSION

This chapter has explained the senses in which fashion and clothing may be
thought of as 'revolutionary', as challenging and criticising prevailing or
dominant class and gender identities. Revolutionary fashion and clothing
were explained in terms of resistance, as a series of ongoing challenges and
oppositions, rather than as one, complete and final revolutionary act. Two
forms of resistance, reversal and refusal, were explained. Fashion and clothing could attempt to challenge dominant conceptions of class and gender by
reversing the privilege accorded class and gender identities, or they could
attempt to escape all forms of class and gender identity as inherently
bourgeois or patriarchal. The problems that each of these strategies faced in
avoiding being incorporated or appropriated by the dominant or prevailing class and gender structures were also outlined. In terms of fashion and
clothing, neither refusal nor reversal, in the forms of punk or early Women's
Liberation Movement feminists, for example, were sufficient to avoid
being appropriated by the dominant or prevailing structures of class and
gender. Partington's description of the ways in which working-class women

inappropriately appropriated the 'New Look' of the late 1940s and early 1950s was explained as a more successful challenge to the identities and positions ascribed to working-class women by the fashion and marketing industries. The strategy of these women, while not necessarily a conscious strategy, was more complex than either refusal or reversal. It also involved confusing the categories with which the dominant groups operated. It may be claimed that it was this that prevented the identities that these women had created from being immediately appropriated by the structures that they were trying to challenge.

FURTHER READING

- Hall, S. and Jefferson, T. (eds) (1976) *Resistance through Rituals*, Routledge, is the *locus classicus* for **cultural studies type accounts of resistance**. Essays in this collection look at various youth subcultures in post-war Britain and contain references to clothing and style and there is a long theoretical essay on ideology, hegemony and related themes.
- For more on the view of **fashion as an endless series of changes**, see Baudrillard, J. (1981) *For a Critique of the Political Economy of the Sign*, Telos Press. Fashion's relation to history and change is dealt with by Ulrich Lehmann in his (1999) essay 'Tigersprung: Fashioning History', in *Fashion Theory*, Volume 3, Issue 3, pp. 297–322. He presents a more discursive and difficult treatment of the connections between fashion, revolution and history in his (2000) *Tigersprung: Fashion in Modernity*, MIT Press. This is not an introductory book by any means but p. 36 may be the place to start.
- On the **relation of punk to gender**, see Evans, C. and Thornton, M. (1989) *Women and Fashion*, Quartet Books. Chapter two of this volume looks at the relation of women to the punk movement, something that the present chapter does not explicitly do.
- Valerie Steele (1985) *Fashion and Eroticism: Ideals of Feminine Beauty from the Victorian Era to the Jazz Age*, Oxford University Press, contains a useful introductory and, in a sense, corrective chapter on **psychoanalytic approaches** to fashion.
- Diana Crane (2000) *Fashion and its Social Agendas*, Chicago University Press, looks at women's use of masculine suits, hats and ties as examples of **resistance to the dominant stereotypes**. She looks mainly at the nineteenth century, but also takes in such twentieth-century examples as Ralph Lauren.
- There is a special edition of *Fashion Theory* (2000), Volume 4, Issue 4, devoted to **masculinities**. It is largely historical, containing essays on eighteenth-century Macaronis, nineteenth-century tailors and the presentation of masculinity in *Playboy* magazine, Hitchcock's *North by Northwest* and in Carnaby Street, for example. A more sociological treatment of masculinity and fashion is found in Tim Edwards' (1997) *Men in the Mirror: Men's Fashion, Masculinity and Consumer Society*, Cassell. This looks at men's magazines, the shopping experience and the politics of consumption. Haug, W. E. (1986) *Critique of Commodity Aesthetics*, Polity, contains interesting sections on men's toiletries and 'Hush Puppy' shoes, for example, and the relation of commodities to socialist politics.
- The website at *www.hiphop-directory.com/* represents a beginning from which to investigate hip-hop in terms of resistance.
- The website at *www.celebritywonder.com* may be searched for images and further information on Courtney Love.

7

FASHION, CLOTHING AND POSTMODERNITY

INTRODUCTION

Chapter five was concerned with the ways in which fashion and clothing signalled and reproduced positions and relations of class and gender, and chapter six considered the ways in which fashion and clothing could be used to challenge or contest those positions and relations. Chapter five was about the ways in which fashion and clothing could be understood as reproductive activities; chapter six looked at the ways in which they could be understood as revolutionary activities. One way of understanding the present chapter would be to think of it as attempting to explain items of fashion and clothing as, in principle, undecidable between these two things, as potentially both reproductive and critical of dominant or prevalent class and gender positions and relations. As will be seen later, items like the stiletto may be taken as objects of women's enslavement (this would be the approach of chapter five), or as items used to construct a new identity (as would have been the approach found in chapter six), or as both at the same time. The present chapter, then, will attempt to explain how an item of fashion or clothing may be considered, at least potentially, undecidable.

Inevitably, this book has already touched on many concerns and topics that some commentators have identified as being peculiar or peculiarly relevant to the various debates surrounding the idea of postmodernity. Topics like meaning, identity and culture, for example, which have all been investigated in previous chapters, are all claimed by someone, at some point, to be central to the matter of postmodernity. Kellner has suggested that one of the distinguishing features of postmodernist art, for example, is the way in which it mixes popular culture with high culture (Kellner 1988: 239) Bauman has suggested that the main feature ascribed to postmodernity is a 'permanent and irreducible *pluralism* of cultures' (Bauman 1992: 102). Wilson contemplates the ways in which postmodernity allows ethnic minorities, women, lesbians and gay men 'to assert, find or retrieve an "identity"' (Wilson 1992b: 7; see also Wilson 1990: 209). Craik presents a view of postmodernity as involving the 'unfettered circulation of free-floating signs' (Craik 1994: 8); in such an economy, she suggests, meaning cannot but be unstable and interpretation cannot but be insecure. Indeed, Anderson goes as far as to suggest that, were it not for postmodernism, or at least the post-structuralist philosophers he holds to be responsible for postmodernism, fashion and clothing would not be proper topics for any kind of serious investigation (Anderson 1983: 42).

It must be acknowledged, then, that some of the topics seen in previous chapters and some of the approaches to those topics will have been informed by the sorts of concerns and arguments to be found in the various debates surrounding postmodernity. This must mean that some of the topics and approaches are not informed by postmodern concerns. It must mean that there are topics and approaches seen in previous chapters that are the products of the sorts of concerns and arguments characteristic of what came before postmodernity. One of the things that the 'post' of postmodernity suggests is that what came before was modernity; one of the things that this chapter must do, therefore, is to give some idea of the main differences between modernity and postmodernity. This 'post' determines that any account of postmodernity must take the definition of modernity into consideration. It also means that the concerns of postmodernism are not always as different from the concerns of modernism as might be imagined and that there is, therefore, nothing like a clean break between the concerns of the two ideas. The present chapter may be seen, then, not as an add-on, as something that introduces a whole new set of interests and relations for fashion, but as proposing another perspective on already existing concerns and relations.

This chapter must also explain how fashion and clothing are described and explained in terms both of modernity and postmodernity. It is to be hoped that these tasks will prove to be as interesting as they promise to be difficult. These tasks promise to be difficult not least because modernists and postmodernists alike claim that fashion and clothing have some sort of special affinity with their theorising, or that fashion and clothing are exemplary of their philosophical positions. They should be interesting, first, because it is often for the same reasons that fashion and clothing are claimed to be especially representative of either modernity or postmodernity and, secondly, because it is occasionally the same person who is making these, apparently contradictory, claims.

For example, Faurschou claims that the main characteristics of postmodernity are 'implicit in the very principles of an expanding fashion culture'. She believes that the chaotic, fragmented and elusive nature of the fashion commodity 'constitutes an exemplary site' for examining the move from modernity to postmodernity (Faurschou 1988: 79). Faurschou seems to be arguing that there is some special affinity between fashion and postmodernity. In contrast, Wilson, whose *Adorned in Dreams* is subtitled 'Fashion and Modernity', is rather ambivalent on the matter. She suggests that ' "Modernity" does . . . seem useful as a way of indicating the restless desire for change characteristic of cultural life in industrial capitalism, the desire for the new that fashion expresses so well' (Wilson 1985: 63). On the same page, however, she also suggests that the eclecticism characteristic of postmodernism 'might seem especially compatible with fashion', which similarly involves constant changes of style. It looks suspiciously as though the same characteristics of fashion are being used to exemplify both modernity and postmodernity. K.W. Back, in a useful essay entitled 'Modernism and fashion', identifies the conscious display of . . . seams, which used to be partially hidden', for example, as one of the characteristic features of modernist fashion. This he suggests is part of the 'mechanics of the message'; as in modernist painting, where the brushstrokes announce that 'This is a picture', or 'This is an oil painting', in modernist fashion, the exposure of seams announces that 'This is clothing' (Back 1985: 12). Drawing attention to the 'mechanics' of the piece, exposing the seams for example, is, of course, one of the trademarks of the work of people like Ann Demeulenmeester and Martin Margiela, who are more commonly or generally presented as postmodern, deconstructionist designers.

Whether they are analysing modernity or postmodernity, one thing that these analysts all tend to agree on is that it is fashion, and not dress or clothing, that is the topic under consideration. Dress and clothing, which have been described above as 'anti-fashion' and which have been seen either to serve those who would contrive to escape class-based society or to indicate a very simple society, are not of interest to modernists or postmodernists. Modern and postmodern societies both being societies in which mobility is both possible and desirable and, as Baudrillard says, fashion only appearing in 'socially mobile societies' (Baudrillard 1981: 49), it is fashion, as opposed to clothing or dress (with their more anthropological connotations), which is the object of these analysts' attention. This is not to say, of course, that there are not a few paradoxical moments when it is clothing or dress that are demanded by the context.

It may be useful, at this point, to distinguish between 'modernity' and 'modernism', and between 'postmodernity' and 'postmodernism'. Boyne and Rattansi (1990), for example, suggest that modernity and postmodernity are social, cultural, economic and political configurations. Modernity and post-modernity and involve relations to science and technology. Modernism and postmodernism, on the other hand, are intellectual or aesthetic projects which form constitutive elements of modernity and postmodernity. They are ways of conceptualising or understanding these configurations. Modernism must be distinguished from modernity, they say, because the former represents an important critique of the latter. Whether postmodernism also constitutes a critique of postmodernity is not entirely clear, although many contemporary theorists are critical of both postmodernity and postmodernism. It should become clear, however, that postmodernism is, like modernism, a critique of modernity.

FASHION AND MODERNITY

Both Wilson (1985) and Faurschou (1988) locate the beginnings of modernity with the rise of industrial capitalism. Both agree that it is only with the rise of industrial capitalism that fashion comes on to the scene. Berman supplies a little more detail: he identifies three stages of modernity. The first, he suggests, lasted from the beginning of the sixteenth century to the end of the eighteenth; in this period, people are just beginning to experience modern life and have little or no sense of themselves as a modern public. The second begins with the 'great revolutionary wave' of the 1790s and lasts until the twentieth century; in this stage, people have a more conscious understanding of the idea that they are living through times of change and modernity. In this stage, the experience of living in a modern world begins to be thought about explicitly. The third consists of the remainder of the twentieth century. In this stage, modernity begins to take in the whole world, and a worldwide culture of modernity is to be found in thought and art (Berman 1988: 37).

Although Wilson suggests that the society of the Renaissance was modern, insofar as it was moving towards a 'secular worldliness' and was becoming preoccupied with the dynamic, ever-changing everyday world, and insofar as it had a wealthy middle class that competed in terms of finery with the nobility, it was not until the industrial revolution that fashion and modernity were fully realised (Wilson 1985: 60). As she says, the industrial revolution sees the beginning of an age of machinery, an age when, for the first time, people's lives are transformed and dominated by machinery. With mechanical help, things could be changed much quicker and with much more accompanying noise; the earth could be mined and harvested and the products of that mining and harvesting could be transformed, made into goods and transported around the country with what must have been at the time the most alarming speed and noise. Wilson insists, and is convincing, on the Janus-faced character of the development of capitalism at this stage; 'the perpetual movement of modernity both thrilled and terrified the new citizens of the great industrial centres' (Wilson 1985: 60). These industrial centres were, of course, the rapidly developing cities. City life, then, is also a part of the experience of modernity; places where people work, where goods are bought and sold, and where people engage in common leisure activities. It should not be forgotten that these experiences would also have been new to people at this time.

As noted in previous chapters, the industrial revolution and the development of capitalism also saw the development of new and different classes. Essentially, in feudal society there had been a group of people who owned the land, the aristocracy, and a group who were permitted to work on it, the serfs. There had also been other classes which rather complicated this structure: there were vassals, guild-masters, journeymen and apprentices, for example. Moreover, as Marx and Engels point out in *The Communist Manifesto*, within

159

each of these classes there were yet more gradations. Industrial capitalism introduced a different social set-up. Marx and Engels suggest that this period of capitalism tended to simplify the social structure, to reduce the class antagonisms to one main antagonism, between the bourgeoisie and the proletariat. There were social groups who owned factories, mines and so on; there were social groups who administered those factories, mines and so on; and there were those who worked the machines in those factories, mines and so on. In turn, all these groups of people, social classes, were still internally subdivided and were also to be distinguished from the old aristocracy. Modernity, then, saw the phenomenon known as the division of labour; different groups of people did different jobs and people did not necessarily consume all that they produced. And, as has also been seen in previous chapters, there was a sexual division of labour. Simply, it was the role of women in industrial capitalism to ensure that the men were cleaned, clothed, fed and rested in order to be in a fit state to work.

It is in the development of this context that fashion itself begins to develop: the origins of fashion are in the origins of modernity, with the growth of industrial capitalism. Faurschou points out that Marx uses the example of 20 yards of linen equalling one coat in his analysis of exchange value in chapter one of part one of *Capital*, and she points out the irony that 'the whole rationalisation process of capital originated with what would seem to have become the most irrational of commodities'. She then begins to account for the place of fashion within modernity and suggests that, in the late nineteenth and early twentieth centuries, dress was 'a commodity produced according to the existing structure or "ideology of needs"' (Faurschou 1988: 80). What this seems to mean is that fashion was advertised and consumed in accordance with the prevailing ideology of needs.

Drawing on Leiss, Kline and Jhally (1990: 6, 130–59), Faurschou argues that at this time capitalism could be described as being in a 'production-oriented phase'. That is, presumably, that it was more concerned to sell goods on the basis of the qualities that went into their production, rather than on the basis of the qualities involved in their consumption, as will be seen to be the case with postmodernity. Capitalism at this time advertised and marketed its goods in a manner based on the qualities of the goods themselves; advertisers claimed in a general way that the products would improve but not substantively change one's way of life (Faurschou 1988: 80). Leiss, Kline and Jhally point out that, besides the qualities of the product, the price and the use to which the product could be put were also used in advertisements around the turn of the century. They suggest that the metaphoric or emotive themes used in advertisements of this period were that the product was useful and that it possessed certain qualities. They also point out that the advertisements tended to be straightforwardly descriptive (Leiss *et al.* 1990: 6).

One example that Leiss *et al.* use is an advertisement for the corsets made by the Worcester Corset Company of Worcester, Massachusetts, which appeared in the *Ladies' Home Journal*. Figure 17 is not the advertisement in question, but it is very similar and may be used for purposes of comparison. The advertisement that Leiss *et al.* refer to is almost entirely given over to descriptions of the construction of these corsets and to pointing out the high quality of the product. For example, the 'Dowager' corset is said to possess 'the maximum of strength and durability': in all corsets, 'the bone strips are double lined, preventing bones punching through and ensuring longer service'. One must assume that it is the bones in the corset that are referred to here, but, to judge from the illustrations, one would also be forgiven for thinking that it is the ribs of the poor women wearing the corsets that are in danger of punching through. Other items of information include the price, the materials the products are made from, and the sizes and colours available. Unless the names of the corsets, the Royal Worcester Corset and the Dowager Corset, with their aristocratic connotations, are included, there is nothing in the advertisement that refers in any way to the sort of values that might be involved in the consumption of these products. Indeed, the Dowager is even referred to as being 'For Stout Figures', something that would surely deter potential customers today (Leiss *et al.* 1990: 56).

In particular, the advertisement conforms to Faurschou's general analysis of this period of capitalist marketing. The ad is emphasizing 'the craftsmanship, traditional values and tastes that were important to the social economy of prestige and class distinction' (Faurschou 1988: 80). It can also be seen that fashion is being sold here mainly on the strength of how useful it is, its 'use' value: the facts that the corsets will work, and that they will work for a long time, are the aspects of the product that are being used to sell it. Reference is also made in the advertisement to 'exchange' value: the corsets are defined in terms of what one would have to exchange for them in order to purchase them. Faurschou summarises: 'in the early twentieth century, modernist objects still retained some capacity for symbolic investment, whether that of use value, prestige or the expression of identity'; there was some reliable connection between the product and its meaning, whether that meaning was to do with class, gender, prestige or the use to which the item was to be properly put (Faurschou 1988: 81).

FASHION AND POSTMODERNITY

Faurschou appeals to Jameson's account of the cultural logic of late capitalism and to Baudrillard's account of the sign in order to explain the 'break' between modernity and postmodernity. Put simply, modernist objects retain the capacity for symbolic investment while postmodernist objects do not. Another way of putting it simply would be to say that, where modernity conceived of the object in terms of production, postmodernity conceives of it in terms of consumption. In modernity, according to Jameson, commodities still retained the trace of the human labour that had produced them: as he says, 'their relationship to the work from which they issued . . . has not yet been fully concealed' (Jameson 1971: 104–5). In post-modernity, that trace of human labour has been lost and the relationship to work has been concealed. In what Jameson refers to as 'postindustrial capitalism', 'the products with which we are furnished are utterly without depth' (Jameson 1971:105). The link with production has been severed in favour of a connection with consumption and, for Jameson, this constitutes 'a historical break of an unexpectedly absolute kind' (Jameson 1971: 105). This severance is a common theme in postmodern writing concerning fashion. Gilles Lipovetsky's (1994) *The Empire of Fashion*, for example, makes a similar point. He does not deny that fashion objects may 'on occasion be social signifiers' or signs of class distinction, but he says that mass consumption of fashion is 'governed chiefly by a process of . . . differentiation' (1994: 145). And Janet McCracken (2001) generalises the point to include all objects of consumption, or all systems of signs, not just fashion items and systems. She says that

> the signs through which we have to live just don't make any sense at all because the production and consumption of signs is entirely divorced in the consciousness of workers and consumers from any conception of ends, whether political, functional . . . [or] aesthetic (2001: 172).

Where there is always the hint of a nostalgia for the projects of modernity in Jameson's account, there appears to be absolutely none in Baudrillard's and Lipovetsky even approves of the proliferation of infinitely differentiated objects as a strengthening of democracy. Baudrillard thinks rather in terms of 'release' and 'liberation' (Baudrillard 1981: 67). The postmodern object, the 'object-become sign', 'no longer gathers its meaning in the concrete relationship between two people. It assumes its meaning in its differential relation to other signs' (Baudrillard 1981: 66). This is much the same move as that described by Jameson above; rather than labour or the relation between people being the origin of the meaning of the object, as in modernity, it is the relation to all other objects, or signs, that generates the meaning of the postmodern object. Baudrillard's rhetoric of 'release' and 'liberation', however, contrasts rather oddly with his general view of fashion as 'entirely governed by the social strategy of class' (Baurillard 1981: 51). Fashion, in his view, is also one of the best ways that capitalism has of restoring cultural inequality and social discrimination; it functions, as Wilson has it, to 'mask the unchanging nature of domination under capitalism' (Wilson 1990: 220).

The modern object must be freed or 'autonomised' from the various logics that surround it in order for it to become the postmodern object, or object-as-sign, at which point it will be 'recaptured by the formal logic of fashion'. This formal logic of fashion is also referred to as the logic of differentiation, as the logic of the sign and as the logic of consumption by Baudrillard and he

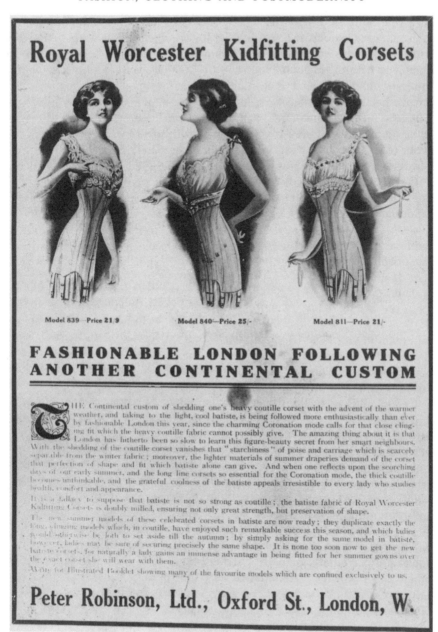

Figure 17 Royal Worcester corset advertisement, nineteenth century

says that it is necessary to distinguish this (fashion/differentiation/sign/ consumption) logic from 'several other logics which habitually get entangled with it' (Baudrillard 1981: 66). There are three other logics which get entangled with the logic of fashion or the sign. The first is a functional logic of use value; it is referred to as a logic of practical operations and utility, and seems to refer to the object when considered as an instrument or as a thing with which to do something. The second is an economic logic of exchange value; this is also referred to as a logic of equivalence or of the market, and seems to refer to considerations of price or commercial exchange. The third is a logic of symbolic exchange; it is also referred to as a logic of ambivalence or of the gift, and seems to refer to considerations involving relationships.

These logics may be characterised as potential sources of the value or meaning of the modernist object: its use, its price and its role in negotiating relations with others. These are not dissimilar from elements of the advertisement analysed above, elements which were held to be representative of that advertisement's modernity. Consequently, Baudrillard argues that

> an object is not an object of consumption unless it is released from its psychic determinations as *symbol;* from its functional determinations as *instrument;* from its commercial determinations as *product;* and is thus *liberated as a sign* to be recaptured by the formal logic of fashion.
>
> (Baudrillard 1981: 67)

Once the object is thus liberated from these logics, it is a sign. As a sign, it exists only insofar as it is different from all other signs and insofar as these differences are coded (Baudrillard 1981: 65). As a sign, it is free to combine with all other signs in the logic of differentiation; in this logic, it is the relation to all other signs that generates meanings.

Baudrillard uses two rings to help illustrate this difference. One is a wedding ring and one is an ordinary ring. The wedding ring is unique and is a symbol of the longevity and indissolubility of a couple's relationship. One would no more change the ring for a different one than one would wear several at a time. In this case, the symbolic logic accounts for the meaning of the ring: fashion, in the forms of difference and substitution, plays no part in the meaning of the ring. 'The ordinary ring is quite different', however (Baudrillard 1981: 66). The ordinary ring is not symbolic of any relationship and may be freely changed or substituted for a different one. Many different ordinary rings may be worn at the same time. As Baudrillard says, 'the ordinary ring takes part in the play of my accessories and the constellation of fashion. It is an object of consumption' (Baudrillard 1981: 66). Here, clearly, the logic of difference generates the meaning or value of the ordinary ring.

Liberated from its determinations as symbol, instrument and product, the sign is determined only by its differences from all other signs: meaning is entirely a product of coded difference. Consequently, postmodern society is a

164

society of consumption, rather than of production. As Faurschou says, post-modern society is a society 'driven to create a perpetual *desire* for need, for novelty, for endless difference' (Faurschou 1988: 82). It is hardly surprising, then, that fashion is often held to have some special affinity with postmodernity. Faurschou goes so far as to say that 'in postmodernity, fashion has become the commodity 'par excellence'' (Faurschou 1988: 82). Were it not a thoroughly modernist, and therefore inappropriate, metaphor, it could be said that both fashion and postmodernity are driven by the engine of difference.

The item of fashion, like Baudrillard's sign, exists only within a network of differences. It is different from all the garments that exist at the same time, that could be worn with it (syntagmatic difference), and it is different from all the garments that come before and after it, that might be worn instead of it (paradigmatic difference). On Baudrillard's account, it might be said that this play of difference is where the item's identity or meaning as fashion comes from. This argument could be developed to suggest that, if its identity or meaning is generated from any other source, it is not fashion, but dress or clothing.

Thus, if the item or garment is considered in terms of its determinations as symbol, instrument or product, it is not fashion. The item or garment may be a wedding ring or a policeman's uniform, a waterproof jacket or a pair of gloves, or a rare and expensive thing, but, considered in these terms, it is not an item of fashion. According to this view, it would be a modern object; it would be dress or clothing. In fact, the way is cleared by this kind of argument for suggesting that 'modern fashion' is actually a contradiction in terms, rather than a tautology. While it is not an argument that could be supported by the Baudrillard of the early 1970s, who is adamant that fashion 'exists only within the framework of modernity' (Baudrillard 1993: 89), his ideas from that time may be used to construct the argument that fashion is properly a postmodern phenomenon. This is one of the paradoxical moments mentioned in chapter one, where what has been presented as fashion appears to turn into something like anti-fashion.

Fashion, however, is different; as soon as one item is exhausted, another takes its place and so on. Another name for this cycle of in-built or planned obsolescence is fashion. Consequently, the desire for another latest model is instantly satisfied by the cycle of fashion in postmodernity. This cycle is the desire for endless difference. Baudrillard refers to fashion as a 'compulsion to innovate signs ... [an] apparently arbitrary and perpetual production of meaning – a kind of meaning drive' (Baudrillard 1981: 79). He points out that neither long nor short skirts have any natural or absolute value: it is only the relation of difference between them that generates any meaning they might have. As he says 'the mini-skirt has nothing whatsoever to do with sexual liberation; it has no (fashion) value except in opposition to the long skirt' (Baudrillard 1981: 79).

What is more disturbing for some people is that, according to Baudrillard's account, it is only this play of difference that produces 'beauty'. The move from long skirts to short skirts has exactly the same fashion value as the opposite move, and both moves 'will precipitate the same effect of "beauty"'. For postmodernity, beauty itself is only a product of difference, and fashion is quite capable of presenting 'the most eccentric, dysfunctional, ridiculous traits' as eminently beautiful, so long as they are sufficiently different from what went before (Baudrillard 1981: 79). There are no absolute values that exist outside the play of fashionable difference to which beautiful things might be compared or from which they might obtain their beauty. For post-modernity, beauty is simply an effect of codified difference. Faurschou summarises this by saying that, for Baudrillard,

> fashion is the epitome of the cynical survival of capitalism. It is the celebration of a perverse, fetishized passion for the abstract code, at the expense of any collective investment in symbolic exchange.
>
> (Faurschou 1988: 83)

Reference was made earlier in this chapter to the way in which Baudrillard's rhetoric of the 'release' and 'liberation' of the fashion sign from its determin-ation as symbol, instrument and product sits uneasily with his general denunciation of fashion as ideology, the mask of social inequality. It may be worth considering whether this 'uneasiness' is another side or aspect of the cultural ambivalence with regard to fashion and clothing that was noted in the Introduction and which will be followed up in the section on 'Fashion and Ambivalence', below. The idea, raised by Faurschou, of celebrating a perver-sion might also be seen as evidence of this ambivalence. For everyday life, if not for Freudian psychoanalysis, perversions are normally the sort of thing to be kept quiet about, not celebrated.

FASHION, ART, PERFORMANCE, MASQUERADE

The ideas of fashion consisting in an endless play of differences which pro-duces effects of identity and beauty and of its being a 'fetishised passion for the abstract code' (Faurschou 1988: 83) raises issues concerning performance, spectacle and masquerade. Masquerade refers to the use of masks and disguise, the three terms being practically interchangeable (see Tseëlon 2001a: 2–3). As Steele points out, and as was seen in the Introduction above, this view of fashion has a long history; the notion of fashion and clothing as bound up in some form of deceit is to be found in eighteenth-century usage while the Bacchanalia and Saturnalia of ancient Greek and Roman civilisa-tions included masked dances in which sexual and social identity were con-structed and performed by means of masquerade (Steele 2001: 73; see also Tseëlon 2001a: 4–5). The use of some artefact, be it mask or textiles, to change, create, hide or enhance appearance, is clearly something that masquerade has in common with fashion and clothing. On such a view of

166

fashion, masquerade has a critical function (Tseëlon 2001a: 3) in that it draws attention to the constructed nature of identity. Efrat Tseëlon (2001b: 108) explains the constructive aspect of masquerade as a 'technology of identity' by means of which the body's covering can conceal and reveal identity and 'create a space from where one can play out desires and fears' (ibid.) The critical, or deconstructive aspect of masquerade is found in its ability to mock and destabilise habit, hierarchy and order (ibid.) Identity may now be thought of as an ongoing performance which is immediately undermined as the 'appearance of authentic identity' (ibid.) and with all the theatrical and spectacular connotations that accompany the idea.

Masquerade also refers to performance. Tseëlon traces the notion of performance back to the work of the philosopher J. L. Austin on what are called performative utterances (things like promises, the naming of ships and saying 'I bet you that . . . ', in which an act is performed in the very speaking of them). Confusingly enough, Austin in turn explains his performatives in terms of masquerade and disguise (Austin 1962: 4). However, when fashion and clothing are considered as masquerade, one performs one's gender and social identities, for example, rather than fashion referring to or reflecting some original and authentic identity. Indeed, Tseëlon explicitly proposes masquerade as an 'alternative to the symbolic role of fashion' (2001b: 103) and points out that in masquerade, 'the actors do not have an essence "behind the performance" . . . they are their performance' (2001b: 107). The way in which Madonna's performance over the last twenty years creates and recreates her image and identity is noted by Caroline Evans (2001: 306) and other pop stars, such as David Bowie and, more recently, Robbie Williams could also be said to have gained a name for transforming their perceived identities through masquerade. Robbie Williams has used fashion and costume to turn his image from that of a cheeky and slightly naughty boy-band boy into a pastiche (see below) of one of the 1960s Rat-Pack. And David Bowie's well-known disguises (from Ziggy Stardust, through The Thin White Duke and appearing on the cover of *Hunky Dory* in a frock to his present incarnation as cybernaut-artist/dealer), may be explained as masquerade, mixing fashion, art, performance and spectacle. Tseëlon argues that masquerade is especially helpful when thinking about fashion and says it is 'particularly suited for "the clothed body"' (2001b: 108). The are various reasons for this. Masquerade is a

> meeting point between the body project and the fashion project. It refers to . . . complete covering (costume) as well as token masking (detail) . . . [and] masking . . . relies as much on visual artefacts as on metaphorical disguise.
>
> (Tseëlon 2001b: 108–9)

Masquerade always already includes the use of visual artefacts (garments, clothes), it can account for whole ensembles or looks as well as the details of individual items making up such ensembles and it is found at the point where the body meets fashion.

That identity is performed and that the result is to be explored and celebrated as a spectacle is a conception that has clear affinities with fashion and fashion shows and it has gained currency in recent years. One consequence of this view is to re-introduce the idea of art, and of performance as art, into the account of fashion although, as Ginger Gregg Duggan says, 'art and fashion have shared a symbiotic relationship in which each discipline simultaneously encourages and competes with the other' at many points throughout history (2001: 243). Duggan explores this relation by looking at how the fashion shows of such designers as Alexander McQueen and John Galliano take on the appearance of the theatre. Galliano's Fall 1997 show, for example, illustrated 'the influence of the theater through the use of decadent set design, props and make-up' (ibid.: 245). On a more critical level, Caroline Evans (2001) places the fashion show as spectacle, in which 'image effaces reality', in the context of capitalism and explains that it could be a paradigmatic case of the way in which 'the fashion show has operated . . . to disguise its commercial origins and goals' (2001: 272). The symbiosis mentioned by Duggan is also seen in the ways in which contemporary artists, like Vanessa Beecroft, have used the trappings of the fashion world in their shows. Beecroft's 1998 performance, sponsored by Gucci, featured 'fifty models, clad in Gucci underwear and stilettos' (Ib.: 244). The relation between art and fashion was also the subject of an 1998 Hayward Gallery exhibition in London. According to Susan Ferleger Brades, the director of the gallery, *Addressing the Century: 100 Years of Art and Fashion* collected examples of art, fashion, photography and theatre design in order to establish and illustrate (in words similar to those of Duggan, above), 'moments when the overlap of art and fashion signals the advancement of a common set of visual discoveries' (Ferleger Brades 1998).

It might be suggested that there is here not so much a relation between fashion and art, however symbiotic, but an identity. Questions such as 'Is it art?', 'Is it design?' and 'Is it fashion?' seem equally impossible to answer with a simple 'yes' or 'no' such is the way one shades into the other. These examples may illustrate exactly the way in which masquerade is both constructive and critical of identity: identity is, again, undecidable in these cases.

FASHION AND ALLEGORY

Baudrillard's account of fashion in general and his comment regarding miniskirts in particular introduce, among other things, the idea of allegory. The idea of allegory is one that is central to the thought of many theorists of postmodernity. It was noted above that the modern object was said to retain its capacity for symbolic investment. It was also said to be conceived of in terms of production: this was an economic determination of the object.

Jameson argued that the modern object retained some trace of the human labour that went into it. All these ways of conceiving of the object are ways of accounting for the meaning of that object, and they are the ways that are discounted by Baudrillard in his account of the meaning of the object. According to Sawchuk, these ways of conceiving of the object are also ways of reducing the object 'to a mere reflection of social and economic developments' (Sawchuk 1988: 64). Considered as either reflections of social movements or as indices of the effects of capitalism, these ways of interpreting the object are reductionist: they reduce a complex phenomenon, like fashion, to an idea that they consider straightforward, like class. They then assume that the former may be satisfactorily explained in terms of the latter. Sawchuk is not alone in wanting to avoid such reductionism.

So, adding to the list of disciplines in terms of which fashion and clothing may be studied (see p.23), Sawchuk suggests that fashion and clothing may be found in a variety of different discourses. They include health, beauty, morality and sexuality, the nation, the economy and location, for example. These discourses may themselves be conceived of as a 'fabric of intertextual relations' and Sawchuk argues that they produce or construct fashion and clothing as things that may be studied and understood. She argues, that is, that fashion and clothing are constituted intertextually, as a result of texts and discourses referring to each other (Sawchuk 1988: 65). On the matter of intertextual constitution, she quotes Derrida, who says that

> no element can function as a sign without referring to another element which itself is not simply present. This interweaving results in each 'element' . . . being constituted on the basis of the trace within it of the other elements of the chain or system. [. . .] Nothing . . . is anywhere ever simply present or absent. There are only, everywhere, differences and traces of traces.
>
> (Sawchuk 1988: 65)

What Derrida is referring to in this quotation is the way in which signs are only meaningful on the basis of their relations to all other signs. It has already been seen in chapter four that signs mean nothing on their own; it is only in relation to other, different signs that they are meaningful. (Moreover, Baudrillard was seen to argue that it is difference that produces or generates the meaning of fashion and clothing, going so far as to say that even beauty is an effect of codified difference.) So, signs are not simply present, as they mean nothing on their own. Only on the basis of relations to other signs, which are different and which are also not simply present, can signs function and be meaningful. The relations to the other signs are called 'traces' by Derrida. He conceives of the meaning of a sign as being produced by its differences from, or its relations to, other signs and by the traces of those differences or relations.

Sawchuk is using this quotation to suggest the way in which fashion and clothing are constituted as elements, as meaningful objects of study. They are produced by their relations to all sorts of other elements (such as health, beauty, etc.) that are themselves not simply present. Fashion and clothing themselves are not simple presences. They are meaningless on their own, and only in relation to all these other discourses, or elements, are they meaningful as objects of study. This may seem an unnecessarily complicated way of saying that fashion and clothing are produced or constituted by their relations to other discourses, that they are constituted intertextually, but Sawchuk thinks that Derrida's version of intertextuality can help escape reductionist accounts of fashion and clothing. She also thinks that it is 'theoretically related' to the concept of allegory, as 'developed' by Benjamin (Sawchuk 1988: 65).

Although Sawchuk never specifies who she has in mind when she refers to 'the standard Marxist and feminist' accounts (Sawchuk 1988: 65), what such reductionist accounts of fashion and clothing do is to explain the meaning of fashion and clothing in terms of economics or class, in the case of Marxism, or in terms of sex, in the case of feminism. To do this is to determine or fix the meanings of fashion and clothing in terms of only class, economics or sex, for example. It is to fix meaning in a manner akin to the way in which Baudrillard's object was determined as symbol, product or instrument. According to Sawchuk, to do this is to understand the products of language and culture as 'symbolic . . . fixed within the chain of signification or in relationship to the "signified"'. Benjamin's concept of allegory, which she sees as related to Derrida's notion of intertextuality, may be used to critically examine this idea of cultural production as symbolic or expressive (Sawchuk 1988: 66). So, to reduce fashion and clothing to class or sex, for example, is to fix their meanings as symbolic or expressive. For Sawchuk, fashion and clothing (and women) cannot be seen in this way. They cannot be seen 'as objects determined simply by two variables, sex and class, for they are constructed in this fabric of intertextual relations' (Sawchuk 1988: 65).

It is not immediately clear that Benjamin's version of allegory will do the things that Sawchuk wants it to do. As Buck-Morss points out, for Benjamin, the notion of fashion is 'specific to capitalist modernity' (Buck-Morss 1989: 97); it seems odd to use his ideas as especially appropriate to the analysis of postmodernity and postmodern phenomena. Jameson, however, quotes Benjamin saying that the allegorical object 'is incapable of projecting any meaning on its own', and this would fit in with the idea noted above of the object being meaningless on its own; the rest of the quotation seems less helpful. Benjamin continues by saying that the allegorical object 'can only take on that meaning which the allegorist wishes to lend it. He instills it with his own meaning' (Jameson 1971: 71). On one level, this explanation makes allegory sound like the idea of *bricolage* that will be explained later in this chapter. On another level it also seems to reintroduce precisely the element of expression, the fixity of meaning that Sawchuk wants to escape. The idea that meaning is a product of individual expression or intention, which would be indicated by the allegorist's 'wishes', is one which has been seen in chapter four to be not unproblematic. This reading of this quotation is also quite incompatible with Newman's account of allegory, in which allegory allows for the understanding of cultural productions 'without recourse to the notion of a constitutive . . . subject whose intentional meaning, the "signified", is transmitted through . . . the "signifier"' (Newman 1989: 130). It may be that Derrida's notion of undecidability, which will be used later, is more useful here than Benjamin's allegorical object.

Sawchuk, however, has a more favourable quotation, one which holds out the promise of liberating meaning and of being more compatible with Derrida's notion of intertextuality. She cites Benjamin, who says that 'the basic characteristic of allegory . . . is ambiguity, multiplicity of meaning . . . Ambiguity is . . . always the opposite of clarity and unity of meaning' (Sawchuk 1988: 66). The notion of allegory also contains a reference to history, as Jameson points out when he describes it as the 'clumsy deciphering of meaning from moment to moment' (Jameson 1971: 72). Allegorical meaning changes in time, then; it is not fixed in its determination by class or sex, for example. This conception of meaning does seem to fit in with, or be related to, Derrida's version of intertextuality insofar as both will allow changing historical and interpretative circumstances to change the meaning of cultural phenomena. Consequently, Sawchuk argues that cultural phenomena – events, objects and images – must be regarded as allegories 'which do not have one fixed or stable meaning but which derive their significance . . . from their place in a chain of signifiers'. Existing in time and therefore subject to temporal fluctuations, this chain is itself not a stable source of meaning (Sawchuk 1988: 67).

Now, Sawchuk thinks that she has escaped the reductionist accounts of fashion and clothing: 'the "meaning" of cultural phenomena is neither expressive of one or two social relations, nor is it "symbolic"' (Sawchuk 1988: 67). Fashion and clothing are no longer to be reduced to social relations like class or sex. Instead, like Benjamin's allegorical objects, she claims, their meanings are produced by changing social and historical circumstances. Thus, for example, when Baudrillard refers to the mini-skirt as having nothing to do with sexual liberation, he is referring to an allegorical object. To say that the mini-skirt is a symbol is to be reductionist and to ascribe a fixed meaning. Similarly, to say that it either is or is not expressive or indicative of sexual liberation for women is also to be reductionist and to ascribe a fixed meaning to the item. To consider it in terms of its difference from the long skirt, at a particular moment in time, is to see its meaning as at least capable of changing, as potentially ambiguous. To see its meaning as being generated in terms of its relations to, or its differences from, other garments is to see its meaning as being generated intertextually.

Thus the mini-skirt mentioned by Baudrillard, for example, may be seen as

171

an item of liberation for women: that may be what it means at a particular place and time. It may also be seen, at another place and time, as an item that reflects a woman's identification with, or submission to, patriarchy's rules of sexual display. It is not the case that, always and everywhere, the mini-skirt is just one of these things. To suggest this would be reductionist and blind to the intertextual constitution of the meaning of such items. As Sawchuk says, 'one cannot assume that a crucifix worn by Madonna is an expression of her essentially Christian nature' (Sawchuk 1988: 67). Madonna may well be in the business of adopting such an icon ironically and deliberately misappropriating its traditional significance, for the sake of fashion or in order to shock. She may, that is, be using it as an allegorical object, rather than as a symbol.

There are other consequences of this position. As Sawchuk says, if the meaning of garments is generated intertextually in a series of relations to other garments and other discourses that are themselves not simply present, then the questions involved in political or aesthetic judgements are made even more complex. For example, it can no longer be assumed, as Sawchuk says someone like Oakley assumes, that an 'anti-fashion discourse . . . [is] inherently feminist' (Sawchuk 1988: 67). Oakley suggests, for example, that in the late 1880s and 1890s, a period of 'feminist rebellion', 'there was a move towards plainer and more masculine dress' (Oakley 1981: 83). Plainer and more masculine dress means 'feminist' or 'feminist rebel'. Almost a hundred years later, an almost identical meaning is being ascribed to masculine dress by Cassell, who is quoted quite seriously by Oakley. Cassell states that the more radical the ideology of a feminist in the early 1970s, the more recognisable her demeanour. The demeanour included wearing workmen's overalls or denims, a 'man's T-shirt or work-shirt' and 'heavy men's workboots'. It also involved doing what are implied to be essentially masculine tasks, such as carrying heavy loads and changing their own tyres (Oakley 1981: 83). Considering the item of fashion or clothing as an allegorical object in accounts like this, then, means that it can no longer be assumed that the rejection of fashion and the adoption of masculine dress are inherently or essentially feminist gestures.

FASHION AND UNDECIDABILITY

The fact that the object exists within a structure, or a series of structures, of other objects and discourses means that the meaning of that object is essentially ambiguous. Whether this is to understand the item as an allegorical object in the sense intended by, or found in the text of, Benjamin, however, is another question. It could also be claimed that ambiguity is not an especially postmodern phenomenon. Ambiguity or polysemy, the co-existence of more than one meaning, may be seen as a characteristic feature of modernist works as well as a feature of postmodernist works. This section will argue that Derrida's notion of undecidability is a more accurate or useful way of referring to what is happening here. Intertextuality, that is, determines that the meaning of an object is undecidable, that it is both produced and destroyed by its place in those systems of differences.

The idea that meaning is a product of an element's relations to all other elements, and of its place in the various discourses that constitute it is not new and has been seen above in chapter four. The idea that an element's meaning is also destroyed or dissipated by those relations and in those discourses, however, may be new. Meaning or value is destroyed or dissipated in that there is no simple presence in terms of which an element may be said to be meaningful. Meaning is always a product of a relation to things which are not simply present and, to that extent, unambiguous or simple meaning is dissipated or dissolved. It is this relation to things which are absent which destroys any decidable meaning that an element may be thought to have. It is claimed that it is this phenomenon that is a postmodern characteristic or feature, and which determines that elements are radically undecidable in terms of their meanings.

The meaning of signs is both produced and destroyed by its relations to all other signs and by its place in different discourses. Derrida calls this effect 'undecidability' (Derrida 1978a: 99, 103–5); intertextuality means that meaning is always undecidable. As Derrida says, meaning or value is at once produced and destroyed (Derrida 1978b: 271). Wright provides an example of the effects of the undecidability of the object in her analysis of the stiletto heel. Figure 18 shows various women, including Ursula Breuer, in the foreground, wearing stiletto heels at the 1960 Amateur World Ballroom Championships at the Hammersmith Palais. Wright's essay may be used to show how this item may be deemed to be undecidable in terms of meaning; its meaning as either an object of enslavement or an item of liberation is undecidable. These meanings, that is, are both produced and destroyed by the item's relations to other items and by its place in a number of discourses.

The stiletto might at first seem the most inappropriate object to use to illustrate undecidability for, as Wright points out, 'it is seen as being exclusively female', even when worn by men, and has been seen by feminists as 'inherently feminine' (Wright 1989: 7). The stiletto has also, she points out, 'been widely accepted as symbolising female subordination' (Wright 1989: 8). That is, the meaning of the stiletto at first appears to be fixed. It appears to be fixed, moreover, in terms of sex and gender. It is said to be 'exclusively' and 'inherently' female or feminine. It is also said to 'symbolise' female subordination. The meaning of the stiletto has been reduced to a determination of social relations and it has been assumed to be inherently anti-feminist. This sort of case against the stiletto, this sort of determination of its meaning is often supported by quotations from people like David Bailey, the photographer, who said 'I like high heels – I know it's chauvinistic. It means girls can't run away from me' (Bayley 1991: 145). (One may care to speculate on why, if women like Ursula Breuer could perform the sort of dance shown in

Figure 18, which certainly appears to demand fast, athletic movements, they could not run away from men like David Bailey.) The meaning of the stiletto, however, appears to be simply or even naturally female, a reflection or an index of some other thing. In this case, the 'other thing' is sex.

Wright's analysis may be used to show quite clearly how the object exists in a number of different discourses, and how it may also have been seen as a thoroughly 'modern' and rebellious object to wear in the late 1950s and early 1960s. The stiletto is constituted intertextually in that it is the object of medical, moral, fashionable and industrial or technological discourses. Medical discourses condemned the heel for causing back problems and for deforming the foot, for example (Wright 1989: 13). Moral leaders appear to have been alarmed by the body shape imposed by the stiletto, emphasising as it did womanly breasts and bottoms (Wright 1989: 134). An advert for Lilley and Skinner, showing impossibly pointed heels and toes, promised 'fashion on the up-beat' (Wright 1989: Fig. 1.3). Industry and technology had to solve the engineering and material problems involved in constructing a heel that might be four or even six inches high and not break the moment a woman stood on it. They also had the problem of finding stiletto-resistant flooring materials for dance halls, offices, aircraft and even pavements (Wright 1989: 13). The stiletto is produced in all of these discourses in a slightly different way. Its meaning, as it is produced in each one of them, therefore, is slightly different. The meaning of the stiletto is seen here to be constituted intertextually, then; it is the object's relation to all of these different discourses that generates the meanings, not the fixed relation to sex or gender.

Baudrillard's claim, that it is simply as a result of a play of differences and not because of any intrinsic or inherent meaning that an item has the meanings that it does, may also be seen in Wright's account of the stiletto. It is suggested that extreme stilettos were often worn as a gesture of defiance against the establishment; female youth culture is said to be 'redefining itself on its differences rather than its similarities' (Wright 1989: 14). This type of shoe is selected to be worn because it is *not* associated with or worn by 'housewives', for example. As Wright says, the heel was used to represent 'dissatisfaction with the conventional female image'; women sought to 'replace' that image with a different image. There is no inherent meaning that is appealed to; it is only as a result of the play of paradigmatic differences that the shoe comes to have the meaning it does.

So, the stiletto should not be seen as inherently or naturally female or feminine. Nor should it be associated with any particular version of femininity. Wright says of the post-1957 stiletto that it might be more accurate to suggest that it 'symbolised *liberation* rather than subordination'.

From 1957, the stiletto was associated with glamour, with rebellion:
it represented some one who was in some way 'modern' and 'up to

Figure 18 Stiletto heels, 1960

date', and above all, someone who inhabited a world outside the home – a go-getter!

(Wright 1989:14)

The problem with this account is that the use of the words 'symbolising' and 'representing' are part of the modernist account of the modern object. They explain the meaning of the object in terms of stable and fixed relations to identities of class and gender, for example. The account of the postmodern object explains the meaning of the object as being produced intertextually. It explains the meaning of an object in terms of the object's relations to other objects and in terms of its place in various different texts or discourses. Wright's account suggests that the stiletto has another, alternative meaning: that it may be explained as a means of rebellion rather than as an object of enslavement. The present account claims that both of these meanings

175

co-exist, at the same time and alongside all sorts of other meanings, generated by the stiletto's place in all sorts of other discourses.

The stiletto does not only exist in terms of its determination by fixed sex
and gender codes, then. Those sex and gender codes are themselves in flux
and so is the stiletto as constituted by them. It is constituted by its place in all
sorts of discourses and in its differences from other shoes. It is clear that in
Wright's account, the stiletto is constituted as a liberating object, and not just
as an item of enslavement. It is constituted as not conventionally feminine,
indeed it is 'breaking from', and a considerable challenge to, those traditional
ideas of femininity. So far from being the instrument of passive, conventionally feminine, women's enslavement, it seems also, and at the same time, to be
a weapon of a newly aggressive, assertive, independent and 'modern' woman.
It is claimed, however, that even from Wright's account, the object may be
seen to be constituted intertextually, in terms of its relations to both other
objects and to other discourses. The meaning of the stiletto is thus undecidable. It is claimed that, if the stiletto heel may be presented as an undecidable
object, then all items of fashion and clothing may be considered as undecidable objects. In this sense, then, the item of fashion or dress may be seen as an
undecidable object, rather than an allegorical object, as claimed by Sawchuk.

FASHION AND PASTICHE

Pastiche is another word, like 'allegory', which looms large in the writings of
many writers on postmodernism. One or two analysts have suggested that
pastiche may be a useful tool with which to attempt to explain contemporary
fashion and clothing. It would probably be a mistake to say that it figures
originally in the work of Jameson as, no doubt, many other chroniclers of
postmodernity have used it before him. But it would probably not be a mistake to say that the idea of pastiche as an especially or characteristically
postmodern practice, as it is found in Jameson's essay 'Postmodernism, and
the cultural logic of late capitalism', for example, has been very influential.
This section will explain Jameson's case, consider fashion and clothing in
terms of the idea of pastiche and then look at Wilson's critique of Jameson's
argument.

The word pastiche refers classically to a musical or literary medley, in
which either tunes or stories are presented in the style of a well-known author
or composer. Pastiche, says Jameson, is to be sharply distinguished from
parody, which consists in the humorous imitation of an author's or composer's style (Jameson 1984: 64). Pastiche, then, is parody without rhetorical
motivation. It is the imitation of style without any of 'parody's ulterior
motives', without the 'satiric impulse', for example, and without the sense
that outside of the imitation, there is any original style to be imitated. As
Jameson says, pastiche is a 'neutral' practice of the satirical mimicry that is
parody (Jameson 1984: 65). In a move reminiscent of those seen above with

regard to the meaning of the object, Jameson suggests that 'modernist styles
... become postmodernist codes'; what modernity recognised as characteristic styles, postmodernity sees as an endless parade of difference, 'irrational
eclecticism' (Jameson 1984: 64).

This account of pastiche is very closely connected to what Jameson says
about nostalgia or *la mode retro* and to the place he ascribes to the notion of
the simulacrum. Jameson points out that the architectural historians' term
'historicism' may be used to refer to the process in which cultural producers
irrationally cannibalise the styles of the past, and he argues that this 'random
stylistic allusion' is now both 'omnipresent' and 'omnivorous' (Jameson 1984:
66). The entire world, he suggests, has been turned into 'sheer images of
itself'; it is all pastiche. Not just architecture, but all cultural production is the
production of imitations of past styles. He calls the objects that one finds in
such a world 'simulacra'; they are pastiche objects, imitation copies for which
there exist no originals. Consequently, cultural producers can only plunder
the past; history itself comes to be seen as a 'vast collection of images' (Jameson 1984: 66), a repository or museum from which 'dead styles' may be taken
and imitated.

It is interesting that Jameson is unsatisfied with the word 'nostalgia' to
describe this phenomenon, given that previous sections of this chapter have
accused him, precisely, of being nostalgic. He is not happy to describe postmodernism, in its plundering of past styles, as nostalgic. This is surely correct: postmodernism, in this guise, is anything but nostalgic for those styles.
They are simply there to be cannibalised and profited from. But Jameson
himself may be described as nostalgic for a time before or outside of postmodernism, when one could indulge in a 'properly modernist nostalgia'
(Jameson 1984: 66) and when the norms of modernity could satirically be
parodied in a 'not necessarily unfriendly way' (Jameson 1984: 65). Whatever,
Jameson is also surely correct to suggest that the process of cannibalisation
and nostalgia are now generalised throughout all forms of 'commercial art
and taste' (Jameson 1984: 66). He refers to films like *American Graffiti* and
Chinatown as 'nostalgia films', complacently recapturing or recuperating
the styles of the past in order to serve the present. Nostalgia, or retro, is now
a collective social enterprise, according to Jameson; it is now one of the
defining, if not actually compulsory, characteristics of our postmodernity.

It should not be difficult to understand how fashion, if not dress and
clothing, might fit into this account of pastiche and retro. Indeed, it is more
difficult to understand why Jameson does not use fashion as an example,
rather than film. As Baudrillard says, 'fashion is always retro'; fashion is
always an 'immediate and total recycling' of past forms (Baudrillard 1993:
88). This chapter has already noted Wilson's claim that 'postmodernism, with
its eclectic approach to style, might seem especially compatible with fashion'
(Wilson 1985: 63). Fashion, like pastiche, appears to be little else apart
from the appropriation of different styles, often styles from the distant past.

Similarly, it involves the constant changing of those styles. Fashion has gained a reputation for plundering both the past and other cultures for novel styles, often with little understanding or even respect for those past times and other cultures. This thoughtless and offensive attitude to the specificities of other times and cultures may appear to be the result of exactly that unprincipled post-literacy that Jameson calls postmodernity. The 'statue with blind eyeballs', as he describes pastiche, could just as well be the mannequin in the fashion store's window (Jameson 1984: 65).

Wilson has pointed out how, from the late 1960s onwards, pastiche or retro describes very well the workings of the fashion industry. She points out, for example, how in 1989 'the French designer Martine Sitbon was introducing pastiche or "retrochic" versions of 1970s fashions which were themselves a pastiche of the 1940s' (Wilson 1992b: 6). The layers of ironic, postmodernist quotation start to become distinctly vertiginous at points like this. According to Jameson, pastiche is supposed to be parody without any saving graces like satire or humour: it may be suspected that, in such an account, to pastiche a pastiche would not only be graceless but also rather unhealthy. Conceiving of fashion as pastiche, the irrational or random cannibalisation of all the styles of the past, may also explain the puzzlement of 1970s fashion journalists noted by Wilson. Apparently, these journalists could not explain the way in which the orderly evolution of one style into another seemed to end around this time. Clearly, if fashion is conceived of as the random or irrational process described by Jameson's pastiche, explanation will be impossible because that is what random and irrational mean, that they are unavailable to reasonable or reasoned explanation.

The claim that Sitbon was producing pastiches of the styles of the 1970s, which were themselves pastiches of the styles of the 1940s, should raise the question as to whether pastiche is in fact peculiar to postmodernity. It may be the case that fashion, and even dress and clothing, have always produced pastiches of the styles of the past. Wilson has an interesting version of the argument regarding whether Jameson is correct to identify pastiche and retro in fashion as exclusively something that afflicts us today: she asks, 'Is retro so exclusively *de nos jours*?' (Wilson 1990: 224). In answer to this question she suggests that, at least in the industrial period, fashion 'has relied on pastiche and the recycling of styles'. Dior's claim that the actual or basic and underlying shapes of garments changed very little and very slowly before the early twentieth century, is used to support this suggestion. Dior argues that an impression of change and movement was achieved by the clever use of 'superficial decoration' and motifs. Wilson also notes how Liberty catalogues of the early part of the twentieth century advertised gowns in a variety of '"historical" styles: Egyptian, medieval, Elizabethan, Madame de Pompadour' (Wilson 1990: 224).

However, Dior's claim regarding superficial decorations and motifs, even if they are 'often rifled from the past', does not seem strong enough to do the amount of work Wilson wants it to do and it is further undermined by Dior's other claim that the basic shapes of the garments changed very slowly at this time. Clearly, the precise meanings of words like 'slowly' and 'superficial' in a context like this are debatable, especially if the work of people like Richardson and Kroeber (1973) and Young (1973) is taken into account. Richardson and Kroeber suggest that 'the basic dimensions of modern European feminine dress alternate with fair regularity between maxima and minima which in most cases average about fifty years apart' (Richardson and Kroeber 1973: 101). Young, alternatively, proposes that each cycle in women's dress lasts about thirty years (Young 1973: 118). Both of these sets of research seem agreed that within these larger cycles there are smaller variations, although it may be claimed that this talk of larger and smaller begs the same question as the ideas of slow and superficial above.

FASHION AND *BRICOLAGE*

Newman, who provides useful introductions to most of the concepts mentioned so far in this chapter, has suggested that '*bricolage* is a tempting category to apply to the visual arts' (Newman 1989: 133). Levi-Strauss, who may be said to have initiated the anthropological discussion of *bricolage* to which the postmodernists all refer, suggests that it is 'common knowledge' that the artist is something of a *bricoleur* (Levi-Strauss 1966: 22). This section will define *bricolage*, distinguishing it from the notions of pastiche and retro, before explaining how it may be applied to the creative production involved in fashion design.

Levi-Strauss' translator points out that there is no precise equivalent of the word *bricoleur* in English, suggesting that 'he is a man who undertakes odd jobs and is a Jack of all trades' but is not strictly an 'odd job man' or handyman (Levi-Strauss 1966:17). The French term has a slightly derogatory sense and Levi-Strauss proposes 'someone who works with his hands and uses devious means compared to those of a craftsman' (Levi-Strauss 1966: 16–17). The *bricoleur* is also someone who undertakes a wide variety of tasks and who is forever making do, not necessarily using either the correct tools or the proper materials. So, the *bricoleur* uses whatever tools and materials are at hand in order to complete a job. *Bricolage* is contrasted in this text with the craftsman's work and also with the notion of engineering or science. Engineering is often understood as something approaching an exact science. The engineer and the scientist procure tools and materials in the light of the project they are set; they have ideas as to what are the most appropriate tools and materials needed to complete a specific project. The *bricoleur* collects and retains tools and materials on the basis that they may come in handy next time, while the engineer and the scientist, as well as the craftsman, all have specialist tools and the proper materials with which to work (Levi-Strauss 1966: 18).

Bricolage, then, uses the 'remains and debris' of events, 'odds and ends', 'fossilised evidence of the history of an individual or a society', for its constructions (Levi-Strauss 1966: 22). Its present constructions are always made out of things which have already been used in the past: *bricolage* is the 'continual reconstruction from the same materials', materials which have always already been used in the past (Levi-Strauss 1966: 21). Consequently, *bricolage* involves the continual recombination of elements. These elements may be finite in number but they are always 'permutable, that is, capable of standing in successive relations with other entities'. An alteration in the relations in which any element exists will affect all the elements in the structure and change the meaning of each of them (Levi-Strauss 1966: 20). This latter aspect has been seen in the discussion of meaning in chapter three where a change in the syntagmatic or paradigmatic relations in which an element existed changed the meaning of that element.

The notion of *bricolage*, as it has been defined here, bears some resemblances to the notion of pastiche, as discussed by Jameson. *Bricolage* also appears to have certain features in common with the idea of 'retro'. Pastiche and retro, like *bricolage*, employ references to the past; they involve looking to the materials and styles used in the past. While it is extremely difficult to distinguish *bricolage* and retro, there does seem to be a genuine difference between *bricolage* and pastiche. *Bricolage*, like retro, implies the creation of new meanings from the materials and styles taken from the past. Pastiche, however, does not seem to involve the creation of new meanings; it is comparatively nihilistic, at least in Jameson's version. Jameson says that pastiche is parody without the rhetorical motivation, or without the satirical energy, but *bricolage* has a motive: it is interested in creating new meanings. Retro, similarly, does not have the nihilistic undertones of Jameson's pastiche.

It should not be too difficult to see how fashion and clothing design may be viewed as *bricolage*, especially as they have already been discussed in terms of pastiche and retro. The use of materials and styles from the past to create new items of fashion and clothing is straightforwardly the work of the *bricoleur*. It is on the matter of the tools, however, that fashion and clothing design may not want to be associated with the *bricoleur*. It may be that, with all the specialised machinery and with all the specialist paraphernalia, fashion and clothing design will not want to see itself in the position of the *bricoleur*, who has just enough tools to do most of the sorts of things that he may be called upon to do. It may be, that is, that the fashion and clothing designer sees themself as rather more of the craftsman or even the engineer than the *bricoleur*, and it would be in terms of the specialised tools and so on used in the practice of creative production that such an argument could be mounted. This, however, would be highly ironic and it would run counter to most of Levi-Strauss' intentions.

It runs counter to most of Levi-Strauss' intentions because in this essay he is trying to argue that the distinction between the *bricoleur* and the engineer is

180

sometimes less clear than might at first be thought. It would be ironic because, as Derrida says, 'the odds are that the engineer is a myth produced by the *bricoleur*' (Derrida 1978b: 285). As Levi-Strauss points out, for example, both *bricoleur* and engineer are confronted by a 'previously determined set' of practical and theoretical knowledges and of technical means (Levi-Strauss 1966:19); neither is free to do as they wish when presented with a task. It is precisely this point, however, that Derrida uses to make his argument that there is no distinction between the two, at least in the sense in which Levi-Strauss wants there to be a distinction. As Derrida says,

> if one calls *bricolage* the necessity of borrowing one's concepts from the text of a heritage which is more or less coherent or ruined, it must be said that every discourse is *bricoleur*.
>
> (Derrida 1978b: 285)

Derrida even uses cloth as a metaphor to describe the impossibility of escaping heritage and history. He says that nobody can be the origin of their own discourse, nobody can 'construct it . . . "out of whole cloth"' (Derrida 1978b: 285). There is no one, no discourse, that does not have to use the language, the materials and the tools with which they are landed in order to operate, and to this extent, everyone and every discourse is *bricoleur*.

Now, if this is the case, then it makes no sense whatever to claim that fashion and clothing design are not *bricolage* but rather science or engineering, as was suggested above; 'the engineer and the scientist are also species of *bricoleurs*' (Derrida 1978b: 285). It also makes no sense to disparage fashion and clothing design for not being, or for not being more like, engineering or science. It is claimed that this latter argument is relevant to the curious position enjoyed by fashion and clothing design. There are many people willing to dismiss these subjects as not terribly important, as not being as demanding as the so-called 'hard' sciences, for example, and some of these arguments have been discussed earlier in the present volume. If, however, it is the case that the positions of the engineers and scientists are myths, as Levi-Strauss and Derrida claim, then it is illegitimate to dismiss fashion and clothing design as trivia.

The desire to create new meanings, which enables *bricolage* to escape the charge of nihilism, and which may bear interesting comparison to Baudrillard's 'meaning drive' noted earlier, provides another link to what Newman has called the 'theorisation of postmodernism'. Newman suggests that Levi-Strauss' description of the kind of thought characteristic of *bricolage* as 'imprisoned in the events and experiences which it never tires of ordering and re-ordering in its search to find them a meaning' (Levi-Strauss 1966: 22) is actually an 'evocative description of the predicament of the postmodernist artist' (Newman 1989: 133). Levi-Strauss sees the artist as something of a *bricoleur* and Newman sees the postmodern artist as existing in the same predicament as a *bricoleur*. The rest of the passage is also very interesting in that it refers to the way in which the thought that is characteristic of the *bricoleur* 'acts as a liberator by its protest against the idea that anything can be meaningless' (Levi-Strauss 1966: 22). This may be read as referring to the desire to create endless new meanings which distinguished *bricolage* and retro from the meaninglessness of pastiche.

FASHION AND AMBIVALENCE

Throughout this book, fashion and clothing have been described as ambivalent or anomalous. In the Introduction, fashion was said to be both respectable and disreputable, it was both communicative and deceptive. In chapter two, fashion was described as both an art and a design activity. Chapter three presented clothing as having both a modest and an immodest function. And this chapter has argued that the stiletto is at the same time enslaving and liberating for women. Fashion and clothing are also clearly both intensely personal and resolutely political matters: nothing is more intimate or closer to one's own body than the clothes one wears and yet they communicate one's preferences and statuses to the wider society, in public. This situation, in which it is not clear which of two categories the topic belongs to, may be termed ambivalence, or anomaly.

Zygmunt Bauman uses the term 'ambivalence' to describe the 'possibility of assigning an object or event to more than one category' (1991: 1), while Mary Douglas calls anomalous any element 'which does not fit a given set or series' and likens it to 'ambiguity', which refers to any element 'capable of two interpretations' (Douglas 1966: 37). For Bauman, ambivalence is a condition peculiar to postmodernity (and reaches its high point in Derrida's undecidables, as discussed above), but for Douglas any society, at any time may experience, and have to deal with, the anomalous. Both speak of the unease that is generated by the phenomenon. Bauman refers to the 'scandal' (1991: 18ff) and the 'horror' (1990: 146) of ambivalence and indeterminate objects, while Douglas posits an 'anxiety' experienced by those confronting the anomalous (1966: 39). Elizabeth Wilson presents versions of this apprehension in her (1985) *Adorned in Dreams*. Her Introduction catalogues the various ways in which the 'ambiguity' and 'strangeness' of fashion and clothing generate 'uneasiness' (1985: 2). One of her examples is that of 'clothes without a wearer' which, nevertheless, make present the bodies of potential, or past wearers (Wilson 1985: 2). She elucidates this strangeness by referring to the dichotomous concepts noted above: clothing 'links the biological body to the social body, the public to private' but none of the concepts is sufficient to explain clothing on its own. As she says, 'clothing marks an unclear boundary ambiguously and unclear boundaries disturb us' (ibid.).

Both Bauman and Douglas volunteer methods for dealing with ambivalence or anomaly and reducing the unease and anxiety. Bauman offers two basic strategies, fighting indeterminacy or living with it (1990: 151–3 and

1991: 61–73). Fighting indeterminacy includes the reclassification of the ambivalent, so that what is at first ambivalent is subsumed under one or other of the familiar categories. Other aspects of fighting ambivalence include mismeeting it (or denying the ambivalence), eliminating it and assimilating it (ibid.) while 'living with ambivalence' is another name for the condition of postmodernity (1991: 231ff). The translation of Bauman's strategies into terms appropriate to fashion and clothing would not be easy; it would take a whole other essay to perform and here is, perhaps, not the place. Douglas, however, suggests five strategies with which to meet anomaly (1966: 39–40) and, as her strategies are *prima facie* more germane to the topics of fashion and clothing than Bauman's are, this section will look at two of them.

It must be said that Douglas's strategies are not always entirely dissimilar to Bauman's. Her first provision is essentially the reclassification of the anomalous, 'settling for one or other interpretation' (1966: 39). Examples of this approach might include Part Four of Eicher *et al.* (2000) *The Visible Self*, which deals with fashion as a form of art, or Josephine Miller's essay in Conway (ed.) (1987) *Design History: A Students' Handbook*, in which fashion and dress are studied as forms of design. There is little, if any ambiguity about the status of fashion or dress in these examples and any ambivalence is removed. The writers have made a decision and assigned fashion and dress, which have been seen to be problematic, to an unproblematic category. This is probably the most common strategy and the easiest to make sense of. Another of Douglas's approaches is more challenging and involves labelling the anomalous element as 'dangerous' (1966: 39). Quite how this is to be understood in terms of fashion is not immediately clear, but talk of 'fashion victims' does not escape the implication that fashion is something hazardous, to which one might fall prey.

Finally, Bauman's suggestion that 'living with' ambivalence is the name for postmodernity may be unpacked, and simplified, a little. He argues that tolerance, the tolerance 'for the otherness of the other' (1991: 262), is the way to live with ambivalence. The 'other' here is the ambivalent, that which will not, or cannot, be classified using a culture's dichotomous concepts and Bauman seems to argue for accepting and tolerating the strangeness of the other (1991: 236–7). It should come as little surprise when Bauman describes postmodernity, living with ambivalence, as 'a site of opportunity and of danger' (1991: 262). Fashion, which has been explored in this chapter and in this section as a prime example of postmodernity, as the anomalous and the ambivalent, is again described as dangerous.

CONCLUSION

While this chapter has argued that the fashion or clothing object is constituted intertextually, in a network of relations to other objects and to other discourses, it would probably be true to say that fashion and clothing are not experienced as such in everyday life. To paraphrase Derrida, there is no sense in doing away with, or in escaping from, the concepts and experiences of everyday life; it may fairly be claimed that nobody routinely experiences their clothes as undecidable. For the most part, one's clothes are worn and experienced as conventional, or as classic, or as revolutionary, for example; that is why they are worn, and only rarely is it the case that one sets out to construct or experience an outfit as undecidable.

On the other hand, the concept of the *bricoleur* may well be much more familiar to people. It may be that this conforms to and confirms their experience of putting together outfits from garments that they have worn before in other contexts. This aspect of the experience of clothes is consistent with that proposed by Tim Dant in his (1999) *Material Culture in the Social World*. He refers to the fact that, for a lot of people and for a lot of the time, clothes are acquired, chosen and worn in a variety of ways 'that are on the margins of anything approaching a fashion system' (1999: 102). Large parts of people's wardrobes are full of clothes that have been 'gifts' or cast-offs from other people, or which have been 'borrowed' with or without permission. This 'non-cash, non-public, informal economy' (Dant 1999: 102), which he says actually determines what most people wear most of the time, sounds very much like a version of *bricolage*. Moreover, even within the cash-based and 'formal' economy of the high street or shopping mall, it may be that the idea of *bricolage* is highly familiar to people choosing what to buy in a store. The idea of fashion and clothing answering the desire to create and recreate endless new meanings out of the heritage of the past, the idea of fashion and clothing as *bricolage*, that is, may well be both familiar and welcome. Something akin to this sense of *bricolage* may be found in the work of Simmel, who notes the way in which 'fashion repeatedly returns to old forms'. Simmel may be taken as implying that the past can be seen as a sort of storehouse of styles, shapes and textures, which may be re-selected, given the passage of time, once the 'charm of difference' has been restored to them (Simmel 1971: 320).

This chapter has tried to provide an introduction to some of the debates, issues and concepts surrounding fashion, clothing, postmodernity and postmodernism. Fashion and clothing were first explained briefly as relating to modernity and modernism, and in terms of their being either product, symbol or instrument; the corset advertisement was used to illustrate how this item, for example, was sold on the strength of its uses, its symbolising of a certain type of woman and the quality of materials out of which it was made. Baudrillard's 'liberation' of the fashion object from these logics was used to discuss fashion as a postmodern object. In this account, the object functions only as a differential sign and meaning is produced only from the relation to other fashion and clothing signs. Sawchuk's attempt to interpret this in terms of Benjamin's concept of allegory was examined and it was argued that, while Benjamin's concept would not necessarily do the things that Sawchuk wanted, it was possible to explain the fashion object as

184

undecidable. According to this account, the meaning of the object, as either reproductive or revolutionary, for example, was both produced and destroyed by its place in any number of discourses and by its relations to all other fashion objects. For Bauman, the undecidable was responsible for a scandal and this scandal was linked to Douglas's description and treatment of the anxiety generated by anomalous objects or elements, such as fashion. Baudrillard's liberation of the fashion sign may also be responsible for the relation to masquerade, performance and the spectacle, which were discussed in terms of the critique and construction, or the production and destruction, of identity.

So, where chapters five and six presented fashion and clothing as decidable, as either reproductive or revolutionary, this chapter has explained them as undecidable, as both reproductive and revolutionary at the same time. Such an account of the fashion object may be taken as being more consistent with the notion of the active consumer, noted by Partington. Indeed, it may even be questioned whether the notion of the 'consumer' is sufficient when it seems to be the case that such 'consumers' may be said to be producing as much as consuming. This suspicion of the 'active/passive' dichotomy may not be unrelated to the suspicion of the 'simple opposition of dominant and dominated', noted by Derrida (Derrida 1994: 55) which the theory of hegemony both deals in and deconstructs. Finally in this chapter, the use of concepts such as pastiche and *bricolage* was explained in terms of fashion and clothing.

FURTHER READING

- Various works on **fashion and the body** have been neglected here because this book is not about fashion and the body. Elizabeth Wilson's (1992) 'Fashion and the postmodern body' in Ash, I and Wilson, E. (eds) *Chic Thrills: A Fashion Reader*, Pandora, deals with Foucault, feminism and postmodernity. Evans, C. and Thornton, M. (1989) *Women and Fashion*, Quartet, also has at least one chapter explicitly concerned with fashion, feminism and postmodernity, as well as some that are highly relevant to the concerns of the chapter. Joanne Entwistle's (2000) *The Fashioned Body: Fashion, Dress and Modern Social Theory*, Polity Press also concentrates on the body. Entwistle, J. and Wilson, E. (eds) (2001) *Body Dressing*, Berg is a very useful collection of essays which considers the body, fashion and their relation to a host of topics, including consumption, masquerade, gender and the work of Alexander McQueen.
- For more on **fashion and deconstruction**, see Alison Gill's (1998) essay, 'Deconstruction fashion: the making of unfinished, decomposing and re-assembled clothes' in *Fashion Theory*, Volume 2, Issue 1, pp. 25–50. She uses Derrida's work on the idea of deconstruction to explore Martin Margiela's fashion design. The following websites might also prove interesting, on the work of Margiela; *www.bozzi.it/ilsito/margf/marging.html* and *www.fashionlive.com*
- For more on the idea of ***bricolage* and fashion**, see Dant, T. (1999) *Material Culture in the Social World*, Open University Press, pp. 102ff and Hebdige, D. (1979) *Subculture: The Meaning of Style*, Routledge, pp. 102–6.
- Gilles Lipovetsky's (1994) *The Empire of Fashion: Dressing Modern Democracy*,

Princeton University Press develops and extends **Baudrillard's account of fashion** in that he argues that differentiation and consumer choice apply to all products, not just those of fashion and clothing, see pp. 143ff, for example. For more on the notion of the simulacrum, see Baudrillard, J. (1983) *Simulations*, Semiotext(e).

- In a special edition of *Fashion Theory* devoted to the theme of **fashion and performance**, Caroline Evans' (2001) essay 'The Enchanted Spectacle' (in *Fashion Theory*, Volume 5, Issue 3, pp. 271–310), explores performance and identity in relation to fashion shows, considering early mannequins and more recent shows by Kenzo, Theirry Mugler and Yves Saint Laurent. This edition also contains essays on fashion and performance art.

8

CONCLUSION

This book has tried to introduce and explain fashion and clothing as communication. It has taken the relatively uncontroversial notion that the things people wear are significant or meaningful, and it has attempted to explain what sort of meanings fashion and clothing may have, how those meanings are produced or generated, and how fashion and clothing communicate those meanings. It was argued that meanings, like fashions, were not static or fixed. It was argued that even the use of the term 'fashion' was not static or fixed, that it was a product of the context in which it appeared and that an item could function as fashion at one moment and as clothing, or anti-fashion, at another. Non-verbal signs such as items of fashion and clothing, like linguistic signs, then, take their meanings from the context, or syntagm, in which they appear. New items of fashion and clothing change the context, the syntagm, in which they appear and thus alter the meanings of all other items in the syntagm, in the same way as the addition of a word to a sentence, for example, alters the meaning of that sentence. These ideas were developed in chapter seven to explain the idea of undecidability.

Undecidability was presented as the idea that the differential relations which produce or generate meanings also destroy or dissipate those meanings. The stiletto heel, for example, could be explained as both liberating and enslaving; changing the context, changing the relations to other objects and discourses, was seen to change the meaning of the item. The meaning of the item is both produced and destroyed by the relations to other objects and discourses. It might be argued, from a commonsense point of view, that nobody experiences the meanings of the garments they wear as undecidable. People do not perceive the items in their wardrobes or on sale in shops as illustrating the way in which the effect of modesty is created only by reference to revealment. They see garments as too revealing, or too modest, for example, not as the way in which one differentially constructs the effect of the other; there is no undecidability here. It might also be argued, from the same perspective, that nobody sets out to communicate undecidable meanings. For the most part, people put garments together into ensembles that they believe are smart, or formal, or casual or right for a wedding; there is little room for the undecidability of garments here.

And, supposing that they have any choice in this matter, people are surely right to do this. It is not much of a message that says 'both smart and casual'; a communication that contains mutually contradictory statements is not much of a communication. So, for the most part, and for most people, most of the time, fashion and clothing are not undecidable. The interpretation of meanings is largely reliable and finite; as noted above, faced by a friend's shirt we do not think to ourselves, 'I wonder what he means by that', nor do we conjure up endless syntagmatic chains, paradigmatic sets and discourses in which it might be found and in relation to which it might be meaningful. We think, 'That shirt is a mistake; too masculine/feminine or smart/casual, or whatever, for here and now'. A decision is made in favour of one or other of the dichotomous terms, rather than meaning being seen as endlessly deferred and postponed in the differential relation between them. This differential 'play' then, must be arrested or curtailed at some point in order for communication to take place.

To say this is clearly to disagree with Baudrillard on the matters of fashion, communication and meaning. Baudrillard suggests that 'fashion, like language, is aimed . . . at the social', but whereas language 'aims for meaning', fashion 'aims for a theatrical sociality'. Moreover, whereas language *aims* at communication, fashion *plays* at it'; fashion turns communication into the 'goal-less state of a signification without a message' (Baudrillard 1993: 94). While this book has been careful to distance itself from the approach of someone like Lurie, who it was claimed takes the metaphor of clothing as a language (too) literally, fashion and clothing have been explained as communicative phenomena, as non-verbal communication. As suggested above, the differential play of signs must be curtailed in order for communication to take place; people do, after all, do something like communicate with each other. So Baudrillard's goal-less state of signification without a message must also be escaped or curtailed in order for fashion and clothing to communicate, for surely it cannot be denied for very long that they do communicate. The claim that fashion aims at a theatrical sociality is also difficult to uphold. Even if it is assumed that it is fashion, and not clothing or dress that is in question here, it could still be argued that fashion is aiming for meaning no less than language. There is a level at which fashion constitutes the social and at which it communicates something like the desire for social mobility. Fashion is meaningful if only at the level at which it is recognisable as fashion.

It is also claimed, however, that the two versions of the interpretation and communication of meanings noted above may finally help to explain the two profiles of fashion and clothing that have been noted so far. This book began by considering the ambiguous profile that was presented by fashion and clothing in many western capitalist societies at the end of the twentieth century. From one side the profile was attractive and seductive. From the other side the profile, while no less seductive, was seen as trivial and deceitful and therefore much less attractive. Sapir provides an example of the mildest form of this ambiguity, noting that 'fashion may carry with it a tone of approval or disapproval' (Sapir 1931: 139). This curious and ambiguous profile has reappeared at many points and in various forms throughout the book. It was noted with regard to ideology, for example, where it was suggested that those who disapproved of fashion saw and desired the possibility of a beyond or an end to ideology. It was also noted with regard to cultural production, where it was suggested that creativity could be given a positive and a negative value; creativity could be seen as transcendence and inspiration, or it could be seen as akin to madness and feared as a result. So, it seems reasonable to return to the ambiguity of fashion and clothing, and to the ambivalence of many societies towards them, here in the conclusion.

Fashion and clothing exist in the conceptual space or difference between so many oppositions that it is tempting to explain the ambiguous profile that they present as being the product of a sort of generalised undecidability. Fashion and clothing are not simply either private or public phenomena, for example, they are 'on the borderline between subject and object' (Buck-Morss 1989: 97). They represent something like a border or a margin between a public, exterior persona and a private, interior identity. As Wilson says, 'clothing marks an unclear boundary ambiguously, and unclear boundaries disturb us' (Wilson 1985: 2). Chapter three demonstrated how fashion and clothing may not simply be reduced to either a means of concealment or a means of display; garments are both revealing and concealing at the same time. As Barthes says, the erotic in dress is a matter of intermittence:

> the intermittence of skin flashing between two articles of clothing (trousers and sweater), between two edges (the open-necked shirt, the glove and the sleeve); it is this flash which seduces, or rather: the staging of an appearance-as-disappearance.
>
> (Barthes 1975: 9–10)

Lisa Jensen, who designed the clothes worn by Michelle Pfeiffer in the Hollywood film *The Fabulous Baker Boys*, appears to have understood this point. Pfeiffer is playing a sexy singer in this film and her clothes clearly need to establish her as such. Jensen says that, to achieve a sexually attractive effect, it is not necessary to show massive amounts of female flesh; rather, 'you should play hide and seek with the body' (quoted in Davis 1992: 87).

Items of fashion and clothing are themselves neither living nor moving but, especially if they are old or discarded, they seem to hint at the movements of the body or bodies that once moved them around; they inhabit some limbo between the animate and the inanimate. Different garments, different fashions and clothes, also determine the movements that can be made while wearing those garments, fashions and clothes. Indeed, it may be said that it is to some extent precisely the movements that they enable us or force us to make

that are as much the fashion as the garments themselves. Fashion and clothing are the mass-produced means by which individual style is constructed;
somehow we believe that the shirt, or the skirt, which both exist in their
thousands of copies, is 'us'. Mass-produced garments are used to construct
what is thought of and experienced as an individual identity, a way of being
different to everyone else. 'That dress is so you', we say, for example, of a
dress that may be worn by many hundreds of people at that very moment. In
these ways, identity shades into difference, and difference into identity.

In these oppositions, the meaning or value of one of the terms is only
produced or generated on the basis of its containing the other within it. For
example, in the construction of an individual identity, use has to be made of
mass-produced items and of a socially sanctioned code. At the heart of individual identity, then, at the heart of something that is supposed to be specific
to an individual, is the mass-produced, the garment that exists in the form of
hundreds or thousands of copies. Moreover, that identity can only be constructed according to a network of differences which are already understood
and common to a whole community. The most inert and inanimate object, a
garment, already prescribes the sorts of movements that its wearer will be
constrained to make; even before it is worn, this inanimate object contains
determinations of the animate. Concealment and display, disappearance and
appearance, and modesty and seduction do not coincide with the simple
presence or absence of the item of fashion or clothing. The item of fashion
and clothing may be present and yet still display and seduce; as Barthes says,
appearance may occur in the places where the garment gapes, and in the gaps
between garments.

In each of these cases the meaning of the terms is transformed. It is not as
if the movement is between terms that retain a stable meaning, as in the case
of Simmel's dialectic. Thus appearance only makes sense on the basis of it
containing reference to disappearance. There is no essence of display. Display
is only meaningful on the understanding that it contains reference to concealment. Similarly, there is no essence of modesty. Modesty only makes any
sense if the possibility of seduction exists. The meaning of the terms is transformed in such a way that the terms are no longer strictly decidable; they
always already refer to that which was supposed to have been opposed to
them and to have been maintained as separate to or outside of them. Fashion
and clothing then, existing in the gaps or spaces between these conceptual
oppositions, are themselves undecidable in terms of these oppositions.
They are not simply decidable in terms of public/private, subject/object,
appearance/concealment, modesty/ seduction, individual/group and so on.

As noted above, however, this differential play must be arrested or curtailed
at some point in order for interpretation in terms of one or other of these
dichotomous concepts to take place. Finally, then, the curious cultural profile
enjoyed by fashion and clothing may be understood as the result of a conflict
between the desire for there to be a 'beyond' to the process of endless deferral

and differentiation in which the meaning of terms is always a result of a relation to other, different and absent terms, and the realisation that there can be no such beyond. Those who see fashion and clothing as trivial and deceptive, and who bemoan their shallow and exploitative natures, are those who desire such a beyond. They are those who desire an end or an outside to the play of differences because they think that this would lead to stable and fixed meanings. Those who value fashion and clothing positively, who see fashion and clothing as evidence of creativity and cultural production, are those who realise that there is no such beyond and who are happy to enjoy the play of cultural difference as it is found in fashion and clothing. They are those who are happy with the idea that difference produces meanings, and who have no wish to see difference curtailed or escaped. It is claimed, then, that this is the nature of fashion and clothing and that this is the nature of meaning and communication. The structural ambivalence of western capitalist societies towards fashion and clothing may be explained by these conflicting desires, by these two interpretations of interpretation and meaning.

GLOSSARY

These are not offered as highly developed definitions. They are intended merely as simple introductions, to give a working knowledge of the ideas in order that readers may return to the text and make some sense of it.

Bricolage

Using or adapting material which is at hand to perform a function or create an effect. Using 'odds and ends', improvising, putting together found or second-hand items to create a look or ensemble.

Class

'Social classes are . . . groups of people who have a similar relationship to the means of production in society and, as a result, a common social and cultural position within an unequal system of property ownership, power and material rewards' (O'Sullivan *et al.* 1994: 39). The 'means of production' include the machinery, technology and other plant that are used in making commodities. The relationship to this machinery and so on is basically that you either own it, work on it or manage it in some way. The inequality stems from the fact that, according to whether you own, work on or manage it, you will get more or less material reward (money), as a wage and enjoy more or less power as a consequence. The owners will always get the most material rewards because they profit from the surplus value generated by the workers and managers.

Clothing

What people wear. May or may not be fashionable. Roach-Higgins *et al.* (1995: 10) suggest it generally means 'enclosures' (garments) that 'cover the body' and therefore omits bodily modifications, which also may or may not be fashionable.

Communication

The 'negotiation and exchange of meaning' (O'Sullivan *et al.* 1994: 50). A form of social interaction in which individuals are constituted or established as members of a culture. Fashion and clothing are communication because they are ways in which meanings are exchanged and processes through which individuals are established as members of cultural groups.

Connotation

A kind of meaning. The kind of meaning that is born of the associations an item has for someone, or the things it makes someone think or feel. 'Young, free, hardworking, American, active' are some of the connotational meanings of denim jeans identified by Fiske (1989: 2–3).
Cf. Denotation

Consumption

Need (natural) or desire (cultural) for and subsequent obtaining (usually through purchase) and use of commodities produced in capitalist societies. What one consumes and desires to consume is generated by culture. May be theorised as 'passive', in which consumers participate in already created meanings, or 'active', in which consumers generate new, alternative meanings.

Culture

Notoriously difficult word to define. Williams' (1981: 13) definition is used here, that it is 'the signifying system through which ... a social order is communicated, reproduced, experienced and explored'. The signifying system is explained as an economy of institutions, practices, representations and meanings. The social order refers to the way in which different classes, for example, relate to one another in a social structure, higher or lower than other classes. Fashion and clothing are signifying (meaningful) practices which go to make up (the signifying system that is) culture and through which the social order is communicated, reproduced and so on.

Denotation

A kind of meaning. Often referred to as the literal meaning. Can be correct or incorrect. 'Cotton twill weave fabric of white and blue threads which originates from the French town of Nîmes' (O'Hara 1986: 88) is the denotational meaning of denim.
Cf. Connotation

Dress

Like clothing. What people wear. May or may not be fashionable. 'An assemblage of modifications of the body and/or supplements to the body' (Roach-Higgins *et al.* 1995: 7)
Cf. Fashion and Dress

Fashion

'Everybody has to get dressed in the morning and go about the day's business. What everybody wears to do this has taken different forms in the West for about seven hundred years and that is what fashion is' (Hollander 1994: 11). Cf. Fashion and Clothing

Gender

What a culture makes of, or the significance a culture gives to, naturally occurring sexual differences.

Ideology

Complicated Marxist term meaning many, many things. Used here to denote systems of beliefs held by members of classes concerning the world and its contents, including beliefs about the naturalness and rightness of the class's identity and political position. Fashion and clothing may communicate and reproduce the dominant set of beliefs (the dominant ideology), or they may be used to contest and challenge them (resistance).

Myth

Roland Barthes' way of complicating the Marxist term 'ideology'. Myth, connotation and ideology describe basically the same operations in the same domain (Barthes 1977: 49). The connotational meaning of elements (fashion, items of clothing, for example), varies according to class (and also gender, age, ethnic, national and sexual position) and thus bears resemblances to ideology. Myth also resembles ideology in that the denotational meaning of elements appears to be natural and ensures that the connotational meanings of ideology are experienced as natural.

Paradigm

Set of elements from which one element, usually, is chosen in order to combine it with other elements in an ensemble, look or syntagm. From the

paradigm of trousers (jeans, flannels, twills, chinos, etc.), one chooses one pair to wear and combine with other garments into a syntagm.
Cf. Syntagm

Parody

Humourous or satirical (political) mimicry or imitation of a style or look (Jameson 1984: 64–5).

Pastiche

Parody's dim cousin. Gormless aping of a style or look lacking humorous or political motives of parody (Jameson 1984: 64–5).

Reproduction

The process in which a capitalist economy ensures that the status quo is maintained. The status quo here means existing class, gender and ethnic identities and positions, institutions, practices and beliefs.

Resistance(s)

Ways in which the status quo may be challenged or disrupted. Refers to contesting the meaning of elements (items of fashion, conceptions of male or female beauty, etc).

Sign

Unity of signifier (physical or material vehicle) and signified (meaning). If the signifier (material vehicle) is 'a pair of jeans', the signified (meaning) could be 'blue trouser-like garment, with patch pockets, rivets etc.' (denotation) or 'young, free and sexy' (connotation).

Syntagm

Combination or sequence into which elements are combined. Semiological word which can mean 'ensemble' 'outfit' or 'look' when applied to fashion and clothing. Thus, an ensemble might include shoes, socks, trousers, shirt, tie and jacket. One tie would be chosen from the paradigm set of all ties to go to make up the syntagm of the outfit.
Cf. Paradigm.

Undecidability

'Property' of items of fashion and dress meaning different, and often contra-dictory, things at the same time. Effect of the way meaning is produced in different contexts: different contexts will produce different meanings.

BIBLIOGRAPHY

Adorno, T. W. (1967) *Prisms*, Cambridge, Mass.: MIT Press.

Anderson, P. (1983) *In the Tracks of Historical Materialism*, London: Verso.

Appignanesi, L. (ed.) (1989) *Postmodernism: ICA Documents*, London: Free Association Books.

Arnold, M. (1964) *Matthew Arnold's Essays in Criticism*, London: Dent.

Arnold, R. (1999) 'Heroin Chic', in *Fashion Theory*, Volume 3, Issue 3, pp. 279–96.

Ash, J. and Wilson, E. (eds) (1992) *Chic Thrills: A Fashion Reader*, London: Pandora.

Ash, J. and Wright, E. (1988) *Components of Dress*, London: Comedia/Routledge.

Attfield, J. and Kirkham, P. (eds) (1989) *A View from the Interior: Feminism, Women and Design*, London: The Women's Press.

Austin, J. L. (1962) *How To Do Things With Words*, Oxford: Oxford University Press.

Back, K. W. (1985) 'Modernism and fashion: a social psychological interpretation', in Solomon, M. R. (ed.) *The Psychology of Fashion*, Massachusetts: Lexington Books.

Barber, B. and Lobel, L. S. (1952) 'Fashion in women's clothes and the American social system', in Wills, G. and Midgley, D. (1973) *Fashion Marketing*, London: Allen & Unwin.

Barnard, M. (1998) *Art, Design and Visual Culture: An Introduction*, Basingstoke: Macmillan

Barnes, R. and Eicher, J. B. (eds) (1992) *Dress and Gender: Making and Meaning*, Providence, RI and Oxford: Berg.

Barthes, R. (1960) 'Le bleu est à la mode cette année', in Wills, G. and Midgley, D. (eds) (1973) *Fashion Marketing*, London: Allen & Unwin.

—— (1967a) 'The diseases of costume', *Partisan Review*, 34 (1) Winter.

—— (1967b) *Elements of Semiology*, New York: Hill and Wang.

—— (1971) 'Reponses', in *Tel Quel*, No. 47.

—— (1972) *Mythologies*, London: Paladin.

—— (1975) *The Pleasure of the Text*, New York: Hill and Wang.

—— (1977) *Image, Music, Text*, Glasgow: Fontana/Collins.

—— (1983) *The Fashion System*, Berkeley: University of California Press.

Baudrillard, J. (1981) *For a Critique of the Political Economy of the Sign*, St Louis, Mo.: Telos Press.

—— (1983) 'The precession of simulacra', Semiotext(e).

—— (1993) *Symbolic Exchange and Death*, London: Sage.

Bauman, Z. (1990) 'Modernity and Ambivalence' in *Theory, Culture and Society*, Volume 7, pp. 143–69

—— (1991) *Modernity and Ambivalence*, Cambridge: Polity Press.

—— (1992) *Intimations of Postmodernity*, London: Routledge.

197

Bayley, S. (1991) *Taste: The Secret Meaning of Things*, London: Faber and Faber.

Bell, Q. (1976) *On Human Finery*, London: Allison & Busby.

Benjamin, W. (1977) *The Origins of German Tragic Drama*, London: New Left Books.

Berger, J. (1972) *Ways of Seeing*, London: BBC and Penguin.

Berman, M. (1988) 'The experience of modernity' in Thackara, J. (ed.) *Design after Modernism*, London: Thames and Hudson.

Billington, R. *et al.* (1991) *Culture and Society*, Basingstoke: Macmillan.

Bird, J. (1977) 'Art and design as a sign system', in *Leisure in the Twentieth Century*, Design Council Publications.

Bottomore, T. and Rubel, M. (eds) (1961) *Karl Marx: Selected Writings in Sociology and Social Philosophy*, Harmondsworth: Penguin.

Boyne, R. and Rattansi, A. (eds) (1990) *Postmodernism and Society*, London: Macmillan.

Braudel, E. (1981) *Civilisation and Capitalism 15th-18th Century. Volume One: The structures of everyday life: The limits of the possible*, London: Collins.

Brookes, R. (1992) 'Fashion photography; the double-page spread; Helmut Newton, Guy Bourdin and Deborah Turbeville', in Ash, J. and Wilson, E. (eds) *Chic Thrills: A Fashion Reader*, London: Pandora.

Bruzzi, S. and Church Gibson, P. (eds) (2000) *Fashion Cultures: Theories, Explanations and Analysis*, London, Routledge.

Buckley, C. (1986) 'Made in Patriarchy: Toward a Feminist Analysis of Women and Design', in *Design Issues*, Vol. III, No. 2, pp. 3–14

Buck-Morss, S. (1989) *The Dialectics of Seeing Walter Benjamin and the Arcades Project*, Cambridge, Mass. and London: MIT Press.

Carey, J. W. (1988) *Communication as Culture*, London: Routledge.

Carlyle, T. (1987) *Sartor Resartus*, Oxford: Oxford University Press.

Carter, A. (1978) 'Fashion, a feminist view', in *Sunday Times Magazine*, 1 October.

—— (1992) *Nothing Sacred: Selected Writings*, London: Virago.

Chapman, R. and Rutherford, I. (eds) (1988) *Male Order*, London: Lawrence & Wishart.

Chen, T. M. (2001) 'Dressing for the Party: Clothing, Citizenship and Gender-formation in Mao's China', in *Fashion Theory*, Volume 5, Issue 2, pp. 143–72.

Cherry, C. (1957) (3rd edn 1978) *On Human Communication*, Cambridge, Mass. and London: MIT Press.

Clark, K. (1956) *The Nude: A Study in Ideal Form*, New York: Garden City.

—— (1969) *Civilisation: A Personal View*, London: BBC Books and John Murray.

Clarke, R. (1982) 'Norman Parkinson: fifty years of portraits and fashion', *British Journal of Photography Annual.*

Clough, A. (1990) 'Eggar challenged on snub to design', *Design Week*, 5 (44): 3.

Cocks, J. (1988) 'Issey, an essay' in Penn, I. *Issey Miyake*, Boston: New York Graphic Society Book.

Coleridge, N. (1989) *The Fashion Conspiracy*, London: Mandarin.

Conway, H. (ed) (1987) *Design History: A Students' Handbook*, London: Routledge.

Cordwell, J. M. and Schwarz, R. A. (eds) (1979) *The Fabrics of Culture: The Anthropology of Clothing and Adornment*, The Hague: Mouton.

Corner, J. and Hawthorn, J. (eds) (1980) *Communication Studies*, London: Edward Arnold.

Craik, L. (1994) *The Face of Fashion; Cultural Studies in Fashion*, London: Routledge.

Crane, D. (2000) *Fashion and its Social Agendas: Class, Gender and Identity in Clothing*, Chicago: University of Chicago Press.

Crawley, E. (1965a) 'The sexual background of dress' in Roach, M. F. and Eicher, J. B. (eds) *Dress, Adornment and the Social Order*, New York: John Wiley.

—— (1965b) 'Sacred dress' in Roach, M. F. and Eicher, J. B. (eds) *Dress, Adornment and the Social Order*, New York: John Wiley.

Crystal, D. (ed.) (1990) *The Cambridge Encyclopedia*, Cambridge: Cambridge University Press.

Culler, J. (1975) *Structuralist Poetics*, London: Routledge.

Damhorst, M. L., Miller, K. A. and Michelman, S. O. (eds) (1999) *The Meanings of Dress*, New York, Fairchild Publications.

Dant, T. (1999) *Material Culture in the Social World*, Buckingham: Open University Press.

Davis, F. (1985) 'Clothing and fashion as communication', in Solomon, M. R. (ed.) *The Psychology of Fashion*, Mass.: Lexington Books.

—— (1992) *Fashion, Culture and Identity*, Chicago, Ill.: University of Chicago Press.

Derrida, J. (1978a) *Spurs/Eperons*, Chicago, Ill.: University of Chicago Press.

—— (1978b) *Writing and Difference*, Chicago, Ill.: University of Chicago Press.

—— (1994) *Specters of Marx*, New York and London: Routledge.

Design Council Publications (1977) *Leisure in the twentieth century: History of design. Fourteen papers given at the second conference on twentieth century design history 1976*.

Douglas, M. (1966) *Purity and Danger: An Analysis of the Concepts of Pollution and Taboo*, London: Ark Paperbacks.

Douglas, M. and Isherwood, B. (1979) *The World of Goods; Towards an Anthropology of Consumption*, London: Allen Lane.

Duggan, Ginger Gregg (2001) 'The Greatest Show on Earth: A Look at Contemporary Fashion Shows and their Relationship to Performance Art', in *Fashion Theory*, Volume 5, Issue 3, pp. 243–70.

Dyer, G. (1982) *Advertising as Communication*, London: Routledge.

Eco, U. (1972) 'Social life as a sign system' in Robey, D. (ed.) *Structuralism*, London: Jonathan Cape.

Edwards, T. (1997) *Men in the Mirror: Men's Fashion, Masculinity and Consumer Society*, London: Cassell.

Eicher, J. B., Evenson, S. L. and Lutz, H. A. (eds) (2000) *The Visible Self: Global Perspectives on Dress, Culture and Society*, New York: Fairchild Publications.

Eliot, T. S. (1975) *Selected Prose of T. S. Eliot*, London: Faber.

Emberley, J. (1988) 'The fashion apparatus and the deconstruction of postmodern subjectivity' in Kroker, A. and Kroker, M. (eds) *Body Invaders*, London: Macmillan.

Entwistle, J. (2000) *The Fashioned Body: Fashion, Dress and Modern Social Theory*, Cambridge: Polity Press.

Entwistle, J. and Wilson, E. (1998) 'The Body Clothed' in *Addressing the Century: 100 Years of Art and Fashion*, London: Hayward Gallery.

Entwistle, J. and Wilson, E. (eds) (2001) *Body Dressing*, Oxford: Berg.

Evans, C. (2000) 'Yesterday's Emblems and Tomorrow's Commodities; the Return of the Repressed in Fashion Imagery Today', in Bruzzi, S. and Church-Gibson, P. (eds) (2000) *Fashion Cultures: Theories, Explanations and Analysis*, London: Routledge.

—— (2001) 'The Enchanted Spectacle', in *Fashion Theory*, Volume 5, Issue 3, pp. 271–310

Evans, C. and Thornton, M. (1989) *Women and Fashion: A New Look*, London: Quartet Books.

Faurschou, G. (1988) 'Fashion and the cultural logic of postmodernity' in Kroker, A. and Kroker, M. (eds) *Body Invaders*, London: Macmillan.

Ferleger Brades, S. (1998) 'Preface' to *Addressing the Century: 100 Years of Art and Fashion*, London: Hayward Gallery.

Filmer, D. (1992) 'Jeans' in *Clothes Show Magazine*, May.

Fiske, J. (1989) *Understanding Popular Culture*, London: Routledge.

—— (1990) *Introduction to Communication Studies*, London: Routledge.

Flügel, J. C. (1930, 3rd edn 1950) *The Psychology of Clothes*, London: The Hogarth Press and the Institute of Psychoanalysis.

Foote, S. (1989) 'Challenging gender symbols', in Kidwell, C. B. and Steele, V. (eds) *Men and Women: Dressing the Part*, Washington, DC: Smithsonian Institute Press.

Forty, A. (1986) *Objects of Desire*, London: Thames and Hudson.

Foster, H. (ed.) (1983) *The Anti-Aesthetic*, Port Townsend, WA: Bay Press.

Fox-Genovese, F. (1987) 'The empress's new clothes', *Socialist Review*, 17 (1): 7–30.

Freeman, H. (2001) 'From Loafers to Sofas', *The Guardian, G2*, 21 December.

Freud, S. (1977) *On Sexuality*, Pelican Freud Library, vol.7, edited by Angela Richards, Harmondsworth: Penguin Books.

Freudenberger, H. (1963) 'Fashion, sumptuary laws and business', in Wills, G. and Midgley, D. (1973) *Fashion Marketing*, London: Allen & Unwin.

Gaines, J. and Herzog, C. (1990) *Fabrications: Costume and the Female Body*, London: Routledge.

Gamman, L. and Marshment, M. (eds) (1988) *The Female Gaze: Women as Viewers of Popular Culture*, London: The Women's Press.

Garber, M. (1992) *Vested Interests: Cross-dressing and Cultural Identity*, London: Routledge.

Gill, A. (1998) 'Deconstruction fashion: the making of unfinished, decomposing and re-assembled clothes', in *Fashion Theory*, Volume 2, Issue 1, pp. 25–50.

Gombrich, E. (1950) *The Story of Art*, London: Phaidon.

Gordon, B. (1987) 'Fossilized fashion: "old fashioned" dress as a symbol of a separate, work-oriented identity', in *The American Journal of Dress*, 13: 49–59.

Griggers, C. (1990) 'A certain tension in the visual/cultural field: Helmut Newton, Deborah Turbeville and the *Vogue* fashion layout', in *Differences*, 2 (2): 76104.

Hall, S. and Jefferson, T. (1976) *Resistance through Rituals: Youth Subcultures in Post-War Britain*, London: Routledge.

Harrison, M. (1991) *Appearances: Fashion Photography since 1945*, London: Jonathan Cape.

Haug, W. F. (1986) *Critique of Commodity Aesthetics*, Cambridge: Polity Press.

Hebdige, D. (1979) *Subculture: The Meaning of Style*, London: Routledge.

Hirschman, F. C. and Holbrook, M. B. (eds) (1980) *Symbolic Consumer Behaviour*, Proceedings of the Conference on Consumer Aesthetics and Symbolic Consumption. Sponsored by the Association for Consumer Research and the Institute of Retail Management, New York University.

Hollander, A. (1993) *Seeing Through Clothes*, Berkeley: University of California Press.

—— (1994) *Sex and Suits*, New York: Kodansha International.

Holman, R. H. (1980) 'Apparel as communication', in Hirschman, F. C. and Holbrook, M. B. (eds) *Symbolic Consumer Behaviour.*

Honey, N. (1990) *Woman to Woman: Photographs by Nancy Honey*, Bath: Hexagon.

Horn, M. J. and Gurel, L. M. (1981) *The Second Skin: An Interdisciplinary Study of Clothing*, Boston and London: Houghton Mifflin.

Hurlock, B. (1965) 'Sumptuary law', in Roach, M. F. and Eicher, J. B. (eds) *Dress, Adornment and the Social Order*, New York: John Wiley.

i-D Magazine (1985/6), No 32, Dec/Jan.

Imre, T. (1986) 'Pure new wool: a photo campaign for the mid-80s', in *British Journal of Photography Annual*, pp.8–11.

James, S. (1984) *The Princess of Wales Fashion Handbook*, London: Orbis.

Jameson, F (1971) *Marxism and Form*, Princeton: Princeton University Press.

—— (1983) 'Postmodernism and consumer society', in Foster, H. (ed.) *The Anti-Aesthetic*, Port Townsend, WA: Bay Press.

—— (1984) 'Postmodernism and the cultural logic of late capitalism', *New Left Review*, 146 (Fall): 53–92.

Julier, G. (2000) *The Culture of Design*, London: Sage.

Kaplan, E. Ann (1984) 'Is the gaze male?', in Snitow, A., Stansell, C., and Thompson, S. (eds) *Desire: The Politics of Sexuality*, London: Virago.

Keenan, W. J. F. (2001a) 'Introduction: *Sartor Resartus* Restored: Dress Studies in Carlylean perspective', in Keenan (ed) (2001b) *Dressed to Impress: Looking the Part*, Oxford: Berg.

—— (ed.) (2001b) *Dressed to Impress: Looking the Part*, Oxford: Berg.

Kellner, D. (1988) 'Postmodernism as social theory: some challenges and problems', *Theory, Culture and Society*, 5 (2–3).

Kern, S. (1975) *Anatomy and Destiny: A Cultural History of the Human Body*, New York: Bobbs Merril.

Khan, N. (2000) 'Catwalk Politics', in Bruzzi, S. and Church-Gibson, P. (eds) (2000) *Fashion Cultures: Theories Explanations and Analysis*, London: Routledge.

Kidwell, C. B. and Steele, V. (1989) *Men and Women: Dressing the Part*, Washington, DC: Smithsonian Institution Press.

Klein, N. (2000) *No Logo*, London: Flamingo.

König, R. (1973) *The Restless Image*, London: Allen & Unwin.

Kroker, A. and Kroker, M. (1988) *Body Invaders: Sexuality and the Post-Modern Condition*, London: Macmillan.

Larrain, J. (1979) *The Concept of Ideology*, London: Hutchinson.

Laver, J. (1932) *Clothes*, New York: Horizon.

—— 1945) *Taste and Fashion: From the French Revolution to the Present Day*, London: G. G. Harrap.

—— (1949) *Style in Costume*, Oxford: Oxford University Press.

—— (1963) *Costume*, New York: Hawthorne.

—— (1969a) *The Concise History of Costume and Fashion*, New York: Abrams.

—— (1969b) *Modesty in Dress*, Boston: Houghton Mifflin.

Leach, E. (1976) *Culture and Communication: the Logic by which Symbols are Connected*, Cambridge: Cambridge University Press.

Lehmann, U. (1999) 'Tigersprung: Fashioning History', in *Fashion Theory*, Volume 3, Issue 3, pp. 297–322

—— (2000) *Tigersprung: Fashion in Modernity*, Cambridge, Mass.: MIT Press.

Leiss, W., Kline, S. and Jhally, S. (1990) *Social Communication in Advertising*, London: Routledge.

Le Quesne, A. L. (1993) *Carlyle in Victorian Thinking*, Oxford: Oxford University Press.

Levi-Strauss, C. (1966) *The Savage Mind*, London: Weidenfeld and Nicolson.

Light, A. (ed) (1999) *The Vibe History of Hip-Hop*, London: Plexus Publishing.

Lipovetsky, G. (1994) *The Empire of Fashion: Dressing Modern Democracy*, Princeton: Princeton University Press.

Luck, K. (1992) 'Trouble in Eden, trouble with Eve', in Ash, J. and Wilson, E. (eds) *Chic Thrills: A Fashion Reader*, London: Pandora.

Lurie, A. (1992) *The Language of Clothes*, London: Bloomsbury.

McCracken, G. D. (1985) 'The trickle-down theory rehabilitated', in Solomon, M. R. (ed.) *The Psychology of Fashion*, Mass.: Lexington Books.

McCracken, J. (2001) *Taste and the Household: The Domestic Aesthetic and Moral Reasoning*, New York: State University of New York Press.

McRobbie, A. (ed.) (1989) *Zoot Suits and Second-hand Dresses*, Basingstoke: Macmillan.
—— (1998) *British Fashion Design: Rag Trade or Image Industry?* London: Routledge.
Mapplethorpe, R. (1983) *Lady Lisa Lyon*, New York: Viking.
Martin, R. 'Wordrobe: the messages of word and image in textile and apparel design of the 1980s'. Paper presented at the Seventh Annual Conference on Textiles in association with *Ars Textrins* at the University of Maryland on 25 June 1989.
Marx, K. (1954) *Capital*, vol.1, London: Lawrence & Wishart.
—— (1959) *Capital*, vol. 3, London: Lawrence & Wishart.
—— (1975) *The Poverty of Philosophy*, Moscow: Progress Publishers.
Marx, K. and Engels, F. (1968) *Selected Works in One Volume*, London: Lawrence & Wishart.
—— (1970) *The German Ideology*, London: Lawrence & Wishart.
—— (1992) *The Communist Manifesto*, Oxford: Oxford University Press.
Miller, D. (1987) *Material Culture and Mass Consumption*, Oxford: Basil Blackwell.
Miller, J. (1987) 'The Study of Dress and Textiles', in Conway, H. (ed) (1987) *Design History: A Students' Handbook*, London: Routledge.
Modleski, T. (ed.) (1986) *Studies in Entertainment: Critical Approaches to Mass Culture*, Bloomington and Indianapolis: Indiana University Press.
Moore, S. (1988) 'Here's looking at you, kid!', in Gamman, L. and Marshment, M. (eds) *The Female Gaze*, London: The Women's Press.
More, T. (1965) *Utopia*, translated by P. Turner, Harmondsworth: Penguin.
Mulvey, L. (1989) *Visual and Other Pleasures*, Basingstoke: Macmillan.
Nabokov, V. (1991) *The Annotated Lolita*, Harmondsworth: Penguin.
Neustatter, A. (1992) 'Young love, first love', *The Guardian*, 6 January.
Newman, M. (1989) 'Revising modernism, representing postmodernism: critical discourses of the visual arts', in Appignanesi, L. (ed.), *Postmodernism: ICA Documents*, London: Free Association Books.
Oakley, A. (1981) *Subject Women*, Oxford: Martin Robertson.
O'Hara, G. (1986) *The Encyclopaedia of Fashion*, London: Thames and Hudson.
O'Sullivan, T., Hartley, J., Saunders, D., Montgomery, M. and Fiske, J. (2nd edn 1994) *Key Concepts in Communication*, London: Routledge.
Panofsky, E. (1955) *Meaning in the Visual Arts*, Harmondsworth: Penguin.
—— (1955) 'Iconography and iconology: an introduction to the study of Renaissance art' in *Meaning in the Visual Arts*, Harmondsworth: Penguin.
Parker, R. and Pollock, G. (1981) *The Old Mistresses: Women, Art and Ideology*, London: Routledge & Kegan Paul.
Partington, A. (1990) 'The gendered gaze', in Honey, N. *Woman to Woman*, Bath: Hexagon.
—— (1992) 'Popular fashion and working-class affluence', in Ash, J. and Wilson, E. (eds) *Chic Thrills: A Fashion Reader*, London: Pandora.
Penn, I. (1988) *Issey Miyake: Photographs by Irving Penn*, Boston: New York Graphic Society Book.
Perrot, P. (1994) *Fashioning the Bourgeoisie: A History of Clothing in the Nineteenth Century*, Princeton: Princeton University Press.
Plato (1961) *Collected Dialogues*, edited by Edith Hamilton and Huntington Cairns, Bollingen Series LXXl, Princeton: Princeton University Press.
Polhemus, T. (1994) *Streetstyle: From Sidewalk to Catwalk*, London: Thames and Hudson.
Polhemus, T. and Procter, L. (1978) *Fashion and Anti-fashion: An Anthropology of Clothing and Adornment*, London: Thames and Hudson.

Poll, S. (1965) 'The Hasidic community', in Roach, M. F. and Eicher, J. B. (eds) *Dress, Adornment and the Social Order*, New York: John Wiley.

Ribeiro, A. (1992) 'Utopian dress', in Ash, J. and Wilson, E. (eds) *Chic Thrills: A Fashion Reader*, London: Pandora.

Richardson, J. and Kroeber, A. L. (1973) 'Three centuries of women's dress: a quantitative analysis', in Wills, G. and Midgley, D. (eds) *Fashion Marketing*, London: Allen & Unwin.

Roach-Higgins, M. F., Eicher, J. B. and Johnson, K. K. P. (eds) (1995) *Dress and Identity*, New York: Fairchild Publications.

Roach, M. F. and Eicher, J. B. (eds) (1965) *Dress, Adornment and the Social Order*, New York: John Wiley.

Roach, M. F. and Eicher, J. B. (1979) 'The language of personal adornment', in Cordwell, J. M. and Schwarz, R. A. (eds) *The Fabrics of Culture*, The Hague: Mouton.

Robey, D. (ed.) (1972) *Structuralism: The Wolfson College Lectures*, London: Jonathan Cape.

Rosenfeld, L. B. and Plax, T. G. (1977) 'Clothing as communication', *Journal of Communication*, 27: 24–31.

Rouse, F. (1989) *Understanding Fashion*, Oxford: BSP Professional Books.

Sapir, F. (1931) 'Fashion', *Encyclopedia of the Social Sciences*, vol. 5.

Saussure, F. de (1974) *Course in General Linguistics*, London: Fontana/Collins.

Sawchuk, K. (1988) 'A tale of inscription/fashion statements' in Kroker, A. and Kroker, M. (eds) *Body Invaders: Sexuality and the Post-Modern Condition*, London: Macmillan.

Sennett, R. (1986) *The Fall of Public Man*, London: Faber and Faber.

Shakespeare, W. (1951) *The Complete Works of Shakespeare*, edited by P. Alexander, London: Collins.

Sigman, S. J. (1987) *A Perspective on Social Communication*, Mass.: Lexington Books.

Silverman, K. (1986) 'Fragments of a fashionable discourse' in Modleski, T. (ed.) *Studies in Entertainment: Critical Approaches to Mass Culture*, Bloomington and Indianapolis: Indiana University Press.

Simmel, G. (1971) 'Fashion', in Wills, G. and Midgley, D. (eds) (1973) *On Individuality and Social Forms*, Chicago, Ill.: University of Chicago Press.

Smith, J. (1999) 'Kinderwhoring' in Watt, J. (ed) (1999) *The Penguin Book of Twentieth-Century Fashion Writing*, London: Penguin.

Snitow, A., Stansell, C., and Thompson, S. (eds) (1984) *Desire: The Politics of Sexuality*, London: Virago.

Solomon, M. R. (ed.) (1985) *The Psychology of Fashion*, Mass.: Lexington Books.

Sontag, S. (1978) 'The Avedon eye', in *Vogue* (December).

Steele, V. (1985) *Fashion and Eroticism*, New York: Oxford University Press.

—— (1989a) 'Appearance and identity', in Kidwell, C. B. and Steele, V. (eds) *Men and Women: Dressing the Part*, Washington, DC: Smithsonian Institution Press.

—— (1989b) 'Clothing and sexuality', in Kidwell, C. B. and Steele, V. (eds) *Men and Women: Dressing the Part*, Washington, DC: Smithsonian Institution Press.

—— (2001) 'Fashion, Fetish, Fantasy' in Tseëlon. E. (ed) (2001a) *Masquerade and Identities: Essays on Gender, Sexuality and Marginality*, London: Routledge.

Thackara, J. (ed.) (1988) *Design after Modernism*, London: Thames and Hudson.

Thody, P. (1977) *Roland Barthes: A Conservative Estimate*, London: Macmillan.

Tickner, L. (1977) 'Women and trousers', in Design Council Publications.

Triggs, T. (1992) 'Framing masculinity; Herb Ritts, Bruce Weber and the body perfect' in Ash, J. and Wilson, E. (eds) *Chic Thrills: A Fashion Reader*, London: Pandora.

Tseëlon, E. (1992a) 'Fashion and the signification of social order', *Semiotica*, 91 (1 and 2): 1–14.

—— (1992b) 'Self-presentation through appearance', *Symbolic Interaction*, 15(4): 501–13.

—— (2001a) *Masquerade and Identities: Essays on Gender, Sexuality and Marginality*, London: Routledge.

—— (2001b) 'From Fashion to Masquerade: Towards an Ungendered Paradigm' in Entwistle, J. and Wilson, E. (eds) (2001) *Body Dressing*, Oxford: Berg.

Tulloch, C. (1992) 'Rebel without a pause', in Ash, J. and Wilson, E. (eds) *Chic Thrills: A Fashion Reader*, London: Pandora.

Veblen, T. (1992) *The Theory of the Leisure Class*, New Brunswick and London: Transaction Publishers.

Volosinov, V. N. (1973) *Marxism and the Philosophy of Language*, New York: Seminar Press.

Watt, J. (ed.) (1999) *The Penguin Book of Twentieth-Century Fashion Writing*, London: Penguin.

Wilbekin, E. (1999) 'Great Aspirations: Hip-Hop and Fashion Dress for Excess and Success' in Light, A. (ed.) (1999) *The Vibe History of Hip-Hop*, London: Plexus Publishing.

Williams, R. (1961) *The Long Revolution*, Harmondsworth: Penguin/Pelican.

—— (1962) *Communications*, Harmondsworth: Penguin.

—— (1976) *Keywords*, Glasgow: Fontana.

—— (1981) *Culture*, Glasgow: Fontana/Collins.

Williamson, J. (1986) 'Woman is an island: femininity and colonisation' in Modleski, T. (ed.) *Studies in Entertainment: Critical Approaches to Mass Culture*, Bloomington and Indianapolis: Indiana University Press.

Wills, G. and Midgley, D. (eds) (1973) *Fashion Marketing*, London: Allen & Unwin.

Wilson, E. (1985) *Adorned in Dreams: Fashion and Modernity*, London: Virago.

—— (1990) 'These new components of the spectacle: fashion and postmodernism', in Boyne, R. and Rattansi, A. (eds) *Postmodernism and Society*, London: Macmillan.

—— (1992a) 'Fashion and the meaning of life', *The Guardian*, 18 May, p. 34.

—— (1992b) 'Fashion and the postmodern body', in Ash, J. and Wilson, E. (eds) *Chic Thrills: A Fashion Reader*, London: Pandora.

Wittgenstein, L. (1958) *Philosophical Investigations*, Oxford: Basil Blackwell.

Wright, L. (1989) 'Objectifying gender: the stiletto heel', in Attfield, J. and Kirkham, P. (eds) *A View from the Interior: Feminism, Women and Design*, London: The Women's Press.

Young, A. B. (1973) 'Recurring cycles of fashion' in Wills, G. and Midgley, D. (eds) *Fashion Marketing*, London: Allen & Unwin.

Young, M. (1992) 'Dress and modes of address; structural forms for policewomen', in Barnes, R. and Eicher, J. B. (eds) *Dress and Gender: Making and Meaning*, Providence, RI and Oxford: Berg.

INDEX